Dr. Timothy Gatewood's work addresses two problems found at the crossroads of theology proper and epistemology, viz., (a) that God's knowledge cannot be caused by what he has created, and (b) that human knowledge must include what is uncreated and unchanging; and Dr. Gatewood's work does so by retrieving central doctrines of Thomism on these matters that are compatible with Reformed theology, resulting in a theory that safeguards God's aseity while providing an analogical interpretation of human knowledge. It offers a clear and cogent defense that serves the larger agenda of theological retrieval.

THOR MADSEN,
Professor of New Testament, Ethics, and Philosophy,
Midwestern Baptist Theological Seminary,
Kansas City, Missouri

The relationship between God and truth is frequently neglected or assumed in contemporary theology. This well-executed study of a Reformed Thomistic account of divine omniscience fills a gap and shows just how fruitful retrieval theology can be. A helpful and illuminating study that reminds us that truth, goodness, and beauty can never be separated from each other – or God.

GAVIN ORTLUND
Founder, Truth Unites

Modern theology lost its way because it divorced truth not only from Scripture but from God himself. Timothy Gatewood calls us to remember that God is the First Truth. Our triune Lord is the transcendent ground of truth and sovereignly grants access to truth through intellectual participation. *Truth Not Served by Human Hands* is a serious addition to the library being written by an elite cadre of evangelical theologians who recognize the classical tradition, ably advanced by Thomas Aquinas and preserved by his Reformed heirs, requires recovery. If you have even the slightest interest in the truth, you will acquire and consume Gatewood's book.

MALCOLM B. YARNELL III
Research Professor of Theology,
Southwestern Baptist Theological Seminary,
Fort Worth, Texas

R.E.D.S.

REFORMED, EXEGETICAL AND DOCTRINAL STUDIES

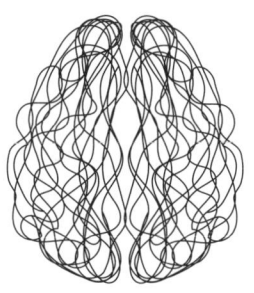

TRUTH NOT SERVED BY
HUMAN HANDS

RETRIEVING THE KNOWLEDGE OF GOD IN REFORMED THOMISM

TIMOTHY A. GATEWOOD

SERIES EDITORS J.V. FESKO & MATTHEW BARRETT

MENTOR

Print ISBN 978-1-5271-1363-3
Ebook ISBN 978-1-5271-1383-1

10 9 8 7 6 5 4 3 2 1

Published in 2025
in the
Mentor Imprint
by
Christian Focus Publications Ltd,
Geanies House, Fearn, Ross-shire,
IV20 1TW, Great Britain.

www.christianfocus.com

Cover design
by Pete Barnsley

Printed by
Bell & Bain, Glasgow

MIX
Paper | Supporting responsible forestry
FSC® C007785

CONTENTS

Dedicated in memoriam to my mother,
Linda Gatewood.

Writing is all about telling the truth, and mama
told me to do my best at both.

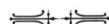

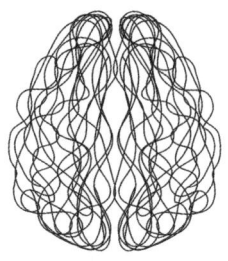

Series Preface

Reformed, Exegetical and Doctrinal Studies (R.E.D.S.) presents new studies informed by rigorous exegetical attention to the biblical text, and engagement with the history of doctrine, with a goal of refined dogmatic formulation.

R.E.D.S. covers a spectrum of doctrinal topics, addresses contemporary challenges in theological studies, and is driven by the Word of God, seeking to draw theological conclusions based upon the authority and teaching of Scripture itself.

Each volume also explores pastoral implications so that they contribute to the Church's theological and practical understanding of God's Word. One of the virtues that sets R.E.D.S. apart is its ability to apply dogmatics to the Christian life. In doing so, these volumes are characterized by the rare combination of theological weightiness and warm, pastoral application, much in the tradition of John Calvin's *Institutes of the Christian Religion*.

These volumes do not merely repeat material accessible in other books but retrieve and remind the Church of forgotten truths to enrich contemporary discussion.

MATTHEW BARRETT
J. V. FESKO

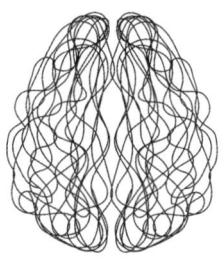

Acknowledgements

All books are products of a specific community. Ideas do not occur in isolation but are the result of dialogue, debate, push-back, and friendship. God reveals truth in a wide variety of ways, but He has made us a communal people designed to reach conclusions through corporate investigation. It seems cliché to confess, but I could not have produced this work, regardless of its quality, without the support, guidance, and occasional insistence from those around me.

First, Drs. Matthew Barrett, Thor Madsen, and J. V. Fesko have been consistent sources of encouragement and wisdom. Dr. Madsen has been on the ground floor of this project from the very beginning and was willing to share his philosophical expertise with a student still discovering how to articulate his questions. Dr. Fesko has provided support since I've moved to Jackson and has graciously recommended this project for publication. Finally, Dr. Barrett has been my dissertation chair, my boss, my pastor, and my friend. This project would be significantly different without his guidance, and I think the same could be said about me. Being one of Barrett's students will have profound effects in my life for years to come – and all he did was tell me who to read!

Second, my family has supported this endeavor for years. Beth has been willing to listen to what must sound like the ravings of a mad man. She has prayed for me, watched the boys while I wrote, and encouraged me when I was overwhelmed. My boys, John Howard and Thomas, have allowed me the time to write and have made my study a happier place due to their presence. Being able to share the finished product with my sons has been one of my biggest motivations to complete this work, especially in the midst of significant changes. I do not know if they will ever read this, but it is for them more than anyone. I hope that one day they will come to love the God who Knows.

In 2021, while I was in the midst of writing my dissertation, my family suffered the loss of my brother, Dr. Benjamin Gatewood. Then, as I was preparing the same work for publication, we lost my mother, Linda Gatewood. This project has witnessed too much loss, multiple home addresses, scheduling delays, job changes, and simply hard days. I genuinely mean it when I say that this book would not have been completed without my family, friends, pastors, students, and the faculty at both Hartfield Academy and Midwestern Baptist Theological Seminary.

This finished work is dedicated to my mother. I cannot begin to guess what she would have thought about the book (I never saw her read a philosophy book in her life), but I know that she would have read every single word. She would have told everyone about it. She would have loved it not because it was good but because it was mine. With support like that, writing becomes an almost possible endeavor. We miss her greatly, but we know that she is currently experiencing truth, beauty, and goodness more than we could ever imagine. Whereas we know the truth, she stares Truth in His face, unveiled and blessed.

Timothy A. Gatewood

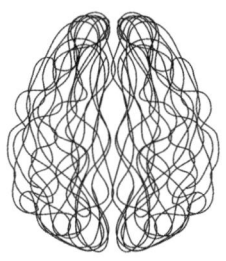

Abstract

This book will recover a Thomistic doctrine of God's independent omniscience to construct a proper definition of metaphysical truth. Specifically, I will argue that the Reformed Thomistic models of the divine intellect and the divine Ideas are the grounds of a participatory theory of truth in which creaturely truth is called such because of its participation in the First Truth, God Himself. As opposed to novel forms of theism which map dependence onto the divine intellect, the Reformed Thomistic model highlights God's transcendent, *a se*, and independent intellect, thus protecting truth's permanence without compromising its intelligibility.

SECTION ONE:

Truth and God

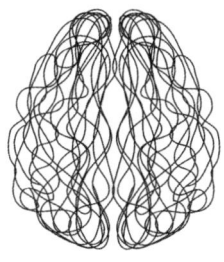

CHAPTER ONE

The Divinity–Truth Connection

Thomas Aquinas begins his most comprehensive theological work, the *Summa Contra Gentiles*, by identifying the final cause of all intellectual endeavors. He writes:

> Now, the end of each thing is that which is intended by its first author or mover. But the first author and mover of the universe is an intellect, as will be later shown. *The ultimate end of the universe must, therefore, be the good of an intellect. This good is truth. Truth must consequently be the ultimate end of the whole universe, and the consideration of the wise man aims principally at truth.* So it is that, according to His own statement, divine Wisdom testifies that He has assumed flesh and come into the world in order to make the truth known: 'For this was I born and for this came I into the world, that I should give testimony to the truth' (John 18:37). (Aquinas, *SCG* 1.1.2)[1]

The chief end of the intellect, then, is to pursue truth. The wise man, however, should not be satisfied by the investigation of any mundane truth but should rather focus his energy on 'that truth which is the origin of all truth, namely, which belongs to the first principle whereby all things are' (Aquinas, *SCG* 1.2.2). For Thomas, this first principle

---

1. Thomas Aquinas, *Summa Contra Gentiles*, Book 1: *God*, trans. Anton C. Pegis (1265; repr. Notre Dame: University of Notre Dame Press, 2014), 60; emphasis added. Anton C. Pegis, in fact, characterizes the *Summa Contra Gentiles* as 'a work devoted to the exposition and defense of divine truth' (Anton C. Pegis, General Introduction to *Summa Contra Gentiles,* by Thomas Aquinas [Notre Dame: University of Notre Dame Press, 2014], 32).

and origin of truth is the God of the Bible 'who is truth one and simple' (Aquinas, *SCG* 1.9.1).

Thomas was not the first theologian to articulate this deep-rooted connection between God and truth,[2] and many thinkers have professed this connection since the Dominican friar's death.[3] Indeed, even secular philosophers such as Simon Blackburn, an outspoken opponent of theism, have noted the connection.[4] Blackburn writes, 'There is an air of divinity that hangs over the concept of truth,' and he frequently uses religious language to describe truth as possessing

---

2. For instance, significant figures in classical theism such as Augustine and Anselm had addressed the relationship between God and truth well before Thomas. For a sample of Augustine's writings concerned with the relationship between God and truth, see Augustine, *Eighty-Three Different Questions*, The Fathers of the Church, trans. David L. Mosher (Washington, DC: The Catholic University of America Press, 1982), 37, q.1; Augustine, *Eighty-Three*, 42, q.9; Augustine, *The Usefulness of Belief*, in *Earlier Writings*, The Library of Christian Classics, ed. and trans. J. H. S. Burleigh (Louisville: Westminster John Knox Press, 2006), 318; Augustine, *The Soliloquies*, in *Earlier Writings*, The Library of Christian Classics, ed. and trans. J. H. S. Burleigh (Louisville: Westminster John Knox Press, 2006), 24; Augustine, *Of True Religion*, in *Earlier Writings*, The Library of Christian Classics, ed. and trans. J. H. S. Burleigh (Louisville: Westminster John Knox Press, 2006), 254. For Anselm's views, see Anselm, *On Truth*, in *Anselm of Canterbury: The Major Works*, Oxford World Classics, ed. Brian Davies and G. R. Evans (Oxford: Oxford University Press, 2008). This principle continued to transcend Thomas as the Westminster Confession of Faith emphasized the relationship between God and truth listed above in sections 1.1, 1.4, 1.5, 2.1, 8.3, 18.2, 21.6, and 23.3 (Westminster Confession of Faith [Carlisle, PA: Banner of Truth Trust, 2015]). This is reiterated in the London Baptist Confession of Faith in sections 1.1, 1.4, 1.5, 2.1, 8.3, 14.2, and 20.6 (The Baptist Confession of Faith 1689 [Carlisle, PA: Banner of Truth Trust, 2012]).

3. Thomas is frequently described as a Dominican monk, but this is technically incorrect. See Thomas Aquinas, *Quodlibetal Questions*, trans. Turner Nevitt and Brian Davies (Oxford: Oxford University Press, 2020), li, lv; Richard J. Reagan, Introduction to *Compendium of Theology*, by Thomas Aquinas (Oxford: Oxford University Press, 2009), 5.

4. In terms of religious affiliation, Blackburn adopts the term 'infidel.' For more information concerning Blackburn's religious opinions, including his campaign for a less religious society and the problems of theism as he perceives them, see Rick Lewis, 'Interview with Simon Blackburn,' in *The God Issue*, *Philosophy Now* 99 (2013). Blackburn has written numerous books concerning truth theory, including Simon Blackburn and Keith Simmons, eds., *Truth*, Oxford Readings in Philosophy (Oxford: Oxford University Press, 1999); Simon Blackburn, *Truth: A Guide* (Oxford: Oxford University Press, 2007); and Simon Blackburn, *On Truth* (Oxford: Oxford University Press, 2018). He also serves as the editor of the *Oxford Dictionary of Philosophy*, which may explain why some definitions within the dictionary have a noticeably anti-theistic bias.

'omnipresence' and 'authority.'[5] Furthermore, he approvingly quoted a pragmatist who entitled the consensus opinion fated to be achieved by researchers as the 'predestinate opinion.'[6]

In secular journalism, the connection between God and truth has been suggested by *Time Magazine*, which featured nearly identical cover photos more than fifty years apart asking the questions, 'Is God Dead?' and 'Is Truth Dead?,' respectively.[7] The editors of *Time* were so committed to drawing this connection between God and truth that they produced the latter cover by hand as they 'could find no modern type foundry which has an exact interpretation of the one used on the original cover.'[8] The lengths that the editors of *Time* were willing to go, to draw a comparison between God and truth suggest that the connection between the two transcends religious adherence and can be recognized across disciplines both sacred and secular. Theologians, philosophers, journalists, and the laity all recognize one common idea – as God goes, so goes truth. As the Lutheran scholar Jordan Cooper writes, 'Once truth is divorced from God, and hence from any value or inherent goodness, its foundation has already collapsed.'[9]

This work will emphasize the aforementioned divinity–truth connection by demonstrating that God is the source and definition of metaphysical Truth and the provider of all creaturely meaning. Unlike humans, God does not receive knowledge from His creatures, but instead knows all things through the knowledge of His own essence. God's comprehensive self-knowledge includes the knowledge of all creation because God knows how His essence is imitated by His

---

5. Blackburn, *On Truth*, 13, 32-33. He continues, 'Deception is an insult to this divinity, as well as an insult to its target. … Sometimes we have to settle for mere opinion or guesswork, but the god of truth is better served by attendant deities, such as reason, justification and objectivity' (Blackburn, *On Truth*, 13).

6. Blackburn, *On Truth*, 40. The full quote from C. S. Peirce reads, 'No modification of the point of view taken, no selection of other facts for study, no natural bent of mind even, can enable a man to escape the *predestinate opinion*. This great law is embodied in the conception of truth and reality.'

7. See 'Is God Dead?' *Time Magazine* 87, no. 14 (1966); 'Is Truth Dead?' *Time Magazine* 189, no. 12 (2017).

8. See D. W. Pine, 'Is Truth Dead? Behind the Time Cover,' *Time*, March 23, 2017, accessed August 27, 2020, https://time.com/ 4709920/donald-trump-truth-time-cover/.

9. Jordan Cooper, *In Defense of the True, the Good, and the Beautiful: On the Loss of Transcendence and the Decline of the West* (Ithaca: Just and Sinner, 2021), 60.

creatures. Creatures receive their being from God and, therefore, receive their perfections by participating in the likeness of the divine essence. If a creature has life, for instance, it is because God has shared pure, unlimited life with the creature as fitting to its finite mode of existence. This rule, known as the *modus principle*, applies to all creaturely perfections – wisdom, truth, beauty, being, etc. Any derivative good that may be found in a creature can first be found perfectly and eminently in the Creator. In this way, creatures receive their truth by participating in the first Truth, God Himself.[10]

The Biblical Case for the Divinity–Truth Connection

That a divinity–truth connection exists cannot be denied by Bible-believing Christians. Scripture presents the God of Israel as one who is 'abounding in lovingkindness and truth' (Exod. 34:6, cf. Gen. 24:27; Pss. 57:3 [LXX 56:4]; 61:7 [LXX 60:8]; 89:14 [LXX 88:15]).[11] This God of truth is ontologically different than man, as He *cannot* lie, does not repent, and always fulfills what He has promised to do (Heb. 6:18, Num. 23:19, 1 Sam. 15:29, Titus 1:1-2).[12] As Thomas Schreiner writes, 'He wouldn't

---

10. Mark McIntosh summarizes this argument as such: 'Few points have emerged more clearly throughout this book than the intense wonder and joy that awaken in the exponents of the divine ideas tradition as they contemplate the Trinitarian ground of all creatures. Moreover for them this wondering joy is really a threefold awareness: first, that in knowing Godself God knows the cherishable and inclusive truth of all creatures; second, that this eternal act of self-knowing is the ground of truth itself, the very source and transformative goodness of all truth; and third, more wonderfully still, this divine act of self-knowing – in which God knows all creatures and in which truth itself is established – is also the basis of God's infinite and inexhaustible joy, the beatitude or happiness that is the very life of God.' See Mark A. McIntosh, *The Divine Ideas Tradition in Christian Mystical Theology* (Oxford: Oxford University Press, 2021), 167.

11. Unless otherwise noted, all Scripture references are retrieved from the New American Standard Bible (NASB) (Grand Rapids: Zondervan, 2002). Some English translations, such as the ESV, render the passages from Psalms with the term 'faithfulness' instead of 'truth,' but the LXX uses *alēthia* rather than *pistis* on each occasion. Truth may necessarily include an aspect of faithfulness, but the LXX translators chose not to employ *pistis* in these passages even though they did elsewhere.

12. For a classical theist's explanation of the divine 'repentance' terminology found in Scripture, see Steven J. Duby, '"For I Am God, Not a Man": Divine Repentance and the Creator-Creature Distinction,' *Journal of Theological Interpretation* 12, no. 2 (2018): 149-69.

be God if he could lie.'[13] This repeated biblical theme suggests that truth, however it may be defined, is grounded in the divine nature.[14]

Indeed, God associates Himself with truth in Isaiah 65. In this passage, God says, '… he who is blessed in the earth will be blessed by *the God of truth*; And he who swears in the earth will swear by *the God of truth*; …' (Isa. 65:16).[15] Blessings from God are elsewhere associated with truth in Psalm 85:

> I will hear what God the LORD will say; For He will speak peace to His people, to His godly ones; … Lovingkindness and truth have met together; Righteousness and peace have kissed each other. Truth springs from the earth, and righteousness looks down from heaven. Indeed, the LORD will give what is good, and our land will yield its produce (Ps. 85:8-12 [LXX 84:11-13]).

Likewise, God brings judgment against those who deny truth. Isaiah 59:14 cites the lack of justice, righteousness and truth within His covenant community as an example of the wickedness that has incited His judgment. Indeed, God desires 'truth in the innermost being' (Ps. 51:6 [LXX 50:8]), and this desire is demonstrated by the commands against lying and false testimony throughout the Old and New Testaments (Exod. 20:16; Prov. 6:16-19; 12:22; 19:9; Col. 3:9-10; Eph. 4:25; Rev. 21:8).[16]

---

13. Thomas Schreiner, *Commentary on Hebrews*, Biblical Theology for Christian Proclamation, ed. T. Desmond Alexander, Andreas J. Köstenberger, and Thomas R. Schreiner (Nashville: B&H Publishing, 2015), 203.

14. Herman Bavinck, citing Augustine, explains this difference by writing, 'He is pure being. *He does not possess but is the truth.* "O Truth, which you truly are!"' See Herman Bavinck, *Reformed Dogmatics*, vol. 2, *God and Creation* (Grand Rapids: Baker Academic, 2004), 209; emphasis added. See Augustine, *Confessions*. Oxford World Classics (Oxford: Oxford University Press, 1998), 10.41, 7.10, 12.25.

15. Of course, it should be noted that according to the evangelical doctrine of verbal plenary inspiration, all the verses cited throughout Scripture would be examples of God's self-identification as the God of truth, even when He is not the explicit speaker. Still, it is noteworthy that in these examples, God explicitly draws this distinction Himself rather than have it applied to Him by others. The 'God of truth' is a title that God freely chooses to apply to Himself.

16. This abbreviated list shows God's command against lying across the testaments. Other verses concerning God's hatred of lying include but are not limited to the following: Lev. 19:11; Pss. 5:6; 31:18; 34:13; 58:3; 101:7; 119:163; 120:2; Prov. 12:5, 19; 13:5; 14:5, 25; 19:5, 22; 21:6; 26:18-19, 28; Jer. 23:32; Hosea 4:2; Zeph. 3:13; Matt. 15:18-20; Luke 16:10; James 3:14; 1 Pet. 3:10. Furthermore, lying is not limited to uttering false propositions but also includes the commands issued against dishonesty in business and ethics such as described in Prov. 11:1.

In one of the most memorable expressions in Scripture, the incarnate Son proclaims Himself to be 'the way, and *the truth*, and the life' (John 14:6). John introduces readers to this Son within the first chapter of his Gospel as one who, like the Father, is 'full of grace and truth' (John 1:14).[17] As such, even though no one has seen the Father, 'the only begotten God' displays two of the former's chief characteristics – grace and truth (John 1:18). It is not surprising that when Jesus explains His kingdom mission by proclamation of the truth, Pilate, who is ignorant of Jesus' true identity, responds with the quintessential postmodern question, 'What is truth?' (John 18:38).[18] 'Jesus is God's embodied truth claim,' writes Kevin Vanhoozer, 'a covenant proposition made personal (John 14:6), whose history displays how things ultimately are (or will be).'[19] Similarly, Thomas described Jesus as *ille homo esset ipsa divina veritas* – 'this human being is divine truth itself.'[20]

Likewise, in three of five passages concerned with the Paraclete, the Holy Spirit is identified as 'the Spirit of truth' (John 14:17; 15:26; 16:13). D. A. Carson explains, 'Coming so soon after 14:6, where Jesus claims to be the truth, "the Spirit of truth" may in part define the Paraclete as the Spirit who bears witness to the truth, *i.e.* to the truth that Jesus is.'[21] Jesus' assertion that the Spirit of Truth will testify about Him

---

17. Some have argued that *alētheia* is used in John's prologue to demonstrate 'covenant faithfulness' or 'steadfastness.' For example, see C. K. Barrett, *The Gospel According to St. John* (Louisville: Westminster John Knox Press, 1958), 139. However, as A. C. Thiselton surveys the Johannine usage of *alētheia*, he concludes, '[T]he evangelist probably took it to mean "divine reality" in a more strongly ontological sense (cf. v. 17) as he understands *alētheia* in 4:23; 8:44; 14:6; 17:17; 18:37d.' See A. C. Thiselton, 'Truth,' *The New International Dictionary of New Testament Theology*, ed. Colin Brown (Grand Rapids: Zondervan, 1978), 3:89. Thiselton is positively quoting R. Schnackenburg, *The Gospel According to St. John* (New York: Herder and Herder, 1968), 1:273.

18. It is interesting to note that some modern and postmodern skeptics proclaim Pilate as the clear winner of this exchange and hero of the narrative. For more info, see Bruce D. Marshall, *Trinity and Truth,* Cambridge Studies in Christian Doctrine 3 (Cambridge: Cambridge University Press, 2000), 1-2.

19. Kevin Vanhoozer, 'Truth,' *Dictionary for Theological Interpretation of the Bible*, ed. Kevin J. Vanhoozer (Grand Rapids: Baker Academic, 2005), 819.

20. Thomas Aquinas, *Commentary on the Gospel of John*, vol. 2, *Chapters 6–12*, trans. Fabian Larcher and James A. Weisheipl, 3 vols., Thomas Aquinas in Translation (Washington, DC: The Catholic University of America Press, 2010), 8.188

21. D. A. Carson, *The Gospel According to John*, Pillar New Testament Commentary (Grand Rapids: William B. Eerdmans Publishing Company, 1991), 500.

strengthens Carson's argument (John 15:26). As such, the triune life is one of consistent proclamation of truth by truth itself.[22] Believers, then, may be pulled into the triune life as Jesus tells His disciples that the 'Spirit of truth' is the divine person who leads them into 'all the truth' (John 16:13). Elsewhere, John contrasts the Spirit of God with the spirit of the antichrist. In so doing, John encourages his readers to listen to the gospel message and differentiate the 'spirit of truth' from the spirit of error (1 John 4:2-6).

As has been shown, Christians cannot separate the concept of truth from the doctrine of God without subverting a wealth of biblical texts. However, while Scripture makes it clear that the divinity–truth connection exists, it does not articulate a specific definition of 'metaphysical' truth.[23] In other words, the Bible expresses truth by teaching readers that which is true, and thus affirms that something called 'truth' exists in some capacity, but it does not explain how best to understand that which it names 'truth.' This observation comes with a host of difficulties and can be linked to heated debates regarding the reality of abstract objects, the different interpretations of nominalism and realism, and what it means for something to 'exist.'

While some of these topics will be briefly discussed in later chapters, the point at this juncture is to acknowledge that the authors of Scripture presupposed that truth meant *something* without explicitly stating exactly what that *something* must entail. Thus, the distinction between truth and that which is true is sometimes quite difficult to parse. Christians, therefore, are left to theological and philosophical argumentation to pinpoint the proper definition of truth in a growing field of options. It stands to reason, however, that due to the strong relationship between

---

22. Augustine writes, '*Truth itself, speaking as a human being* among others, said to those believing in Him: "If you continue in my word, you are truly my disciples; and you shall know the truth, and the truth shall set you free"' (Augustine, *On Free Will*, 59).

23. Biblical scholars and theologians are divided on a biblical theological definition of truth. For the perceived distinction between the Hebrew and Greek understanding of truth, see Charles Hodge, *Systematic Theology* (Peabody, MA: Hendrickson Publishing, 2016), 1:436-37; Wolfhart Pannenberg, *Basic Questions in Theology*, trans. George H. Kehm (Philadelphia: Fortress Press, 1972), 2:3. For a more nuanced view that suggests a greater continuity between the Hebrew and Greek usage, see A. C. Thiselton, 'Truth,'; Norman Geisler, 'The Concept of Truth in the Inerrancy Debate,' *Bibliotheca Sacra* (1980).

divinity and truth as highlighted above, a proper view of God will, at the very least, aid in constructing a proper definition of truth.

If humanity confessed a singular view of God, then perhaps the divinity–truth connection and a correlating definition of truth would be uncontroversial. As it stands, however, various proposed models of God are sometimes accompanied by varying models of metaphysical truth, especially in the latter half of the twentieth century. Claims concerning the nature of God that mainstream Western thought once considered to be self-evident, or at least logically demonstrable, have been called into question due in part, to changes in philosophical presuppositions as the surrounding culture of ideas continues to shift from premodernity to modernity and postmodernity. As such, even the most popular views of God within Christianity can vary significantly, and this diversity of views places any potential Christian consensus on the proper definition of truth on unstable ground.

The Metaphysical–Epistemological Divide

The difficulty in distinguishing 'truth' from 'that which is true' is closely related to the broader conversation concerning the distinction between metaphysics and epistemology. Peter Kreeft provides a helpful definition of 'metaphysics' as the 'philosophical science of being qua being, i.e., the science of the most universal principles that hold true of everything that is.'[24] Thomas Joseph White further identifies the subject matter of metaphysics as 'every categorical mode of created being (substances, with their various qualities, quantities, etc.) as well as the transcendental characteristics of created beings (their existence, goodness, unity, truth, etc.).'[25] Metaphysics, then, could simply be called the philosophical investigation of *being* – a subject's most basic act of existence.[26]

---

24. Peter Kreeft, ed., *Summa of the Summa: The Essential Philosophical Passages of St. Thomas Aquinas' Summa Theologica Edited and Explained for Beginners* (San Francisco: Ignatius Press, 1990), 44n30.

25. Thomas Joseph White, *The Trinity: On the Nature and Mystery of the One God*, Thomistic Ressourcement Series 19 (Washington, DC: The Catholic University of America Press, 2022), 229.

26. For the definition of 'being' as an act, see Andrew Davison, *Participation in God: A Study in Christian Doctrine and Metaphysics*, paperback ed. (New York: Cambridge University Press, 2020), 182, 218.

Metaphysics, as such, is the business of 'is-ness.'[27] To approach truth as a metaphysical enterprise, then, would be to ask questions concerning truth's being: What *is* truth? How can it be defined and categorized? What are the components essential to its nature? Does it possess genuine existence? If so, is its existence independent of man or dependent on an intellect? Throughout the following chapters, we will focus on the theological metaphysics of truth by examining the nature of truth in light of certain commitments related to the classical doctrine of God. Questions related to epistemology and truth, while important and legion, will not be the primary concern of this work, although they will be addressed when appropriate.

As distinguished from metaphysics, epistemology is the 'enquiry into the nature and grounds of knowledge.'[28] The topics epistemologists investigate include 'the origin of knowledge, the place of experience in generating knowledge, and the place of reason in [generating knowledge].'[29] The basic and most fundamental epistemological question is, 'How do we know what we know?'[30] If metaphysics is concerned with truth's *being*, then epistemology is concerned with truth's verifiability and justification.[31]

---

27. Richard Muller's definition of metaphysics is quite thorough: 'Metaphysics, or as it is also called, first philosophy, is by definition the philosophical knowledge concerned with the understanding of "being" in the most general sense; thus it is the science of being simply as being, or the science of all beings considered as beings. It includes the discussion of first causes, universals, or essences as the ground of the existence of particulars.' See Richard A. Muller, '*Metaphysica*,' *Dictionary of Latin and Greek Theological Terms: Drawn Principally from Protestant Scholastic Theology*, 2nd ed. (Grand Rapids: Baker Academic, 2017), 218. The *Routledge Dictionary of Philosophy* provides a non-theological treatment of metaphysics and ontology: 'This [discipline] studies being and, in particular nowadays, what there is, e.g. material objects, minds, persons, universals, numbers, facts, etc.' See *The Routledge Dictionary of Philosophy* (2010), s.v. 'metaphysics,' 248. For a skeptical view concerning the validity of metaphysics, see *Oxford Dictionary of Philosophy* (2016), s.v. 'metaphysics,' 303.

28. *The Routledge Dictionary of Philosophy* (2010), s.v. 'epistemology,' 118.

29. Simon Blackburn, *Oxford Dictionary of Philosophy* (2016), s.v. 'epistemology,' 158.

30. For a good introduction to epistemology from an evangelical perspective, see James K. Dew Jr. and Mark W. Foreman, *How Do We Know? An Introduction to Epistemology* (Downers Grove: IVP Academic, 2014). For a thorough representation of the type of topics studied within epistemology, see Ernest Sosa et al., eds., *Epistemology: An Anthology* (Malden, MA: Blackwell Publishing, 2017).

31. Bruce D. Marshall explains this distinction: 'Accounts of truth and accounts of justification can and in practice do vary independently of one another. That is, one might

It may be appropriate to visualize truth as a bridge between metaphysics and epistemology. Hans Urs Von Balthasar summarizes this idea well when he writes:

> This particular question – whether or not truth exists – is the principle concern of critical epistemology, and it is certainly serious enough to warrant a thorough investigation of its own. Ontology [a subset of metaphysics], too, should have pride of place in dealing with this issue, because truth is not just a property of knowledge but transcendental quality of being as such.[32]

This statement from Von Balthasar, however, contains several contested affirmations. For instance, if one adopts a realist framework of metaphysics, such as Platonism or Aristotelianism, then truth has an objective identity apart from any creaturely interpretation. On a realist framework, human thoughts do not create truth but are measured against 'the truth' and are thus determined to be correct or incorrect according to their relation to an objective standard. Furthermore, truth as presented by Von Balthasar is held as a 'transcendental,' a quality of being that is functionally synonymous with being itself. These transcendentals thus 'transcend' all categories and are applied to creatures universally, albeit in various degrees. Not only are such metaphysical beliefs contested in the current philosophical age, but the validity of metaphysics as a legitimate discipline is also called into question.

According to John Milbank, the current philosophical age could be termed the 'epistemological era.' Milbank explains that the epistemological era 'assumes that the true is that which is fully graspable by human reason.'[33] As such, anything beyond physical

---

argue that for beliefs to be true is for them (a) to correspond to reality, or (b) to cohere with other beliefs, or (c) to be among those sentences we will find ourselves warranted in asserting at the ideal end of inquiry, or (d) to be what comes out of the barrel of a gun, that is, what we can compel other people to accept, or (e) to be none of the above. ... But one might also argue that any one of these is the proper or primary criterion for deciding which beliefs are true, and further items may be added to the list, such as (f) to be tied with logical necessity to beliefs which are self-evidently true, which has regularly been invoked as the paradigm of justification, if not as a candidate for an adequate characterization of truth. ... Many, for example, argue that truth is a version of (a), while justification is a version of (b), or perhaps (c).' See Marshall, *Trinity and Truth*, 9.

32. Hans Urs Von Balthasar, *Theo-Logic: Theological Logical Theory*, vol. 1, *Truth of the World*, trans. Adrian J. Walker (San Francisco: Ignatius Press, 2000), 23.

33. John Milbank et al., eds., *Radical Orthodoxy: A New Theology* (New York: Routledge, 1999), 5-6.

verifiability and human mastery cannot be justified as true in the strict sense of the word. An objective standard of truth which is applicable to all human knowledge for all time beyond human testability, then, is considered unreachable and is functionally eradicated. In this sense, the theory of knowledge, *epistemology*, and the theory of what lies beyond the physical world, *metaphysics*, has been separated. Milbank traces this separation between metaphysics and epistemology to medieval scholastic debates:

> Hence while [John Duns] Scotus and [William of] Ockham, like Aquinas, were still interested mainly in human knowledge in so far as it reflected and afforded clues to divine knowledge, in the case of the former two thinkers the 'pious' conjecture that god might so dispose things that what *appears* to humans has no connection to the truly real itself opens the space for the emergence of the modern 'epistemological' focus.[34]

Milbank describes a belief known as theological voluntarism, in which God's will is understood to be radically free, and His omnipotence exists without restrictive parameters. In this view, God's will has primacy over all things, including the divine intellect. God, then, does not have to adhere to any type of order and is free to create any type of world, including one where human knowledge does not align with reality. It is plausible, in this framework, that God is like Descartes's evil genie who creates sense experience to toy with his creation.[35]

Indeed, it was Descartes who, according to Jordan Cooper, first created a system of philosophy built on epistemology rather than metaphysics.[36] Topics such as theological voluntarism, Descartes's subjectivism, and later David Hume's skepticism set the stage for the Godfather of the epistemological age, Immanuel Kant. Cooper writes:

> According to Kant, reality can be divided into two distinct realms: the noumenal and the phenomenal. The noumenal is what Kant calls the 'thing-in-itself.' This is a thing as it actually is, objectively. ... According

---

34. ibid., 6.

35. Cooper, 43. To be clear, Descartes did not consider this evil genie to be God. Cooper explains Descartes's thought, 'If God had created us with this inherent belief [that the senses grasp real things], and it was not true, this would make God deceptive. Descartes's argument for God's existence earlier was based upon the idea of God's perfection, and if God is a perfect being, he cannot be deceptive' (Cooper, 45).

36. ibid., 43.

to Kant, this noumenal realm is completely inaccessible. In other words, humans cannot state with certainty what reality in itself is.[37]

For theologians living post-Kant, the rift between metaphysics and epistemology is often unnoticed, a collective unquestioned assumption present in the philosophical air of the current age.

The metaphysical–epistemological rift had great effects on the doctrine of God in modern theology. If epistemology is separated from metaphysics, then God's transcendence is a severe liability for religious knowledge. The less God is like the created order, the less creatures can know about Him. Rather than abandoning God, the natural tendency for post-Kantian theologians is to describe Him in more understandable and, therefore, creaturely terms. Soon, the doctrine of God collapses into pure immanence, in which God is not only a co-laborer with creation, but sometimes dependent upon it, and other times indistinguishable from it.

In Milbank's estimation, theological voluntarism within some streams of the Scholastic doctrine of God, in which an unrestrained will serves as the defining characteristic of divinity, paved the way for the modern preoccupation with epistemology to the detriment of metaphysics. Milbank's thesis is not novel nor is it limited to Christian thinkers; and if Milbank is correct, the study of metaphysical truth would best be served by premodern thinkers who lived before the metaphysical–epistemological divide.[38] Milbank reaches the same conclusion and thus promotes a movement known as Radical Orthodoxy, which is primarily concerned with theological and philosophical retrieval.

---

37. ibid., 49.

38. For other Christian thinkers who make similar claims, see Hans Boersma, *Heavenly Participation: The Weaving of a Sacramental Tapestry* (Grand Rapids: William B. Eerdmans Publishing Company, 2011); Jordan Cooper, *In Defense of the True, the Good, and the Beautiful: On the Loss of Transcendence and the Decline of the West* (Ithaca: Just and Sinner, 2021); Sebastian Morello, *The World as God's Icon: Creator and Creation in the Platonic Thought of Thomas Aquinas* (Brooklyn: Angelico Press, 2020); Paul Tyson, *Returning to Reality: Christian Platonism for Our Times,* Kalos 2 (Eugene: Cascade Books, 2014). For an excellent historical survey of the function of theological voluntarism in the dawning of the Enlightenment from a non-religious perspective, see Michael Allen Gillespie, *The Theological Origins of Modernity* (Chicago: The University of Chicago Press, 2008).

Theological Retrieval

Movements such as Radical Orthodoxy are examples of the growing trend known as theological retrieval or ressourcement.[39] Craig Carter broadly defines 'ressourcement' as 'the act of remembering the past,' but more specifically, theological retrieval is the act of returning to premodern sources to better address contemporary philosophical and theological problems without modern presuppositions.[40] It should be noted, of course, that retrieval is not simply done for retrieval's sake but rather to improve the state of contemporary conversations. Retrievalists do not seek to return to the past but to help create a better future. As John R. Betz writes, '[O]ur purpose is not to bring everything back to Aristotle and Plato ... but in order to do metaphysics better, having learned from all of these philosophical and theological critiques and lines of inquiry.'[41] We look to the past because we think these figures have something to say about our present.

As Carter writes, '[I]n order for *ressourcement* to succeed, it is necessary to refuse the presuppositions of modernity and to challenge the very rules of the game rather than trying to play it more skillfully than one's opponents.'[42] To accomplish this task, evangelical Christians are exhibiting a welcomed and growing interest in patristic and medieval scholarship. While theological retrieval is not limited to any particular premodern thinker, the thorough and comprehensive theology of Thomas Aquinas makes him a prime candidate. Furthermore, if the ailments of modernity are traceable to medieval scholastic debates and the theology

---

39. Ressourcement technically refers to a specific form of theological retrieval, but the term has also been used to characterize theological retrieval as a whole. For more, see Gavin Ortlund, *Theological Retrieval for Evangelicals: Why We Need Our Past to Have a Future* (Wheaton: Crossway, 2019), 18.

40. Craig Carter, *Contemplating God with the Great Tradition: Recovering Trinitarian Classical Theism* (Grand Rapids: Baker Academic, 2021), 47. See also Craig Carter, 'The Liberal Project v. Ressourcement,' accessed July 1, 2021, https://craigacarter.substack.com/p/the-liberal-project-v-ressourcement, in which he lists Thomas Oden, Richard Muller and John Webster as prominent Protestant examples of scholars engaging in ressourcement. Carter has also offered a fuller definition of ressourcement, which reads 'the recovery of treasures from the past that can enrich our witness and common life in the present and the future' (Carter, *Contemplating God*, 306).

41. John R. Betz, *Christ the Logos of Creation: An Essay in Analogical Metaphysics* (Stubbenville, OH: Emmaus Academic, 2023), 39.

42. Carter, *Contemplating God*, 296.

of Duns Scotus and William of Ockham, as Milbank suggests, then the alternative stream of medieval thought, best represented by Thomas, serves as a logical starting point of investigation.[43]

It is not surprising, of course, that Thomas is of prime interest with the Catholic project of retrieval. The concept of ressourcement is fundamentally attached to Thomism and is indivisible from the movement known as the *nouvelle théologie*. The *nouvelle théologie* questioned the neo-scholastic interpretation of Thomas made popular by such thinkers as Francisco Suarez and Thomas Cajetan. Rather than viewing Thomism as a completed body of work, as the new-scholastics did, the *nouvelle théologie* placed Thomas 'under the spotlight' and invited a wave of critical investigation of the interpretive tradition of Thomas.[44] Indeed, *nouvelle théologie* was the pejorative term applied to these thinkers by their opponents, while 'ressourcement' was the name these thinkers applied to themselves.

While the rediscovery and study of Thomas in Catholic theology seems like a natural progression, some may be skeptical about the rediscovery of Thomas within Protestant theology, even though, as John Bolt points out, these same 'doubting Thomists' may not likewise question the use of other premodern sources, such as Augustine.[45] Yet, while it may seem

---

43. Milbank, of course, is not the only scholar to notice the medieval influence of modernity. See, for instance, Paul Tyson who calls Duns Scotus and William of Ockham the 'great architects of modernity' (Paul Tyson, *Returning to Reality: Christian Platonism for Our Times,* Kalos 2 [Eugene: Cascade Books, 2014], 75).

44. Andrew Davison, *The Love of Wisdom: An Introduction to Philosophy for Theologians* (London: SCM Press, 2013), 129.

45. John Bolt engages these 'doubting Thomists' in John Bolt, 'Doubting Reformational Anti-Thomism,' in *Aquinas among the Protestants,* ed. Manfred Svensson and David VanDrunen (Oxford: Wiley Blackwell, 2018), 129, 131. Indeed, some posit that a rediscovery of Thomas's Augustinianism has influenced the current resurgence of modified Thomism in evangelical thought. See Manfred Svensson and David VanDrunen, 'Introduction: The Reception, Critique, and Use of Aquinas in Protestant Thought,' in *Aquinas among the Protestants,* ed. Manfred Svensson and David VanDrunen (Oxford: Wiley Blackwell, 2018), 6; Michael Dauphinais et al., eds., *Aquinas the Augustinian* (Washington: Catholic University of America Press, 2007). This emphasis of Thomas's Augustinianism is somewhat ironic considering that Thomas's modified Aristotelianism was considered to be theologically dangerous in his time particularly because it broke away from the Neoplatonic tradition as displayed in Augustinianism. See Edward Feser, *Aquinas: A Beginner's Guide,* Oneworld Beginner's Guides (2009; repr. London: Oneworld Publications, 2020), 5. Still, as Carter attests, '[Thomas] quotes Augustine more than Aristotle and does not hesitate to correct Aristotle when necessary' (Carter, *Contemplating God,* 252).

strange for Protestant scholars to adopt the methodology and theology of the Catholic Church's premier theologian, there is good precedent for doing so, especially in light of current philosophical trends.

The influence of Thomas on Protestants will be investigated at length in Chapter 3, but for now it is appropriate to offer a broad overview of what could be called Reformed Thomism. Many of the Reformers and Protestant Scholastics were exposed to Thomistic theology and positively incorporated Thomistic ideas into their writings. According to David Sytsma, this list of Thomistic Reformers includes but is not limited to Martin Bucer, Heinrich Bullinger, Peter Martyr Vermigli, Girolamo Zanchi, Huldrych Zwingli, and Johannes Oecolampadius.[46] While some historians focus only on Martin Luther's total and emphatic rejection of Thomas, others have noted a positive, albeit critical, accommodation of Thomism in the writings of the Reformed Orthodox tradition. In fact, some scholars have identified the existence of a historical stream of 'Calvinist Thomism' from the time of the Reformation onward.[47]

Scholars such as John Patrick Donnelly have noted that a twentieth-century 'Thomist revival' mirrors that of the sixteenth century.[48]

---

46. David Sytsma, 'Thomas Aquinas and the Reformed Biblical Interpretation: The Contribution of William Whitaker,' in *Aquinas among the Protestants*, ed. Manfred Svensson and David VanDrunen (Oxford: Wiley Blackwell, 2018), 51.

47. John Patrick Donnelly, 'Calvinist Thomism,' *Viator* 7 (1976): 441. While Donnelly's work is the most influential source, other scholars have also identified the concept of Calvinistic Thomism. For instance, see Systma, 51; Frank A. James III, 'Peter Martyr Vermigli: At the Crossroads of Late Medieval Scholasticism, Christian Humanism and Resurgent Augustinianism,' in *Aquinas among the Protestants*, ed. Manfred Svensson and David VanDrunen (Oxford: Wiley Blackwell, 2018), 63. Likewise, Michael Allen and Craig Carter discuss and promote the tenets of Reformed Thomism. See Michael Allen, 'The Active and Contemplative Life: The Practice of Theology,' in *Aquinas among the Protestants*, ed. Manfred Svensson and David VanDrunen (Oxford: Wiley Blackwell, 2018), 190-203; Carter, *Contemplating God*. Richard Muller has also been influential in the promotion of this idea. See Richard A. Muller, *Post-Reformation Reformed Dogmatics: The Rise and Development of Reformed Orthodoxy, ca. 1520 to ca. 1725*, vol 3: *The Divine Essence and Attributes* (Grand Rapids: Baker Academic, 2003); and Richard A. Muller, *Divine Will and Human Choice: Freedom, Contingency, and Necessity in Early Modern Reformed Thought* (Grand Rapids: Baker Academic, 2017).

48. Donnelly, 'Calvinist Thomism,' 441. Examples of Protestant theological retrieval are plentiful in contemporary literature. For examples, see Michael Allen and Scott R. Swain, *Reformed Catholicity: The Promise of Retrieval for Theology and Biblical Interpretation* (Grand Rapids: Baker Academic, 2015); Michael Allen and Scott R. Swain, eds., *Christian Dogmatics: Reformed Theology for the Church Catholic* (Grand Rapids: Baker Academic, 2016); Carter, *Contemplating God*; Craig A. Carter, *Interpreting Scripture*

Manfred Svensson and David VanDrunen pinpoint three reasons why contemporary Protestants are motivated to retrieve the theology of Thomas. First, Protestants have gained, or rediscovered, an appreciation of their historical roots. Second, ecumenical conversations between Protestants and Roman Catholics have increased in recent memory. Third, and most pertinent to this current investigation, 'Christians of various confessions have looked for helpful resources to address the challenges of postmodernism and secularism,' which would include contemporary discussions of truth.[49] The rise of postmodernist theories of truth affects both Protestants and Catholics equally, as both share a heritage that assumed an objective and metaphysical definition of truth. In this sense, the rise of Reformed Thomism within evangelicalism may be an example of the popular phrase, 'The enemy of my enemy is my friend.'[50]

Likewise, the use of Thomas by Protestants to defeat philosophical or cultural foes is not novel. Reformed Scholastic Girolamo Zanchi referenced Thomas for similar reasons. Donnelly explains that Zanchi made use of Thomas 'because the standard scriptural arguments had been used and reused to the point that there was a stock answer to every proof text.'[51] Therefore, '[T]heological controversy in the later sixteenth century increasingly stressed showing the metaphysical absurdities and

---

with the Great Tradition: Recovering the Genius of Premodern Exegesis (Grand Rapids: Baker Academic, 2018); James E. Dolezal, *All That Is in God: Evangelical Theology and the Challenge of Classical Christian Theism* (Grand Rapids: Reformation Heritage Books, 2017); Dolezal, *God without Parts: Divine Simplicity and the Metaphysics of God's Absoluteness* (Eugene: Pickwick, 2011); Steven J. Duby, *Divine Simplicity: A Dogmatic Account*, ed. John Webster, Ian A. McFarland, and Ivor Davidson, T&T Clark Studies in Systematic Theology 30 (New York: T&T Clark, 2016); Steven J. Duby, *God in Himself: Scripture, Metaphysics, and the Task of Christian Theology*, Studies in Christian Doctrine and Scripture, (Downers Grove: IVP Academic, 2019); J. V. Fesko, *Reforming Apologetics: Retrieving the Classic Reformed Approach to Defending the Faith* (Grand Rapids: Baker Academic, 2019); Ortlund, *Theological Retrieval for Evangelicals*; Carl R. Trueman, *The Creedal Imperative* (Wheaton: Crossway, 2012).

49. Svensson and VanDrunen, 16.

50. 'Reformed Thomism' and Donnelly's 'Calvinist Thomism' are virtually synonymous. The point of both terms is to highlight the influence of Thomistic thought in the Reformed tradition following John Calvin. The phrase 'Reformed Thomism,' however, will be prioritized throughout this work to emphasize Thomas's general influence over various movements in Protestantism rather than limiting the movement to specific streams of Calvinism.

51. Donnelly, 'Calvinist Thomism,' 450.

ancient heresies implicit in an opponent's position.'[52] As such, there is precedent in the Protestant use of Thomas to examine significant cultural and philosophical presuppositions.

The need for theological retrieval to combat certain modern philosophical trends is made clear by Carter's earlier remarks concerning the 'rules' of modernity. Bruce D. Marshall offers a particularly insightful summation of modernity's theological project. In an effort to defend their right to believe religious doctrines while still maintaining modernity's epistemic expectations:

> Christian thinkers, both theologians and philosophers, have often attempted to respond to this challenge by taking over distinctively modern notions of truth and epistemic justification. Great intellectual ingenuity has gone into this effect. ... But it has persistently tended to yield unsatisfying results.[53]

Modern theologians have sought an 'approximate middle between giving up central Christian beliefs as false and failing to accept the epistemic demands of modernity.'[54] In other words, when theologians attempt to combine classical Christian doctrine with modern philosophical parameters, then the final product typically fails to meet the standards of either Christian theology or secular philosophy. This failure is not due to Christian doctrine's inability to meet the high standards of intellectual pursuits but because the epistemic tools that Christians are adopting were never intended to assess such metaphysical claims. As such, theologians will benefit from retrieving sources that predate the metaphysical–epistemological divide in order to evaluate doctrine within a more appropriate philosophical framework.[55]

To that end, we will seek to recover a Thomistic doctrine of God's independent omniscience, historically affirmed by Protestants, in order to construct a proper definition of 'metaphysical truth.' Specifically,

---

52. ibid.

53. Marshall, *Trinity and Truth*, 4.

54. ibid.

55. Hans Boersma, a major proponent of theological retrieval, refers to this metaphysical–epistemological divide as the tearing of a sacramental tapestry in which heaven and earth have been torn asunder. See Hans Boersma, *Heavenly Participation: The Weaving of a Sacramental Tapestry* (Grand Rapids: William B. Eerdmans Publishing Company, 2011). Boersma also looks to Thomas, among other premodern theologians, to help bridge the gap between metaphysics and epistemology.

I will argue that the Thomistic model of the divine intellect and the divine Ideas are the grounds of a participatory theory of truth in which creaturely truth is called such because of its participation in the First Truth, God Himself. In this way, the bridge between metaphysics and epistemology – truth – can be rediscovered to better suit the needs of Christian theology and overcome modernity's one-sided emphasis. It will be shown that novel forms of theism, henceforth referred to as 'theistic mutualism,' invite alternative models of truth into their systems because they have compromised divine transcendence by mapping dependence onto the divine intellect.

When the divine intellect is understood to be dependent upon external sources for the content of its knowledge, then the divinity–truth connection is ruptured and the metaphysical–epistemological divide is allowed to remain. It will be shown that a Thomistic model of the divine intellect necessitates that divine Truth be independent of creation but knowable by creatures through their grasp of the divine Ideas. The divine Ideas, then, link divine metaphysics with creaturely epistemology. Ironically, the best way to bridge the metaphysical–epistemological divide will be to rediscover and emphasize the divide between Creator and creature. As Etienne Gilson wrote, 'Today our only choice is not Kant or Descartes; it is rather Kant or Thomas Aquinas. All the other positions are but halfway houses on the roads which lead either to absolute religious agnosticism or to the natural theology of Christian metaphysics.'[56]

Classical Theism as Compared to Theistic Mutualism

The Creator-creature divide, which will be discussed at length in future chapters, is inseparably linked to the doctrine of aseity. Positively speaking, 'aseity' means that God is full of life, self-satisfied, and that He contains all perfections in Himself. Negatively speaking, 'aseity' means that God is without need and cannot receive anything He lacks. Divine independence, transcendence, and absoluteness are the defining characteristics of classical theism and are all extensions of divine aseity.

---

56. Gilson, Etienne. *God and Philosophy,* second edition (New Haven, CT: Yale University Press, 2002), 114.

The doctrines of aseity and transcendence as applied to the divine intellect must be retrieved. Indeed, before one can appreciate the diversity among the various models of God, one must first understand this key point of the classical definition. James Dolezal offers the following definition of 'classical theism':

> The approach of classical Christian theism is what one discovers in older Protestant confessions such as the Belgic Confession, Thirty-Nine Articles of Religion, Westminster Confession of Faith, and Second London Confession of Faith. This approach is basically in keeping with the view of God as found in the works of patristic and medieval Christian theologians such as Athanasius, Augustine, Anselm, and Aquinas. It is marked by a strong commitment to the doctrines of divine aseity, immutability, impassibility, simplicity, eternity, and the substantial unity of the divine persons. *The underlying and inviolable conviction is that God does not derive any aspect of His being from outside Himself and is not in any way caused to be.*[57]

Despite its roots in historical creeds and confessions, classical theism is met with increasing skepticism in contemporary theological conversations, especially as it concerns God's absolute independence.

Classical theism's portrayal of God and truth must be considered the standard understanding for both within Christianity despite claims to the contrary. Opponents, such as Clark Pinnock, prefer the term 'conventional theism' because '[t]he term "classical theism" is a recent neologism that conveys more respect than is deserved and implies more agreement among its exponents than there is.'[58] Pinnock, however, then spends the majority of his book explaining his view specifically in contrast to the claims of classical theism. Additionally, the term 'conventional theism' and other alternate titles still convey the reality that these claims have been typical, even normative, throughout church history.

It is true, however, that some evangelicals have preferred the term 'traditionalism' over 'classical theism.' For instance, Chad Owen Brand distinguishes traditionalism or 'traditional Christian orthodoxy' from classical theism in that traditionalism allows God to have a 'genuine relationship' with the world while maintaining God's

---

57. Dolezal, *All That Is in God*, 1; italics added. cf. Carter's definition, which reads, '[T]he historic, orthodox doctrine of God [as the] simple, immutable, eternal, self-existent, First Cause of the cosmos' (Carter, *Contemplating God*, 14).

58. Clark Pinnock, *The Most Moved Mover* (Grand Rapids: Baker Academic, 2001), 6n14.

immutability, whereas classical theism, in Brand's view, does not allow such relationship.[59] Much of the debate depends on how one defines 'genuine relationship,' and, as such, Brand's distinction between the two terms is not necessary. Indeed, classical theism has historically affirmed God's interaction with His creation, a point which Brand does not address in his description of traditionalism. Still, the point remains the same regardless of terminology – that which is classical is also conventional, which is also traditional, which should also be considered the standard.

Opposed to this standard, theological movements arose during the twentieth century that were defined by give-and-take relationships between God and His creatures. These alternative models of God emphasized the necessity of dependence on the Creator's side in order to protect a specific definition of genuine relationality.[60] The essential difference between classical theism and theistic mutualism is the extent to which the Creator is seen as affected by His creatures.

Classical theists hold 'to the absoluteness of God with respect to His existence, essence, and activity.'[61] Indeed, Herman Bavinck believes that aseity 'may be called the primary attribute of God's being.' Indeed, 'By this perfection he is at once essentially and absolutely distinct from all creatures.'[62] The Creator-creature distinction requires divine independence, and classical theists have affirmed this independence in all senses of the word, including how it pertains to the divine intellect. A further investigation of how theistic mutualism differs from classical theism in this regard will be the focus of Chapter 2.

---

59. See Chad Owen Brand, 'Orthodoxy and Open Theism and Their Connections to Western Philosophical Traditions,' in *Beyond the Bounds*, ed. John Piper, Justin Taylor, and Paul Kjoss Helseth (Wheaton: Crossway, 2003), 44n1.

60. For a summary on how World War II served as the impetus of such trends see Stanley J. Grenz and Roger E. Olson, *20th Century Theology: God and the World in a Transitional Age* (Downers Grove: InterVarsity Press, 1992), 170.

61. Dolezal, *All That Is in God*, 10.

62. Herman Bavinck, *Reformed Dogmatics* (Grand Rapids: Baker Academic, 2004), 2:124, 152. Note that Bavinck uses the terms 'aseity' and 'independence' almost interchangeably. While the context of the first quote is in relation to aseity, the context of the second quote further explains the interwoven relationship between the two concepts. 'While aseity only expresses God's self-sufficiency in his existence, independence has a broader sense and implies that God is independent in everything: in his existence, in his perfections, in his decrees, and in his works' (Bavinck, *RD*, 2:152).

Conclusion

God is the Truth, the whole Truth, and nothing but the Truth. The Old and New Testaments, a host of major historical Christian confessions, and even the works of secular philosophers affirm this reality. Regardless of how one defines 'truth' and 'God,' it is clear that the definition of one will affect one's understanding of the other. In order to better understand the divinity–truth connection, theologians should make use of theological retrieval – the examination of premodern texts in order to better address modern and postmodern theological and philosophical conundrums. Specifically, the Thomistic model of the divine intellect will be examined and seen to support a participatory theory of truth, which, in turn, helps to bridge the post-Enlightenment divide between metaphysics and epistemology. For now, Chapter 2 will further examine why theologians need to pursue theological retrieval by highlighting a few examples of theistic mutualism that rose in popularity throughout the latter half of the twentieth century. These new models of theism depict the divine intellect as dependent upon entities external to God, an option that classical theism firmly denies.

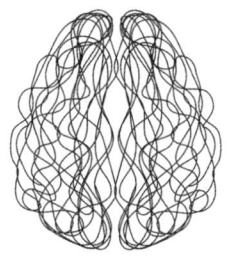

CHAPTER TWO

Truth and Divine Omniscience

Models of Omniscience

Chapter 1 argued that the rift between metaphysics and epistemology combined with contemporary models of God that collapse the Creator-creature distinction have obscured the proper relationship between divinity and truth. Furthermore, it was proposed that a retrieval of a Thomistic understanding of the divine intellect – one in which the content of God's knowledge is independent from creation – could serve as the basis of a participatory theory of truth. Now, we may compare the Thomistic articulation of divine omniscience with various models of the divine intellect within theistic mutualism. Theistic mutualism, though existing in various forms with a wide array of emphases, attributes dependence to God's omniscience. While a short synopsis of a premodern view of omniscience will be given in this chapter, a full definition of Thomas Aquinas's (Thomas's) portrayal of the divine intellect will be offered in Chapter 4.

In addition to discussing a few definitions of divine omniscience, this chapter will provide a broad overview of the most significant theories of truth in contemporary debate. Numerous models of metaphysical truth exist, but only the most popular will be defined: the correspondence theory, the coherentist theory, and the pragmatist theory. Additionally, this chapter will examine a novel approach to the problem of truth that has grown increasingly popular within the last few years, the post-truth theory. The participatory theory of truth, which does not fall neatly into any of the previously mentioned categories, will be addressed and explained in Chapter 5.

One important note should be kept in mind. This project is not a polemical nor a strictly philosophical endeavor. Rather than arguing against certain schools of thought, I will put forth a classical view of truth and let the merits of such a position stand on its own. Additionally, while there are numerous philosophical and epistemological strengths and weaknesses of the various models of truth, this work will focus on the relationship between truth and the doctrine of God. Whether a certain model is to be preferred in strictly philosophical terms over a separate model is best reserved for a different discussion. With this distinction in mind, the present discussion can turn to the various models of divine omniscience.

Omniscience in Classical Theism

As previously stated, classical theists believe that God does not derive any aspect of His being from His creation. In the classical model, God is *a se*, absolute, transcendent, and independent. He does not grow, change, or adapt. Furthermore, His divinity is marked by simplicity, meaning that God is without parts and that everything in God, is God.[1] God's knowledge, therefore, is not something He possesses but is the divine essence itself. God is His knowledge, and as such, if His knowledge undergoes change, then the divine essence undergoes change. This type of substantial change, in which a potentiality within the divine essence is actualized, is an impossibility within the bounds of classical theism. As such, it is impossible for God to learn or to even think discursively within the classical model.

---

1. The doctrine of divine simplicity, or DDS, has been a popular target of critique within theological and philosophical circles. Clark Pinnock, an open theist, who will be examined below, writes, 'Simplicity is, along with impassibility, one of the most alien of the Greek influenced attributes of God. It prevents us from adopting a social model of the Trinity and appreciating the dynamism of it' (Clark Pinnock, *Most Moved Mover* [Grand Rapids: Baker Academic, 2001], 84). For more information, see Alvin Plantinga, *Does God Have a Nature?* (Milwaukee, Marquette University Press, 1980); For a Reformed Thomistic defense of DDS in light of modern and postmodern critiques, see James Dolezal, *All That Is in God* (Grand Rapids: Reformation Heritage Books, 2017); James Dolezal, *God without Parts: Divine Simplicity and the Metaphysics of God's Absoluteness* (Eugene: Pickwick Publications, 2011); Steven J. Duby, *Divine Simplicity: A Dogmatic Account* (London: T&T Clark, 2016).

Thomas's position on this topic is clear. 'Since God's knowledge is his substance,' writes Thomas, 'his knowledge must be altogether invariable just as … his substance is altogether unchangeable' (Aquinas, *ST* 1.14.15). The relationship between simplicity and the divine intellect will be further expounded in future chapters, but it is clear at this point that, for Thomas, any change in the content of divine knowledge would constitute a substantial change and not an accidental change. God cannot learn, and the content of God's knowledge is eternally fixed. Furthermore, God's primary object of knowledge is not external to Himself, which would make Him dependent on creatures, but is instead His own divine nature. Again, Thomas is helpful. He writes, 'God's act of knowing, which is self-subsistent, is the knowing of itself, not a knowing of something else, which would involve proceeding *ad infinitum*' (Aquinas, *ST* 1.14.4 ad 2). Since God knows Himself exhaustively, He knows everything that He could do or has done. Therefore, God has exhaustive knowledge of His creatures without learning from creation. Thomas concludes:

> It is not the substance of the thing known that is the completion of the knower, but its likeness, by which it is in the intellect as the latter's form and completion: the stone is not in the soul, but its likeness, as we read in Aristotle. Things other than God are known by God *because his essence contains their likeness*, as we have just said. So it does not follow that something other than the essence of God is the completion of the divine intellect. (Aquinas, *ST* 1.14.5 ad 2)

It is essential to understand that classical theism, and specifically Thomas, teaches that the *a se* God is a completely independent divine intellect. God's exhaustive knowledge is not perfected in any way by creation because God's being is in no way perfected by creation. Truth, therefore, as the final end of all intellects, including the divine, must be grounded in the divine nature and not something external to God.

Omniscience in the Theologians of Hope

Theistic mutalists of various forms and flavors reject this full-fledged commitment to an independent divine intellect. These mutalists suggest that God's knowledge is relational in nature, and they reject the idea of God's independent omniscience. Craig Carter defines 'theistic mutualism':

The view that God and the world coexist in a two-way relationship in which each affects the other for good or for ill. This view is a type of post-Christian, neopaganism that is not the same as ancient mythological worldviews, but it shares one key point in common with them that makes it more like mythology than the biblical doctrine of God – namely, the rejection of transcendence. The soft version of this view, in which God sovereignly allows creation to cause change in him although he is not forced to do so, is increasingly popular among evangelical theologians, including conservative Reformed ones.[2]

James Dolezal distinguishes soft mutualism from hard mutualism. Dolezal writes, 'The harder sort regards God as a person who allows other beings to function as first causes or absolute originators of actions, events, or objects and who Himself stands as an onlooker within creation, susceptible to an increase in knowledge.'[3] While open theists and process theologians are typically seen as the chief representatives of this group, other movements and even some evangelical theologians also fall into this category. Softer theistic mutualists tend to reject the proposal that God learns from His creation, but they often suggest that 'God undergoes changes in relation and in those alleged intellectual and emotive states of His that are thought to correlate to His changing relations with creatures.'[4]

God's knowledge may be eternally fixed in these soft mutualistic models as a corollary of His eternity, for instance, but creation is still seen as the source of the divine knowledge. One evangelical proponent of theistic mutualism, John C. Peckham, prefers the term 'covenantal theism,' which he defines as 'descriptive of the covenantal God of Scripture envisioned in much traditional Christian worship and prayer – The God who acts in the world, intervenes, speaks, communes, and covenants with his people.'[5] According to Peckham, the modifier 'covenantal' 'conveys that God enters into real back-and-forth relationship with creatures but does so voluntarily, remaining transcendent even as he condescends to

---

2. Craig A. Carter, *Contemplating God with the Great Tradition: Recovering Trinitarian Classical Theism* (Grand Rapids: Baker Academic, 2021), 182.

3. Dolezal, *All That Is in God*, 3.

4. ibid.

5. John C. Peckham, *Divine Attributes: Knowing the Covenantal God of Scripture* (Grand Rapids: Baker Academic, 2021), 37.

be with us (immanent).'[6] In Peckham's model, divine immutability and impassibility must be qualified, but he claims that covenantal theism still upholds omniscience as well as aseity and self-sufficiency. While covenantal theologians, or 'theistic mutualists' as I will refer to them, may use the language of classical theism, the concepts they support are far removed from the classical understanding. The following brief survey of various forms of theistic mutualism will begin with one group of soft mutualists – the theologians of hope.

While they are neither open theists nor process theologians, Wolfhart Pannenberg and Stanley Grenz were two influential twentieth-century theistic mutualists. Both were highly inspired by Jürgen Moltmann's 'panentheism,' and yet both have had great influence in evangelicalism.[7] Pannenberg, for instance, served as Milliard Erickson's 'post-doctoral mentor,' and Erickson's systematic textbook, a staple in evangelical theological classrooms, was dedicated to Pannenberg.[8] Both Pannenberg and Grenz are good test cases for the current investigation, as both writers have expressed concern over the traditional doctrine of divine

---

6. Peckham, 37. Peckham's use of 'transcendence' communicates that God existed before the world, does not need the world for survival, and is entirely unique. Peckham, however, rejects the view of God as *actus purus* and is willing to follow a 'moderate classical theism' in support of a qualified Creator-creature distinction in which God's independence is voluntarily restricted in order to enter into a give-and-take relationship with His creatures (Peckham 2, 23, 42n11).

7. Moltmann's 'panentheism' represented the trend of divine dependence that took place over the twentieth century. Grenz and Olson write, 'A major key to understanding Moltmann's doctrine of God in its distinction from classical theism and process theology is his idea of God's *self-limitation*. Without question Moltmann posited a reciprocal relationship between God and the world. In his immanence God is in some way dependent on the world, although the world's dependence on God remains greater' (Stanley J. Grenz and Roger E. Olson, *20th Century Theology: God and the World in a Transitional Age* [Downers Grove: InterVarsity Press, 1992], 181). Moltmann writes, '*How do I experience God?* What does God mean for me? How am I determined by him? We must also ask the reverse questions: *how does God experience me?* What do I mean for God? How is he determined by me? Of course the relationship between God and man is not a reciprocal relationship between equals. But if it is not a one-sided relationship of causality and dependency either – if it is a relationship of covenant and love – then for man's experience of himself this question is not merely valid; it is actually necessary' (Jürgen Moltmann, *Trinity and the Kingdom* [Minneapolis: Fortress Press, 1993], 3-4).

8. See Millard J. Erickson, *Christian Theology*, 3rd ed. (Grand Rapids: Baker Academic, 2013). According to Pannenberg's endorsement of the book, the work 'constitutes an excellent example of the evangelical outlook on the Christian faith. ...' Pannenberg is a frequently cited source of inspiration throughout the book.

omniscience, to the point of redefining the doctrine, and they have clearly articulated their views concerning metaphysical truth.

Pannenberg believes that eternal comprehensive foreknowledge, often considered a necessary component of divine omniscience, prohibited libertarian human freedom according to which a person's acts are determined by himself apart from exterior causes.[9] Pannenberg writes, 'An almighty and omniscient being thought of as existing at the beginning of all temporal processes excludes freedom within the realm of his creation.'[10] In order to eliminate this controversy, Pannenberg does not specifically attack God's omniscience, nor His omnipotence, but rather His eternal existence and independence.[11] Pannenberg continues:

> An *existent* being acting with omnipotence and omniscience would make freedom impossible. But such a being would also not be God, because it could not be the reality which determines everything, for the reality of freedom, of human subjectivity, would remain outside its grasp. ... [I]f Christian theology is nowadays to think of God as the origin of human freedom, then it can no longer think of him as an existent being.[12]

Pannenberg does not intend to suggest, however, that God is not real or present. Rather, Pannenberg interprets both God and truth through an eschatological lens.[13] According to Pannenberg, then, God's divinity

---

9. 'In Pannenberg's view, a God who knows all things in advance of time or a God who fashions a plan for the world before time begins or *a God who is thought of as perfect and complete in himself at every point of past or present is a God who in the end leads to atheism,* for such a God renders the autonomy of man unthinkable.' (John O'Donnell, 'Pannenberg's Doctrine of God,' *Gregorianum* 72, no. 1 [1991]: 92). For an overview of the various views of free will from an evangelical perspective see Norman Geisler, 'Freedom, Free Will, and Determinism' in *Evangelical Dictionary of Theology,* second edition (Grand Rapids: Baker Academic, 2001), 467.

10. Wolfhart Pannenberg, 'Speaking about God in the face of Atheist Criticism,' in *The Idea of God and Human Freedom* (Philadelphia: Westminster Press, 1973), 108.

11. John O'Donnell writes, 'Thus, from the moment of creation God has placed himself in relation and therefore *he has made his divinity dependent* on his creation' (O'Donnell, 84). Pannenberg made the startling claim that 'in a restricted but important sense God does not yet exist' (Pannenberg, *The Idea of God and Human Freedom*, 53, 110).

12. Pannenberg, *The Idea of God and Human Freedom*, 109-10.

13. 'Whereas the past can always be thought of as formerly existent, as though the basis of its reality were that it was once existent, the future in particular seems to offer an alternative to an understanding of the real which is concentrated entirely upon what is existent. For what belongs to the future is not yet existent, and yet it already determines present experience, at least the present experience of beings who – like man – are oriented

will not be proven, nor truly established in full, until God's promises are accomplished in time.

The eschatological motif of Pannenberg's theology is a pillar of his systematic work. However, the question most pertinent to the present discussion is, 'How does Pannenberg uphold God's omniscience without compromising human freedom?' For Pannenberg, this balance is reached by limiting omniscience to its bare essentials. He writes, 'When we speak of God's knowledge we mean that nothing in all his creation escapes him. All things are present to him and are kept by him in his presence. This is not necessarily knowledge in the sense of what is meant by human knowledge and awareness.'[14] According to John O'Donnell, 'Pannenberg intends to interpret the language of divine intellect and will in a metaphorical way.'[15] Pannenberg believes that biblical passages describing God's intellect or will are anthropomorphisms and that readers should understand that God's knowledge simply means that nothing 'escapes [H]im' and that all things are 'present to [H]im.'[16] As such, 'divine omniscience' is nearly synonymous with 'God's omnipresence' and empirical in kind. All things are eternally present to God who correctly interprets and analyzes all external events before Him. The content of the divine intellect, therefore, is dependent on objects of

---

towards the future and always experience their present and past in the light of a future which they hope for or which they fear' (ibid., 110). Pannenberg continues, 'Thus the reality of the future and that of freedom belong together, by contrast with what exists here and now. Neither exist themselves, but they have power over what exists here and now' (ibid., 111). Again, compare this to Jürgen Moltmann who writes, 'The "future" must be considered as the mode of God's being.' (Jürgen Moltmann, 'Theology as Eschatology,' in *The Future of Hope, Theology as Eschatology*, ed. Frederick Herzog [New York: Herder & Herder, 1970], 10).

14. Wolfhart Pannenberg, *Systematic Theology* (Grand Rapids: William B. Eerdmans Publishing Company, 1991), 1:379-80.

15. O'Donnell, 89. Pannenberg's metaphorical understanding should not be confused with Thomas's use of analogical predication, which Pannenberg specifically denies. See Pannenberg, *Systematic Theology*, 1:344n14. Pannenberg later wrote, 'It is just as metaphorical to speak of the intellect of God as to call God the "rock" of our salvation or the "light" on our path, or to speak of the Word of God' (Pannenberg, *Systematic Theology*, 1:379).

16. O'Donnell, 90. Stanley Grenz supports this interpretation of Pannenberg's works. Grenz writes, 'Pannenberg offers a metaphorical understanding of the attributes of reason and will. God's knowing, or omniscience, he suggests, refers to the inescapable nature of the presence of God' (Stanley J. Grenz, *Reason for Hope: The Systematic Theology of Wolfhart Pannenberg*, 2nd ed. [Grand Rapids: William B. Eerdmans, 1990], 79).

knowledge external to the divine essence.[17] Creatures, in Pannenberg's view, must contribute to divine knowledge if any autonomy or freedom is to be granted to creation. The source of God's knowledge, then, resides in creation.

Stanley Grenz, a follower of Pannenberg, makes a similar argument based on the eschatological view of God. Grenz describes omniscience:

> The medieval theologians generally viewed [omniscience] in the abstract. For this reason, they debated whether God not only knew all actual but also all possible events. We have concluded, however, that the attributes are *relational terms*. Consequently, in declaring 'God is omniscient' we are not intending to make a claim concerning God's theoretical knowledge, but to affirm his perfect cognition of the world. God is cognizant of all things precisely because they are present to him immediately and as themselves.[18]

Omniscience, in this view, is thus not an abstract term describing the hypothetical content of God's theoretical knowledge but is instead a relational term. God knows all things because He stands in relation to all things as their Creator and sustainer. This relational aspect of God is critical to understanding Grenz's conception of the immanent Trinity as essentially social and communal. According to Grenz, 'The God we know is none other than the Triune One, the eternal community of Father, Son, and Holy Spirit, and consequently the God who is love. ... The God we know is internally and externally relational.'[19] Indeed, 'Because God is triune – the Father, Son, and Spirit in eternal

---

17. O'Donnell continues, 'For the relation between God and the world, this means that God lets the world be the world, hence be autonomous, but God embraces the world within his own infinite life. God is distinct from the world but not separate from it' (O'Donnell, 91). One can recognize the influence of Moltmann's panentheism in such a claim.

18. Stanley J. Grenz, *Theology for the Community of God* (Grand Rapids: William B. Eerdmans Publishing Company, 2000), 92.

19. Grenz, *Theology for the Community of God*, 27. Grenz's social Trinitarianism, which he specifically affirms in *Theology for the Community of God*, 78, is another example of Pannenberg's and Moltmann's influence (See Moltmann, *Trinity and the Kingdom*). For O'Donnell's description of Pannenberg's Trinitarianism, see O'Donnell, 87-88. Concerning Grenz's Trinitarianism, it is interesting to note that he specifically mentions Thomas as an example of Trinitarian decline: 'Thomas Aquinas, for example, was more interested in setting forth what could be deduced from the world concerning the one God who is its First Cause than delineating the finer points of the doctrine of the Trinity' (Grenz, *Theology for the Community of God*, 63).

relationship – our quest to speak of the being and attributes of God actually constitutes an attempt to characterize the relational nature of God – God in relationship.'[20] Grenz's relational emphasis, placed on the doctrine of the Trinity, led him to discount or deny God's thorough independence as seen through his denial of classical doctrines such as impassibility and immutability.[21] The key idea to notice is that divine omniscience for both Pannenberg and Grenz is dependent upon objects of knowledge external to God, whereas Thomism holds that the primary object of divine knowledge is the divine essence itself.

Soft Theistic Mutualism within Evangelicalism

Theistic mutualism is not limited to a bygone era. Indeed, many contemporary authors, even those who self-identify as evangelical, continue to argue for the dependence of the divine intellect. For example, Katherin Rogers follows an impressive survey of divine omniscience with an unexpected conclusion. After describing the classical arguments for an independent omniscience, Rogers nevertheless concludes, 'Our free choice *produces* God's knowledge of that choice. ... God's foreknowledge *depends* upon my actual choice.'[22] Considering that Rogers had previously defended the doctrine of divine simplicity in relationship to divine omniscience, it is difficult to see how Rogers can avoid the conclusion that creation has a profound causal effect on the divine essence and thus, in some way, contributes to the being of God.[23]

Evangelicals can also consider the project of Ronald Nash who sought a 'mediating concept of God [between Thomism and process theology] that would preserve the legitimate concerns while avoiding the most serious difficulties of both concepts of God.'[24] After suggesting that God's omniscience is tied to His power running through the free choices

---

20. Grenz, *Theology for the Community of God*, 77.

21. ibid., 91.

22. Katherin A. Rogers, *Perfect Being Theology*, Reason and Religion (Edinburgh: Edinburgh University Press, 2000), 86; emphasis added.

23. Rogers, 75.

24. Ronald H. Nash, *The Concept of God: An Exploration of Contemporary Difficulties with the Attributes of God* (Grand Rapids: Zondervan, 1993), 36. This goal is similar to the basis of John S. Feinberg's work on the doctrine of God, which also lends itself to theistic mutualism at times. See John S. Feinberg, *No One Like Him: The Doctrine of God*, Foundations of Evangelical Theology (Wheaton: Crossway, 2001).

of creatures, Nash writes, 'The Christian theist can recognize a sense in which even an immutable and perfect God can change. Human beings can make a difference to God.'[25] As such, even conservative theologians who attempt to uphold classical doctrines can still find themselves at a loss when describing the proper object of God's knowledge, thus lending themselves to the tone of theistic mutualism.[26] It is worth noting that Clark Pinnock, an open theist discussed below, lists Ronald Nash as an evangelical thinker who embraces a certain relationality within his doctrine of God while still attempting, unsuccessfully to Pinnock, to maintain a classical understanding of God's attributes. Pinnock also lists Millard Erickson, Norman Geisler, Bruce Ware, and Wayne Grudem as further examples.[27]

A contemporary evangelical advocate for theistic mutualism, or covenantal theism as he prefers, is John C. Peckham. Indeed, Peckham may very well represent the ideal evangelical version of theistic mutualism. While Peckham is unafraid to distance himself from the classical definitions of divine immutability, impassibility, and strict simplicity, he also claims that his version of theistic mutualism maintains many classical doctrines, including divine omniscience. Indeed, Peckham's

---

25. Nash, *The Concept of God*, 105.

26. Other examples could be included. Consider, for instance, the work of Bruce A. Ware who, even in his polemics against open theists, supports a modified version of classical doctrines. For examples of Ware modifying doctrines associated with God's radical independence, see Bruce A. Ware, *God's Lesser Glory: The Diminished God of Open Theism* (Wheaton: Crossway, 2000); Bruce A. Ware, 'Modified Calvinist Doctrine of God,' in *Perspectives on the Doctrine of God: Four Views* (Grand Rapids: B&H Academic, 2008), 76-120. Consider also Timothy George's description of omniscience, which is closely linked to the doctrine of omnipresence. See Timothy George, 'The Nature of God: Being, Attributes, and Acts,' in *Theology for the Church*, ed. Danny Akin (Nashville: B&H Academic, 2007), 176-241. George writes, 'God's omniscience … is a corollary of his *eternity*. … Everything is open and laid bare to his eyes, even those things which are yet to come into existence through the free actions of his creatures' (George, 231). In this view, God knows everything because He sees everything. God is omniscient because God has always been present. While it is certainly true that eternity and omniscience walk hand-in-hand, and this imagery reflects biblical language, this description *could* make it seem as if God is only omniscient because He is the perfect observer. God's knowledge, however, precedes the existence or free choices of His creatures. George's description of omniscience is distanced from Thomas who believes 'God sees everything in one, that is, *in himself*. … Hence he sees everything at once and not successively' (*ST* 1.14.7).

27. Clark Pinnock, *Most Moved Mover* (Grand Rapids: Baker Academic, 2001), 75-77.

most popular work includes a thoroughly biblical presentation of divine omniscience and a defense of God's exhaustive foreknowledge against open theists and process theologians.[28] However, Peckham's description of the divine intellect resembles other theistic mutualists more than the classical presentation.

Peckham affirms libertarian freedom, which is not in and of itself contrary to the Thomistic model of the divine intellect, and his arguments concerning necessity and contingency are in line with the Reformed Orthodox.[29] Peckham's rejection of divine simplicity, however, allows him to posit ideas about God that would have seemed foreign to the great tradition, despite the use of the same terminology.[30] In Peckham's covenantal theism, one source of divine knowledge would be the free acts of creatures; thus God's knowledge is dependent upon that which is external to Him. Indeed, Peckham does not offer any classical alternative to his viewpoints and seems to think that his model of the divine intellect is the conservative, evangelical, and classical model.[31] Molinism is a genuine option for Peckham, but he is unwilling to commit to any explanation concerning *how* God's knowledge operates in relation to human freedom and is rather content to affirm simply God's exhaustive knowledge and man's libertarian freedom in faith. Regardless, it is clear from his work that Peckham, an evangelical scholar supported by evangelical publishers and a regular presenter for the Evangelical Theological Society, believes that the divine intellect is dependent upon the acts of creatures despite his regular use of such classical theological terms as 'aseity,' 'self-sufficiency,' and 'transcendence.' Indeed, Peckham's model of the divine intellect would probably be intuitive to many evangelical laymen, and they likewise would assume that they were espousing the long-held classical model.

---

28. Peckham, 111-40.

29. Peckham, 128. Compare Peckham's argument with Richard A. Muller, *Divine Will and Human Choice: Freedom, Contingency, and Necessity in Early Modern Reformed Thought* (Grand Rapids: Baker Academic, 2017).

30. Peckham, 241.

31. See, for instance, ibid., 114. Peckham's research is thorough, and footnotes are plentiful in his work, but his chapter on omniscience only includes two references to classical thinkers. It seems unlikely that this is an oversight considering the depth of his research. Rather, it seems that he does not cite classical works because he believes he is arguing for the classical view in his own work.

Omniscience in Open Theism

Whereas some forms of theistic mutualism attempt to balance God's dependence with man's independence, other forms tilt the scales in man's favor. See, for instance, the words of Pinnock:

> God, in grace, grants humans significant freedom to cooperate with or work against God's will for their lives, and he enters into dynamic, give-and-take relationships with us. The Christian life involves a genuine interaction between God and human beings. ... *God takes risks in this give-and-take relationship*, yet he is endlessly resourceful and competent in working towards his ultimate goals. ... God does not control everything that happens. Rather, he is open to receiving input from his creatures.[32]

Possibly the two most popular forms of theistic mutualism are open theism, represented by such thinkers as Clark Pinnock and Gregory Boyd, and process theology, such as that promoted by John B. Cobb Jr. and Charles Hartshorne. Indeed, the push for divine dependence runs so deep throughout both of these movements that they are often conflated.[33]

Although the accusation is frequently lobbed in their direction, open theists reject the claim that they deny divine omniscience. Rather, they suggest that their argument concerns creation, as in what is knowable, rather than the Creator, the one who knows.[34] For an open theist, God

---

32. Clark Pinnock et al, *The Openness of God: A Biblical Challenge to the Traditional Understanding of God* (Downers Grove: InterVarsity Press, 1994), 7.

33. Both open theists and process theologians deny this familial relation. See, for instance, Gregory A. Boyd, *God of the Possible* (Grand Rapids: Baker Books, 2000), 31 and Gregory A. Boyd, 'The Open-Theism View,' in *Divine Foreknowledge: Four Views* (Downers Grove: IVP Academic, 2001), 43. Likewise, Timothy George offers a helpful qualification: 'Such thinkers [who advocate for the open view of God] are not pure process theologians, for they agree with the historic Christian tradition that God created the world out of nothing. They also say that God has exhaustive knowledge of all that has happened in the past and of everything that is going on now, including the motives and intentions of every human being' (George, 232). Regardless, it is undeniable that both qualify, and would identify, as theistic mutualists.

34. Boyd writes, 'Those who oppose the open view of God on the grounds that it compromises God's omniscience are simply misguided. The debate between the open and classical understandings of divine foreknowledge is completely a debate over the nature of the future. Is it exhaustively settled from all eternity, or is it partly open? *That* is the question at hand, nothing else' (Boyd, *God of the Possible*, 17). It is pertinent to note, however, that the open-theist description of omniscience requires a redefinition or denial of a plethora of classical doctrines such as immutability, impassibility, eternity, and simplicity. While their description of omniscience may focus on creation, it most certainly has profound implications on their doctrine of the Creator.

knows everything that is possible to know, but it is not possible for any being to know the future since it currently does not exist. Since God is not expected to know that which is unknowable, they argue that the open view maintains God's omniscience while affirming the total freedom of creatures. Unlike classical theists, then, open theists believe that God's knowledge is in a constant state of change, as He continually learns what His creatures freely choose to do.

This open view of the future does not mean that God is in a total state of ignorance concerning what is to come since, as Boyd explains, 'much of [the future], open theists concede, is settled ahead of time, either by God's predestining will or by existing earthly causes, but it is not *exhaustively* settled ahead of time.'[35] To argue for this partly opened future, Boyd points out several biblical motifs that suggest God reacts and adapts to new information. These motifs include God's regret over historical events, God's questions concerning the future, God's repeated surprise over the sin of Israel, God's repeated tests to determine the faithfulness of His people, and numerous examples of reversed divine intentions.[36] According to Boyd, if these motifs do not communicate a God reacting to previously unknown information, then it is unclear what they could possibly communicate.[37]

A critical component of open theism is a particular definition of divine love. Richard Rice believes that the open view of God is built on two basic convictions: 'love is the most important quality we attribute to God, and love is more than care and commitment; it involves being sensitive and responsive as well.'[38] Indeed, Rice continues, 'From a Christian perspective, *love* is the first and last word in the biblical

---

35. ibid., 15.

36. Boyd, *God of the Possible*, 53-87. For an evangelical and classical explanation of these motifs, see Steven J. Duby, '"For I Am God, Not a Man": Divine Repentance and the Creator-Creature Distinction,' *Journal of Theological Interpretation* 12, no. 2 (2018): 149-69.

37. Boyd writes, 'If this text [Jeremiah 26] does not teach that God may really change his mind, what would a text that *did* teach this say? ... If his saying "I may change my mind" in Scripture isn't enough to convince us that God may in fact change his mind, then nothing would be' (Boyd, 'The Open-Theism View,' 34).

38. Richard Rice, 'Biblical Support for a New Perspective,' in *The Openness of God: A Biblical Challenge to the Traditional Understanding of God* (Downers Grove: InterVarsity Press, 1994), 15.

portrait of God.'[39] Pinnock reiterates this idea by writing, 'Love is the very essence of His being. ... Love is more than an attribute; it is God's very nature.'[40] As such, love necessitates that God relinquish divine independence in order to have a dynamic relationship with His creation. By Pinnock's and Rice's definition, any other route results in a non-loving God.

In many ways, Pinnock's form of open theism is more extreme than Boyd's or Rice's view.[41] Pinnock writes, 'According to the openness model, God in grace sovereignly granted humans significant freedom to cooperate with or to work against God's will for their lives and to enter into dynamic, give-and-take relationships with himself.'[42] Furthermore, 'Personhood, relationality, and community are more central to our understanding of God than independence and control.'[43] Pinnock is also honest with the fact that reducing God's independence means raising the level of independence creatures have from their Creator.[44] God's knowledge, therefore, is dependent on a correct interpretation of creatures external to Himself. Pinnock makes that clear when he writes:

> God is not independent of the world in every sense. ... He is, therefore, dependent on it, at least in the sense of knowing about it. God takes account of what is happening in the world and responds appropriately.

---

39. ibid., 18. He continues still, 'Love is the essence of the divine reality, the basic source from which *all* of God's attributes arise. This means that the assertion *God is love* incorporates all there is to say about God' (ibid., 21).

40. Pinnock, *Most Moved Mover*, 81.

41. While much of Pinnock's work is comparative to Boyd's, Pinnock is willing to apply the openness hermeneutic to a greater number of biblical passages than Boyd. As a result, Pinnock is willing to suggest that God has a body, must be ignorant of the vast majority of the future rather than a small portion, and is frequently proven to be mistaken through incorrect prophecies. For Pinnock's explanation of unfulfilled prophecy, see Pinnock, *Most Moved Mover*, 51n66-67.

42. ibid., 5. It should also be noted that Pinnock sees significant similarities between the openness model and the theologians of hope in that both 'recognize a God who limits himself in creating a world which has the capacity to affect him without his losing his lordship over it' (ibid., 12). Similar to Grenz, Pinnock believes that Thomas contributed to doctrinal decline by building his theology on a pagan inheritance. See ibid., 70-72.

43. ibid., 29.

44. ibid., 29. Pinnock writes elsewhere, 'The world is dependent on God but God has also, voluntarily, made himself dependent on it in some important respects' (ibid., 31).

Thus, in a sense, God is dependent on the world for information about the world. … New information flows in, and God takes account of it.[45]

The open view of the divine intellect, then, is just as dependent upon creation as a human intellect.

Omniscience in Process Theology

Process theologians depart most radically from classical theism. For them, God's being is marked by ontological dependence on creation. The world needs God to exist, and God needs the world to exist. 'In process thought,' writes Royce Gordon Gruenler, 'there is no social Trinity of Father, Son, and Holy Spirit apart from our world, as Christian orthodoxy has taught from earliest times; rather, God has no real existence apart from us and the extensive continuum of finite entities in the universe that are independent of him.'[46] Likewise, an independent omniscience separated from a give-and-take relationship is presented within process theology as an oxymoron. Douglas Pratt explains:

> Omniscience is indicative of the immanent relationality of God. Knowledge involves necessary mutual interrelationship. Omniscience, in other words, is a function of God's immanence: it implies supreme relational presence to all of reality. In [Charles] Hartshorne's understanding, God's omniscience signifies cognitive relationality, as a constitutive ontological element of deity.[47]

Charles Hartshorne, like Grenz and Pinnock, believes that the theologians of the Middle Ages overstate the abstract and exhaustive qualities of

---

45. Clark Pinnock, 'God Limits His Knowledge,' in *Predestination and Free Will: Four Views* (Downers Grove: IVP Academic, 1986), 147. Pinnock did not choose the title of this chapter and has elsewhere expressed displeasure at the editor's choice. Pinnock does not believe that God limits His knowledge because the only things God does not know are ontologically unknowable. God could not know the future free choices of His creatures even if He desired to do so.

46. Royce Gordon Gruenler, *The Inexhaustible God: Biblical Faith and the Challenge of Process Theism* (Eugene: Wipf & Stock, 1983), 7. He continues to explain, 'God needs the world and his power is not sovereign but only persuasive' (Gruenler, 10). At the time of writing, Gruenler was a 'recovering' process theologian. His ideas concerning social Trinitarianism do not reflect the views of classical theism expressed throughout this project but rather suggest a holdover from his previous theological tendencies. It is also worth noting that Gruenler thanks Pinnock for offering valuable suggestions on the book's original manuscript (Gruenler, 12).

47. Douglas Pratt, 'Charles Hartshorne on Theological Mistakes,' *Colloquium* 26, no. 1 (1994): 63-64.

divine omniscience.[48] For process theologians like Hartshorne, random chance is an undeniable aspect of life that is completely unpredictable by man or God.[49] Divinity is not marked by sovereignty or control but the ability to direct random chance to beneficial ends, which God sometimes accomplishes and sometimes fails to accomplish. The free action of humans 'enriches the divine life' by providing the building blocks of creative freedom.[50] Rather than defining omniscience by exhaustive knowledge, Hartshorne argues that the term applies to God because He knows *more* than any other being could possibly know.[51]

Fellow process theologian, and follower of Hartshorne, John B. Cobb sounds very similar to the mutualists previously described. He roots divine omniscience in God's ability to correctly interpret a reality external to Himself. Cobb writes, 'I cannot understand how there can be truth beyond the multiplicity of perspectives except as there is an inclusive and adequate perspective. The error in my perspective is its deviation from that perspective. I understand that perspective to be final, unsurpassable, truth. I call it God.'[52] Divinity, however, is not a requirement for omniscience, as Cobb admits that 'Buddha might do as well as God.'[53] Simplicity, causation, and omnipotence play no role in Cobb's model of omniscience. Rather, all that a being needs to be

---

48. Charles Hartshorne, *Omnipotence and Other Theological Mistakes* (Albany: State University of New York Press, 1984), 3.

49. 'Since any possible world, other than an utterly dead one (if that even makes sense, and some of us doubt it), must involve a multiplicity of individuals each making its own decisions, it follows (though for two thousand years it was not considered proper to say so) that there is an aspect of real *chance* in what happens. Aristotle and Epicurus knew this, and Plato implied it. But classical theism, supported by the Stoics among the Greeks, held that chance is merely a word for our ignorance of the ways of God. ... The new idea is that causal order is not absolute but statistical. It admits an element of chance or randomness in nature. Many of the leading physicists of recent times are quite explicit about this. But they were preceded in principle by some great Greek philosophers, some French philosophers of modern times, and the three most distinguished of purely American philosophers, Charles Peirce, William James and John Dewey' (ibid., 15-16). It should not be overlooked that the three American philosophers listed by Hartshorne are often portrayed as the fathers of American pragmatism.

50. ibid., 27.

51. ibid.

52. John B. Cobb Jr., 'Ultimate Reality: A Christian View,' *Buddhist-Christian Studies* 8 (1988): 55.

53. ibid.

omniscient is the correct perspective of an impressive amount of external data. This view of divine omniscience would, if true, make the content of divine knowledge dependent on the actions of creatures.

Evangelicals may not recognize the names associated with process theology, but the concepts these men taught may feel familiar. Certain evangelical authors promote forms of divine process while explicitly rejecting the process theology movement. John Frame, for instance, acknowledged that, 'My approach bears a superficial resemblance to process theology, which *also* recognizes two modes of existence in God, transcendent and immanent, sometimes called the "primordial" and "consequent" natures of God.'[54] Granted, Frame only acknowledges a superficial resemblance to the movement, and Frame is clear that he rejects process theology. Still, the passing resemblance may foster an ecumenism between the two camps.

A Broad Overview of Truth

Classical theists do not hold a monopoly on theism. Theistic mutualism grew in influence over the span of the twentieth century and has continued to have a foothold in modern and postmodern theological debates. Changes to theology proper, however, do not occur in a vacuum. Once God is deemed dependent on the created order, then the natural world is seen in a different light. If we, as good Websterians, believe that theology is the 'study of God and all things in relation to God,' then a shift in our understanding of God will affect our understanding of 'all things.'

In light of the divinity–truth connection, it is not surprising that a variety of theistic models has been accompanied by a variety of truth theories. Neither a common definition of God nor truth can be assumed, and while this may have always been the case, the reality of this assertion has been amplified during the nineteenth and twentieth centuries. It is helpful at this juncture to provide a general framework for a few models of truth most popularly adopted in our changing theological context. This survey will focus on four theories: correspondence, coherentism, pragmatism, and post-truth theory, and the preferred model – participatory theory of truth – will be examined in greater depth in a later chapter.

---

54. John Frame, *Doctrine of God*, 572.

The Correspondence Theory of Truth

Truth is a primary concern for epistemologists because the traditional definition of knowledge has been 'justified *true* belief.'[55] In order for a belief to be considered knowledge, it must not only meet certain standards of epistemic justification but also must possess the characteristic of being true.[56] Often times, however, one's definition of truth is assumed rather than rationally defended. Truth is accepted as intuitive for most people, and the definition of 'truth' is frequently assumed to be self-evident. Nonetheless, it has become increasingly clear that assumed definitions of truth vary greatly, even within the same cultural, philosophical, or theological community.

James Emery White has highlighted some significant views of truth drawn from twentieth-century evangelicalism's brightest minds, including Francis Schaeffer and Carl F. H. Henry. As a result of his study, White concludes that the majority of evangelical voices have championed a correspondence theory of truth. This theory describes that which is true as that which corresponds to reality.[57] Likewise, D. K. Clark, writing from an evangelical perspective, explains, 'The word *truth* denotes something that conforms to actuality, is faithful

---

55. Even though this definition of knowledge can be traced back to Plato, its comprehensiveness has been challenged recently by epistemologists. The philosopher Edmund Gettier gained notoriety by questioning the traditional definition of knowledge in an article entitled 'Is Justified True Belief Knowledge?' The effects of this three-page article are still being felt within the field of epistemology as philosophers attempt to answer the difficult questions posed by Gettier. The conclusion is that knowledge must be at least justified true belief, but additional factors must be considered to account for coincidental knowledge and truth-making conditions. As such, the traditional definition of knowledge as justified true belief still provides a necessary foundation, even if it must be supplemented. Justified true belief is often the assumed definition of knowledge within evangelical circles and will be used throughout this paper. For more information, see Edmund Gettier, 'Is Justified True Belief Knowledge?' http://fitelson.org/proseminar/gettier.pdf; originally published in *Analysis* 23, no. 6 (1963): 121-23.

56. For an introductory premier on 'justified true belief,' or JTB, see James K. Dew Jr. and Mark W. Foreman, *How Do We Know? An Introduction to Epistemology* (Downers Grove: IVP Academic, 2014), 20-30.

57. James Emery White, *What Is Truth? A Comparative Study of the Positions of Cornelius Van Til, Francis Schaeffer, Carl F. H. Henry, Donald Bloesch, and Millard Erickson* (Eugene: Wipf & Stock, 1994), 1, 33, 206. Simon Blackburn notes, 'The first natural thing to say about true beliefs is that, like portraits or maps, they too should correspond with something. They should correspond with the facts – the way the world is' (Simon Blackburn, *On Truth* [Oxford: Oxford University Press, 2018], 17).

to a standard, or involves sincerity or integrity. The ground for truth is reality itself.'[58] Notice that Clark specifically cites 'reality' as the ground for truth. A true statement, according to the traditional understanding of the correspondence theory, is one that captures the nature of objective reality. This definition, however, can be affirmed without any belief in theism, due to the vagueness of what constitutes reality. Indeed, it could be used to argue for the divine intellectual dependence promoted by theistic mutualism. If God wants to say something true, then He must make sure His thoughts conform to the external data.

This theory of truth is not limited to evangelicalism and has been supported for millennia. It was Aristotle who wrote, 'To say of what is that it is, or of what is not that it is not, is true.'[59] Likewise, men such as James Barr recognize the correspondence theory of truth as a necessary presupposition of conservative biblical exegesis.[60] In White's estimation, the correspondence theory of truth is the presupposed force behind watershed evangelical doctrines such as inerrancy and inspiration. Indeed, even though this view is the mainstream understanding of truth, White even suggests that 'this theory gives Evangelical theology much of its distinctiveness.'[61]

There is much to be applauded about the correspondence theory of truth, and the participatory theory is largely similar, but the correspondence theory is incomplete without a proper theological basis. The main difference between the participatory account and the correspondence view is that in the former objective reality is explicitly defined through the lens of God's ultimate causation and independence. Once that theological presupposition is affirmed, then a correspondence between thought and external world can function accordingly. Otherwise, the correspondence theory could serve to widen

---

58. D. K. Clark, 'Truth,' *Evangelical Dictionary of Theology*, 2nd ed., ed. Walter A. Elwell (Grand Rapids: Baker Academic, 2001), 1219. It is noteworthy that the first sentence concerning 'truth' within the leading evangelical dictionary promotes the correspondence theory of truth as an absolute fact.

59. Aristotle, *Metaphysics*, in *The Complete Works of Aristotle*, ed. Jonathan Barnes (Princeton, NJ: Princeton University Press, 1984), 4.7.1011b.25-28, 1597. See Blackburn, *On Truth*, 17; Lee McIntyre, *Post-Truth*, The MIT Press Essential Knowledge Series (Cambridge, MA: MIT Press, 2018), 7.

60. James Barr, *Fundamentalism* (Philadelphia, PA: Westminster, 1978), 40-55.

61. White, 35.

the metaphysical–epistemological divide. Classical theism, therefore, offers an improvement on the correspondence theory without rejecting it altogether.

Coherentism

Philosophical shifts following the work of Immanuel Kant have prompted some thinkers to reject the basis of the correspondence theory. If a man's thoughts only reveal his experience of the world rather than the world as it is in itself, then there is no way to know if his experience truly corresponds to reality.[62] The metaphysical–epistemological divide, then, requires new models of truth that better reflect humanity's relation to the natural world. Indeed, even some Christians, especially those who espouse theistic mutualism, are offering new suggestions for a proper definition of truth. The following survey highlights two theories that are potential Christian alternatives to the correspondence theory – coherentism and pragmatism – and one relatively new theory that has yet to be Christianized – post-truth theory.

The first alternative view of truth that will be considered is the coherentist perspective. After rejecting theories of knowledge linked to the Enlightenment, some Christians have adopted post-foundationalism, a theory of knowledge that rejects the idea of a foundational belief on which all other beliefs are built.[63] Instead of viewing knowledge as a building erected on a foundation of primary epistemic beliefs, these Christians understand the nature of knowledge to be an interconnected web of beliefs. The entirety of one's interconnected system of beliefs is understood to be ontological truth.[64] Within this model, justification of a belief is dependent on how well a new truth claim fits into an individual's overall system of belief. Of course, this 'fitting' includes avoiding contradictions, but coherentism involves more than mere conflict aversion. Rather, the system as a whole, full of interconnected

---

62. Some thinkers have moved away from the correspondence theory of truth because they believe the correspondence theory is 'pernicious, insinuating a false picture of the way the mind relates to the world' (Blackburn, *On Truth*, 23).

63. Compare this to Thomas's understanding of theology as *scientia* – 'the discovery of reasons in light of first truths that are necessary.' See Rik Van Nieuwenhove, *An Introduction to Medieval Theology*, 2nd ed. (Cambridge: Cambridge University Press, 2022), 267-68; Aquinas, *ST* 1.1.2.

64. Blackburn, *On Truth*, 27.

beliefs, should possess logical implications and explanatory power of the world. This system sets all beliefs on equal footing and defines 'truth' in regard to how well accepted propositions relate to one another. Alan White describes the coherentist view of truth as follows:

> [T]o say that a statement (usually called a judgment) is true or false is to say that it coheres or fails to cohere with a system of other statements; that it is a member of a system whose elements are related to each other by ties of logical implication as the elements in a system of pure mathematics are related.[65]

This theory can apply both to individual systems of belief as well as corporate schools of thought. On one hand, coherentists could compare views such as theism and naturalism and evaluate their truth claims based on internal logical consistency and external explanatory power. The school of thought that proves to be the most coherent would have epistemic justification in claiming truth. Likewise, individuals may use coherentism to test their individual system of belief. When a person encounters a new propositional truth statement, he is not required to conduct extensive research before being epistemically justified as accepting the statement as true. Rather, if a statement logically coheres with his current epistemic web of belief, and if it offers explanatory power in his personal context, that individual is justified for including the statement into his system. If a new 'judgment' makes sense within one's system, then that judgment is the truth.[66] In this sense, various complete systems of thought, including those that contradict one another, can all be considered the truth. Indeed, within this model, many communities, and even many individuals within these communities, can possess their own truth.

Pragmatism

A further alternative truth theory used by post-foundational theists is pragmatism. While pragmatism is colloquially known for viewing the truth as 'that which works,' the technical definition is more nuanced.

---

65. Alan R. White, 'Coherence Theory of Truth,' in *Encyclopedia of Philosophy*, ed. Paul Edwards (New York: Macmillan, 1967), 1:130; originally discovered in W. Jay Wood, *Epistemology: Becoming Intellectually Virtuous*, Contours of Christian Philosophy, ed. C. Stephen Evans (Downers Grove: IVP Academic, 1998), 117.

66. It should be noted that some coherentists reserve the term 'truth' as the 'real truth belonged not to individual beliefs but only to the interlocking, godlike "whole truth" that we shall never obtain' (Blackburn, *On Truth*, 28).

Pragmatists such as Charles Sanders Peirce and Williams James believe that 'truth' should be defined as that which advances factual inquiry and promotes academic investigation. 'The opinion which is fated to be ultimately agreed to by all who investigate,' writes Peirce, 'is what we mean by the truth, and the object represented in this opinion is the real.'[67] For William James, this means that '[t]he truth of an idea is not a stagnant property inherent in it. Truth *happens* to an idea. It *becomes* true, is *made* true by events.'[68]

Inherent in both pragmatism and coherentism is the subtle belief that ultimate reality is unknowable or, at least, unprovable.[69] If human beings are incapable of escaping their cultural interpretive lenses, then a correspondence theory of truth does not offer any practical value. It is meaningless to require truth to reflect reality if human beings cannot justifiably know reality. The concept of timeless, rational principles that are true for all people, in all cultures, throughout all of history free from cultural presuppositions and biases is seen as archaic at best, if not completely naïve and pernicious. This mistrust of truth's attainability has led some to abandon the search for genuine truth altogether, resulting in the idea known as post-truth theory.

Post-Truth Theory

'Post-truth' is defined as 'relating to or denoting circumstances in which objective facts are less influential in shaping public opinion than appeals to emotion and personal belief.'[70] In the political realm, this term has become associated with phrases such as 'alternative facts' and 'fake news.' Adam McDuffie recalls an illuminating CNN interview with Newt Gingrich. McDuffie describes:

---

67. Charles Sanders Peirce, 'How to Make Our Ideas Clear,' in *Selected Writings (Values in a Universe of Chance)*, ed. Philip P. Wiener (New York: Dover, 1958), 133.

68. William James, *Pragmatism: A New Name for Some Old Ways of Thinking*, repr. ed. (New York: Longmans, Green and Col., 1928), 218.

69. 'If we can know fact only through the medium of our own ideas, the original forever eludes us' (Brand Blanshard, *The Nature of Thought* [London: Allen & Unwin, 1939], 2:268). Henri Renard referred to the idea that ultimate reality is unknowable as the 'shipwreck of all knowledge' (Henri Renard, *The Philosophy of Being* (Milwaukee, WI: The Bruce Publishing Company, 1947), 8.

70. Oxford Languages, 'Word of the Year 2016' accessed February 6, 2020, https://languages.oup.com/word-of-the-year/2016/

When pressed on statistics pointing to a nationwide decline in crime, Gingrich dismissed them as unrepresentative of the feeling of Americans. He argued that 'the average American ... does not think crime is down,' and rejected the statistics outright, saying that he would 'go with what people feel' over the arguments of 'theoreticians.'[71]

When pushed, Gingrich referred to the statistics as the 'view' of the interviewer and, while admitting the data may be theoretically correct, denied that it was 'where human beings are.'[72] Shortly after the 2016 election of President Donald Trump, the *Oxford Dictionary* announced 'post-truth' as its word of the year.

According to several truth theorists, postmodern academics have initiated the post-truth age.[73] While 'fake news' has supposedly existed longer than journalistic news, terms like 'alternative facts' are becoming increasingly common.[74] If interpretation is limited to the linguistic boundaries of a community, then no one narrative can transcend its local context.[75] All narratives thus receive equal treatment and are judged

---

71. Adam McDuffie, 'Searching for Truth in a Post-Truth World: The Southern Baptist Schism as Case Study in the Power of Narrative for the Construction of Truth,' *Baptist History and Heritage* 52, no. 2 (2017): 75. The interview can be accessed at https://www. cnn.com/videos/tv/2016/12/01/gingrich-camerota-crime-stats-newday.cnn. Gingrich states that 'as a politician, I will go with how people feel.' McDuffie is also helpful when he points out that Gingrich's use of 'theoreticians' in opposition of the feeling of the general public is another subtle attack against the relevancy of statistical data.

72. A transcript of Gingrich's conversation can be found in McIntyre, 3-4.

73. McIntyre, 123. Post-truth theory, while rooted in philosophical postmodernism, is frequently discussed within the political realm. Recently, *The Atlantic* has even referred to the 2020 Republican National Convention as the 'post-truth convention.' See McKay Coppins, 'A Carnival of Disinformation: Republicans Warmly Welcomed Voters into Their Post-Truth Convention,' *The Atlantic*, August 28, 2020, https://www.theatlantic. com/ politics/archive/2020/08/ trumps-rnc-was-loaded-disinformation/615838/.

74. On the claim that fake news predates objectively verified 'news,' see Jacob Soll, 'The Long and Brutal History of Fake News,' *Politico Magazine*, December 18, 2016, https:// www.politico.com/magazine/story/2016/12/fake-news-history-long-violent-214535. Soll writes, 'Fake news took off at the same time that news began to circulate widely, after Johannes Gutenberg invented the printing press in 1439. "Real" news was hard to verify in that era. There were plenty of news sources – from official publications by political and religious authorities, to eyewitness accounts from sailors and merchants – but no concept of journalistic ethics or objectivity.'

75. Michiko Kakutani, *The Death of Truth* (New York: Tim Duggan Books, 2018), 47-48. See also McIntyre, 123-150. McIntyre dedicates an entire chapter to the postmodern roots of the post-truth age, which concludes with him naming postmodernism as the 'godfather of post-truth' (McIntyre, 150).

by the cultural influence of their adherents.[76] For many, this equality among narratives means that a scientific fact is no longer a universal truth but is just one narrative offered by one community, scientists, who are limited by their own internal biases, historical positioning, and cultural lenses. The real question is not whether a scientific narrative is true, but rather if it wields power and influence.

This post-truth age is marked by a rise of what Harry G. Frankfurt refers to as bull****. Frankfurt defines the essence of bull**** as the 'indifference to how things really are.'[77] With the rise of a contextualized understanding of knowledge comes individuals who are simply 'unconnected to a concern with the truth.'[78] These individuals may not be malicious, and their assertions may even be correct.[79] Instead of mal-intent, the chief characteristic of these individuals is that they simply do not consider, nor care, whether their views represent reality. According to Frankfurt, '[A bull******] does not care whether the things he says describe reality correctly. He just picks them out, or makes them up, to suit his purpose.'[80] Whereas a liar must respect the truth in some regard, as he hopes that his lie will cohere with the overall body of knowledge, a bull******* is free to proceed with his narrative despite numerous proven contradictions. It does not matter if he is right; it only matters if he wins.

While the will to ignore truth for personal gain is not a new idea, there now exists a philosophical platform for this general mindset. If mankind cannot know reality other than through the defining narratives of their communities, then it cannot be determined whether statements

---

76. One side effect of this supposed equality is what Tom Nichols calls the 'death of expertise.' In a post-truth age, experts are seen as villains who pompously reject the narrative of the uninformed, even though all opinions are supposedly equally valid. See Tom Nichols, *The Death of Expertise: The Campaign against Established Knowledge and Why It Matters* (Oxford: Oxford University Press, 2017).

77. Harry G. Frankfurt, *On Bull**** (Princeton, NJ: Princeton University Press, 2005), 34. Blackburn offers a succinct summary of a post-truth culture: 'A post-shame environment would imply a post-trustworthy environment, which would in turn lead to a post-trust environment' (Blackburn, *On Truth*, 8). Likewise, McIntrye writes, 'The prefix "post" is meant to indicate not so much the idea that we are "past" truth in a temporal sense (as in "postwar") but in the sense that truth has been eclipsed – that it is irrelevant' (McIntyre, 5).

78. Frankfurt, 30.

79. ibid., 47-48.

80. ibid., 56.

reflect objective reality or not. Indeed, the subjective narrative may come to constitute reality itself.[81] As such, the concept of truth is not opposed, nor rebelled against, but entirely ignored as a fictitious entity. It is no wonder that Frankfurt concludes that this movement is 'a greater enemy of the truth than lies are.'[82]

The Various Models of God and Metaphysical Truth

A Thomistic view of God's independent omniscience is the surest guarantee for the existence and knowability of metaphysical truth. However, in their attempt to emphasize God's relationality and dependence on the free action of creatures, various theologians inadvertently compromise the ground of truth itself. Some alternative voices actively and admittedly redefine truth, often embracing the alternative views mentioned above. Other theistic mutualists attempt to maintain the correspondence theory in spite of their novel depictions of God, but then fall victim to philosophical critique. Thomas's model of divine omniscience, however, grounded in God's simple essence and independence, provides Protestants with a sure defense against the abandonment of objective metaphysical truth.

Theistic Mutualism and a Redefinition of Truth

The alternative models of God are not monolithic and neither are their views of truth. Holding to a non-classical view of God does not necessarily mean that one will hold to a coherentist or pragmatic view of metaphysical truth. However, some theistic mutualists indeed opt for a postmodern definition of truth that better aligns with their view of God. For instance, Pannenberg is well-known for his acceptance of the coherentist view of truth. In fact, Grenz concludes, 'Perhaps no theologian has exemplified more clearly the application to theology

---

81. McIntyre writes, 'Post-truth also exists in an even more virulent form. This is when self-deception and delusion are involved and someone actually believes an untruth that virtually all credible sources would dispute. In its purest form, post-truth is when one thinks that the crowd's reaction actually does change the facts about a lie' (McIntyre, 9).

82. Frankfurt, 61. For more information on bull****, see Evan Davis, *Post-Truth: Why We Have Reached Peak Bull**** and What We Can Do about It* (Boston: Little, Brown, & Company, 2017) and James Ball, *Post-Truth: How Bull**** Conquered the World* (London: Biteback, 2018).

of the noncorrespondence epistemological theories of the modern coherentists and pragmatists than Wolfhart Pannenberg.[83]

Pannenberg believes that God must be the unifying aspect of all meaning. If all creation is unified in God, then truth's distinguishing characteristic must be internal coherence. If all things are unified in God, then contradiction is the chief opponent of human knowledge. Pannenberg writes:

> The proof and confirmation [of dogmatics] come chiefly by way of the form of systematic presentation itself as a connection is shown between the various Christian doctrinal statements and also between these statements and whatever else is regarded as true. ... Claiming that the content of Christian doctrine is true in detail, proclamation implicitly presupposes its inner coherence and its coherence with all that is true. ... The systematic investigation and presentation itself entails also a very specific understanding of truth, namely, *truth as coherence*, as the mutual agreement of all that is true. Systematic theology ascertains the truth of Christian doctrine by investigation and presentation of its coherence as regards both the interrelation of the parts and the relation to other knowledge.[84]

This coherentist understanding of truth was adopted by Pannenberg's follower Grenz. He writes, '[C]ontemporary philosophers remind us that knowledge is not a collection of isolated factual statements arising directly from first principles. Rather, our beliefs form a system in which each belief is supported by its neighbors and, ultimately, by its presence within the whole.'[85] Grenz continues, 'We ought to view Christian doctrine as comprising a "web of belief" and see theology, in turn, as the exploration of Christian doctrine viewed as an interrelated, unified whole.'[86] After comparing knowledge to a mosaic rather than a 'collection of beads on a string,' Grenz encourages his readers to reconstruct the world by moving to a 'communitarian theological method.'[87]

---

83. Stanley J. Grenz, *Beyond Foundationalism: Shaping Theology in a Postmodern Context* (Louisville: Westminster John Knox Press, 2001), 43.

84. Pannenberg, *Systematic Theology*, 1:18-22.

85. Stanley J. Grenz, 'Beyond Foundationalism: Is a Nonfoundationalist Evangelical Theology Possible?,' *Christian Scholar's Review* 30, no. 1 (2000): 78.

86. Grenz, 'Beyond Foundationalism,' 78.

87. ibid., 78-79.

While Grenz acknowledges that objective reality exists outside of local communities, he denies the possibility of knowing reality 'as it is.'[88] Instead, Christians may only interpret reality through the lens of their immediate culture. 'The simple fact is,' Grenz writes, 'we do not inhabit the "world-in-itself"; instead, we live in a linguistic world of our own making.'[89] Just as a proposition's truth can only be determined in its context, so can doctrine only be affirmed or denied within a local religious community. In this way, Grenz follows another one of his mentors, George Lindbeck, and compares doctrines to rules of grammar. To ask whether the rules of grammar are 'true' or 'false' 'involves a fundamental misunderstanding of the type of proposition the rule in fact is. It entails ripping the assertion out of its context and treating it apart from its regulative role within the language itself.'[90] Likewise, in a coherentist model of truth, doctrinal truth claims should be evaluated based on their context within a local community's web of belief and their effectiveness in bringing about God's eschatological kingdom.[91]

Other mutualistic voices, such as Hartshorne, subscribe to a pragmatic model of truth. Hartshorne frequently cited American pragmatists such as James, Peirce, and Dewey, and he shared a special relationship with one of the more influential American pragmatists in recent memory, Richard Rorty.[92] Hartshorne writes,

> I entirely agree with pragmatists that a philosophy or theology that *cannot be lived by* is not acceptable. James was also right, again in agreement with Peirce, in rejecting causal determinism. Not only is it unprovable, there is no good reason to hope it is true. Predicting details of the future is not the aim of life, moreover if the causal past determines individuals' behavior, then they are no more responsible for their actions than were their remote predecessors.[93]

---

88. ibid., 80.

89. ibid.

90. ibid., 73.

91. Grenz, 'Beyond Foundationalism,' 81-82. Notice that an affirmation of pragmatism is implicit within this statement. Coherentism and pragmatism are not necessarily opposed to one another and can be frequently seen as linked.

92. For more information on Hartshorne's influence on Rorty, see Daniel A. Dombrowski, 'Rorty Versus Hartshorne, or, Poetry Versus Metaphysics,' *Metaphilosophy* 38, no. 1 (2007): 88-110.

93. Charles Hartshorne, 'My Religious Beliefs,' *Process Studies* 40, no. 1 (2011): 157.

For Hartshorne, an omniscient God whose knowledge is set in stone is not only philosophically suspect but is morally inferior to an open future. Furthermore, Hartshorne consistently rejected doctrines that offered him no practical value in life, such as God's aseity or simplicity, and he devoted his time to those doctrines that could, in his estimation, have practical benefit.[94]

Theistic Mutualism and an Inconsistent Commitment to the Correspondence Theory of Truth

While some theistic mutualists choose to redefine truth to align with their theology, others attempt to maintain a commitment to a correspondence theory of truth. These thinkers, however, leave themselves vulnerable to philosophical doublespeak. Pinnock, for example, claimed to affirm the correspondence theory of truth, but some scholars have rebutted this claim. Rex Koivisto noted a shift in Pinnock's understanding of truth as Pinnock increasingly adopted open theism. Koivisto writes, 'Thus whereas the correspondence theory of truth loomed large in Pinnock's early works [before he was an open theist], the pragmatic theory has been blooming in his later works.'[95] Koivisto continues, '[Pinnock] now apparently holds to a pragmatic view of truth in the place of the correspondence theory of truth. It is the effectiveness of the Bible that is important rather than its self-claims.'[96] To defend his claims, Koivisto draws upon a wide range of Pinnock's works demonstrating a shift in epistemological and metaphysical commitments as well as a change in doctrinal conclusions.

Pinnock, however, has dismissed these claims. Pinnock states that '[p]eople of the Koivisto position tend to exaggerate any shifts that occur in neo-evangelical thought in order to keep the lines of dogmatic clarity clear.'[97] Pinnock continues, 'I would say that I have included in my model of rationality such items as what Koivisto calls pragmatism, but not that

---

94. ibid., 155-57.

95. Rex Koivisto, 'Clark Pinnock and Inerrancy: A Change in Truth Theory?,' *Journal of the Evangelical Theological Society* 24, no. 2 (1981): 150.

96. ibid., 149.

97. Clark Pinnock, 'A Response to Rex A. Koivisto,' *Journal of the Evangelical Theological Society* 24, no. 2 (1981): 153.

I am aware of having dropped out my earlier concerns for logic and evidence.'[98] To defend this claim, Pinnock cites his work *Reason Enough*, which, indeed, promotes pragmatic principles. It is unclear how this defense helped Pinnock, since this work was published during the period of time that Koivisto observed a shift occurring in Pinnock's thought. In *Reason Enough*, Pinnock defines truth by the correspondence between the impressions in human minds and the reality of nature.[99] However, he builds on this definition by stressing both the coherence of truth and the pragmatic value of truth.[100] As such, Pinnock writes:

> I believe the gospel is 'true' in various ways. It is the true end to our quest for meaning and our quest for the intelligibility of the world, true to the religious longings of our heart, true to the biblical record, and true to the moral intuition that we need a new kind of human community on this groaning planet.[101]

While there is much to be admired in the preceding sentiment, it is still a far cry, for better or worse, from a correspondence theory of truth, which would suggest that the gospel is true because it happened.[102]

Reformed Thomism: A Needed Correction

As opposed to theistic mutualism, the Thomistic model of God understands the object of divine knowledge stands apart from creation.

---

98. ibid., 155.

99. Clark Pinnock, *Reason Enough* (Eugene: Wipf & Stock, 1980), 16.

100. ibid., 13-17.

101. ibid., 15.

102. Compare this to the claims of Moltmann who claims that theologians need not be either systematic or consistent. See Grenz and Olson, 175. 'In fact, there is reason to doubt whether [Moltmann] has a coherent theological method in any traditional sense. This lack of systematic approach arises partly from his lack of interest in correct doctrine.' See Moltmann's definition of 'truth' and 'lies': 'What constitutes a lie? I assume it means that someone knows the truth and yet states an untruth, because they assume it to be more useful to them. This we call a "lie," because we do not consider this to be good, but bad. We impose the moral standards "good and bad" on the statements of the person. ... Under abnormal circumstances and in times of dictatorship, lies often become "good," if it means saving other people. I am thinking of the time of the persecution of the Jews by the Nazi dictatorship in Germany. Back then, saying the truth concerning Jews in hiding meant death, and lying saved lives. "Truth and falsehood" cannot be judged in abstract terms, but rather must be considered in concrete life situations' (Jürgen Moltmann, 'The Spirit of Truth,' *Theology Today* 77, no.1 [2020]: 49).

Truth, argues Thomas, is not something external to God to which He is held accountable. Rather, God is the First Truth in which all creaturely truth participates. Thomas writes,

> God's knowledge is the measure of things, not as a quantitative measure, which infinites do not admit, but because it measures the essence and the truth of a thing. For every thing possesses the truth of its own nature in the measure in which it *imitates* the divine knowledge, just as the artist's product does in so far as it corresponds to his art. (Aquinas, *ST* 1.14.12 ad 3)

Whereas the correspondence theory popular in evangelical circles emphasizes the link between an idea and the reality external to a mind, a participatory theory of truth emphasizes the relationship between creatures and the divine essence.[103] For Thomas, God shares truth with His creatures via the divine Ideas.

Like Augustine before him, Thomas believed that all creatures have the divine Ideas as their exemplar cause.[104] Thomas repeatedly references the divine Ideas and their importance to a proper understanding of truth. 'Every thing is said to be true in the absolute sense,' writes Thomas, 'because of its relation to a mind on which it depends' (Aquinas, *ST* 1.16.1). Thus, '[N]atural things are called true when they bear a likeness to the types in the divine mind; e.g. true stone is stone that has the nature proper to stone as it is conceived first in the divine mind' (Aquinas, *ST* 1.16.1). The truth of created reality, then, is measured by the divine mind, but the inverse is not true.

---

103. Brian Davies's summary of Thomas's thought is helpful. He writes, '[Thomas's] idea is that God and what God knows are indistinguishable. He thinks that the subject and object of divine knowledge cannot be thought of as two different things and that God knows himself simply by being God.' See Brian Davies, *The Thoughts of Thomas Aquinas* (Oxford: Clarendon Press, 1993), 130.

104. For more information on Augustine's understanding of the divine Ideas, see Lawrence F. Jansen, 'The Divine Ideas, in the Writings of St. Augustine,' *The Modern Schoolman* 22, no. 3 (1945): 117-31; Mark McIntosh, 'The Maker's Meaning: Divine Ideas and Salvation,' *Modern Theology* 28, no. 3 (2012): 365-84. Both of these authors see a strong similarity between Augustine's views of the divine Ideas and Plato Forms. To read Plato on his Forms, see Plato, *Republic*, Plato: Complete Works, ed. John M. Cooper, trans. G. M. A Grube and C. D. C Reeve (Indianapolis: Hackett Publishing Company, Inc., 1997), 971-1223; Plato, *Timaeus*, Plato: Complete Works, ed. John M. Cooper, trans. Donald J. Zeyl (Indianapolis: Hackett Publishing Company, Inc., 1997), 1224-91.

Thomas's position stands in stark contrast to the definition of omniscience frequently discussed in contemporary theological conversations. A robust understanding of God's independent omniscience, however, ensures a strong commitment to the existence of metaphysical truth, a much-needed corrective for theology in a postmodern world. A proper model of God's omniscience can defend Christians against the dangers of post-truth theory and can bolster the theological parameters for an accurate theory of truth. Once it is seen that a classical understanding of God's intellect is the accurate model, then a commitment to the participatory theory of truth will be seen as a natural and logical implication. It is a deeper definition and understanding of Reformed Thomism to which we now turn.

SECTION TWO:

Thomas, Protestantism, and Thomism

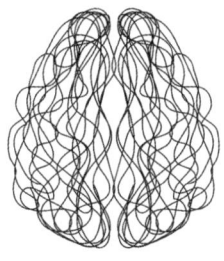

CHAPTER THREE

A Historical and Conceptual Survey of Reformed Thomism

Chapter 1 examined the often-assumed connection between divinity and metaphysical truth. This divinity–truth connection is found repeated throughout Scripture and is a commonsense presupposition for many Christians. Indeed, it was shown that even secular authors sometimes treat truth as a quasi-divine being. Once this connection was considered, the need for theological retrieval was emphasized. The metaphysical–epistemological divide that occurred at the onset of modernity has led many to mistrust truth's attainability. Theological retrieval can help contemporary theologians address the philosophical dilemmas caused by their modern assumptions by drawing attention to presuppositions that are often left unexamined. Specifically, the idea of an *a se,* and therefore independent, divine intellect was proposed as a prime candidate of theological retrieval due to its connection to the concept of truth in classical theology, specifically in the works of Thomas Aquinas.

Chapter 2 then contrasted a classical theistic model of God with various subcategories of theistic mutualism. The main point of contention between these models of theism concerns the nature of God's relationship with His creation. Classical theism emphasizes the transcendence of God, whereas theistic mutualism, in an effort to defend a give-and-take relationship between creation and its Creator, proposes various degrees of divine dependence. Additionally, Chapter 2 provided a broad overview of the most popular models of truth, including the correspondence, coherentist, pragmatic, and post-truth theories. It was proposed that a Thomistic understanding of the divine intellect defines truth via the doctrine of participation, in which creaturely truth shares in the First Truth. This theory will be examined at length in Chapters 6–8.

Before moving on to a defense and fuller explanation of a Thomistic model of divine omniscience, however, it is helpful to highlight the legitimacy of a Protestant retrieval of Thomistic doctrine. There are two major ways to define and defend what has been called Reformed Thomism. First, one could trace the historical development of thought through the work of some of the movement's key figures. Second, one could identify some of the distinctive theological and philosophical ideas associated with the movement. The first method solidifies Reformed Thomism as a legitimate school of thought within the streams of historical Christianity. The second method identifies the boundaries of belief marked by Reformed Thomism in order to identify contemporary representatives. This chapter will address Thomas's influence on the historical development of Protestant thought and will then focus on the distinctive Thomistic ideas contemporary theologians must understand in order to appropriately retrieve a Thomistic model of the divine intellect.

Thomas Aquinas, the Man

No theological system is developed in a vacuum. To understand the theological and philosophical thought of Thomas, one must first grasp the historical context of the man. Born Tommaso d'Aquino in 1226, Thomas was the youngest of at least six children.[1] He was born to an

---

1. Fergus Kerr, *Thomas Aquinas: A Very Short Introduction* (Oxford: Oxford University Press, 2009), 1, 3. There is some debate concerning the origins of the name 'Aquinas.' Some suggest that it stems from the county of Aquino, Thomas's birthplace. However, as Turner Nevitt and Brian Davies suggest, 'The "Aquinas" in "Thomas Aquinas" (*Tommaso de Aquino*) seems to flag the name of his family, not the place of his birth' (Turner Nevitt and Brian Davies, 'Introduction,' in *Quodlibetal Questions*, by Thomas Aquinas, trans. Turner Nevitt and Brian Davis [Oxford: Oxford University Press, 2020], xxviin16). It should also be noted that the date of Thomas's birth, much like many of the details of his life, is debated, but is typically cited as 1224–1225. See, for instance, Ralph McInerny, *St. Thomas Aquinas* (Boston: Twayne, 1977), 13. Simon Tugwell, however, makes a good argument for 1226 based on the existent primary documents in Simon Tugwell, ed., *Albert and Thomas: Selected Writings* (New York: Paulist Press, 1988), 291ff. Additionally, Norman Geisler notes that the number of Thomas's siblings typically ranges between six and fourteen (Norman Geisler, *Thomas Aquinas: An Evangelical Appraisal* [Eugene: Wipf & Stock, 2003], 26).

aristocratic family who expected Thomas to pursue a life of nobility, most likely in hopes of him attaining the position of Abbot at Benedictine Abbey in Monte Cassino.[2] This desire, however, was doomed from the start as, according to family tradition,

> [a] local hermit visited [Thomas's mother, Theodora] at Roccasecca and prophesied that she would give birth to a son called Thomas, who would be unrivalled in holiness and knowledge and that, in spite of his family's intention that he should be a monk at Monte Cassino, he would join the Dominicans.[3]

Thomas's family was displeased when this prophecy was fulfilled as the newly founded Dominicans' commitment to poverty and material simplicity did not match the family's lofty aspirations.[4] To dissuade Thomas from joining the Dominican order,

> [s]eemingly at his mother's behest, Thomas was kidnapped by a squad of Frederick II's soldiers, including his brother Rinaldo, and kept prisoner for over a year, probably at Roccasecca, until, seeing his determination (he resisted the prostitute whom they introduced into his apartment), he was allowed to return to the Dominicans.[5]

---

2. Edward Feser, *Aquinas: A Beginner's Guide*, Oneworld Beginner's Guides (2009; repr. London: Oneworld Publications, 2020), 3; Tugwell, 202. McInerny writes, 'There are grounds for thinking that his family had high hopes for the small boy they brought to the neighborhood monastery, that they saw in him a future abbot of Monte Cassino, with everything that such a position involved. Indeed, it is not unlikely that the then abbot, Landolfo Sinnibaldo, was a distant relative' (McInerny, 14).

3. Tugwell, 201. Tugwell argues that this legend is probably amended to reflect Thomas's entrance into the Dominicans, but Tugwell is unwilling to assume Theodora invented the entire story. The story is reflected in some of the earliest biographies of Thomas by William of Tocco.

4. Feser, *Aquinas*, 3. Healy writes, 'Unlike priests, [the Dominicans] did not settle in a parish under the authority of a bishop, nor, unlike the various orders of monks, did they devote themselves to contemplation and manual labor within the walls of a monastery. Instead they dedicated themselves to a more itinerant and unusually independent life of "preaching in poverty"' (Nicholas M. Healy, *Thomas Aquinas: Theologian of the Christian Life*, Great Theologian Series [Burlington: Ashgate, 2003], 2).

5. Kerr, 11. Feser offers further information: 'Notoriously, [Thomas's family] even went to the extent of sending a prostitute into his room on one occasion, but he chased her away with a flaming stick from the fireplace, which he used afterward to make the sign of the cross on the wall. As the story has it, he then kneeled before the cross and prayed for the gift of perpetual chastity, which he received at the hands of two angels who girded his loins with a miraculous cord' (Feser, *Aquinas*, 3–4).

To make the most of his house arrest, Thomas 'spent the time committing to memory the entire Bible and the four books of the *Sentences* of Peter Lombard.'[6]

As a Dominican friar in Naples, Thomas studied under and served as secretary for one of the most significant scholars of the Middle Ages – Albert the Great.[7] Albert was one of the biggest influences for Thomas's critical use of Aristotle, a practice that would bring Thomas great notoriety and controversy.[8] Albert would go on to recommend Thomas for a lecturer position at the University of Paris where Thomas spent most of his professional career.[9]

Thomas was a prolific author even though all his works were written in a relatively short twenty-year span.[10] Nevitt and Davies divide Thomas's works into five categories: discussions of theological and philosophical matters, commentaries, shorter polemical works, treatises, and the disputed questions.[11] His *Summa Theologiæ*, a systematic explanation of doctrine designed for the training of Dominican preachers, is often

---

6. Feser, *Aquinas*, 3. See also Tugwell, 206.

7. Kerr, 13. cf. Nevitt and Davies, xxix. It was under the tutelage of Albert Magnus that Thomas supposedly inherited the nickname 'the Dumb Ox' due to his heavy stature and quiet demeanor. According to tradition, Albert said: 'We call this lad a dumb ox, but I tell you that the whole world is going to hear his bellowing.' See Kenelm Foster, ed., *The Life of Saint Thomas Aquinas: Biographical Documents* (Helicon Press: London, 1959), 33. Quoted in Brian Davies, *The Thought of Thomas Aquinas* (Oxford: Clarendon Press, 1993), 5. See also Tugwell, 209.

8. Feser refers to Albert as 'the foremost thinker of this Aristotelian revival' (Feser, *Aquinas*, 4). Davies acknowledges that Albert the Great is often seen as a major influence on Thomas's so-called Aristotelianism but denies that Albert introduced Aristotle to Thomas. Davies writes, 'Given the situation at Naples when Aquinas arrived there, it cannot be the case that it was Albert who introduced him to Aristotle. He must have encountered the latter's work before he met Albert. One of his teachers at Naples, Peter of Ireland, was a noted disciple and interpreter of Aristotle' (Davies, *The Thought of Thomas Aquinas*, 3). McInerny repeats this sentiment but concludes, 'What is of the greatest importance is the likelihood that Thomas began at Naples the reading of Aristotle and the other more traditional strands of intellectual influence into a new and coherent synthesis' (McInerny, 15). See also Tugwell, 203.

9. Feser, *Aquinas*, 4. Davies describes the University of Paris as 'one of Europe's chief centres of learning and a well-established training ground for students of theology and philosophy' (Davies, *The Thought of Thomas Aquinas*, 5).

10. Anton C. Pegis, 'General Introduction,' in *Summa Contra Gentiles*, vol. 1, *God*, by Thomas Aquinas, trans. Anton C. Pegis (Notre Dame: University of Notre Dame Press, 1975), 16.

11. Nevitt and Davies, xxxi–xxxiii.

described as his magnum opus and still holds a profound impact on theologians within Catholic and Protestant circles.[12]

Thomas frequently used a modified Aristotelian philosophy to explain and defend Christian theology. According to some, 'The most important of St. Thomas's commentaries are those that he wrote on almost all the works of Aristotle, beginning with the psychological writings and including the Aristotelian treatises in ethics, politics, physics, metaphysics, and logic.'[13] Of course, Thomas's modified Aristotelianism was controversial since, as Feser explained, 'More traditional theologians regarded Aristotelianism as theologically dangerous, and preferred the Neoplatonic tradition in general, and Augustinianism in particular, as more suited to the needs of Christian theology.'[14] Of special note regarding the controversy surrounding Thomas's use of Aristotle is the condemnation of 1277 wherein the bishop of Paris condemned 219 propositions, many of which were based on Aristotelian principles, including a few from the writings of Thomas.[15] While this condemnation may not have stemmed directly from Thomas's writings, other polemical works certainly addressed the Dominican friar personally. According

---

12. See, for instance, Brian Davies, *The Thought of Thomas Aquinas* (Oxford: Clarendon Press, 1993), ix.

13. Pegis, 17.

14. Feser, *Aquinas*, 5. Thomas, however, was not opposed to Augustinianism, and the contemporary research highlights this fact. Manfred Svensson and David VanDrunen write, 'Since the Reformation itself is frequently described as an Augustinian movement, this change in Aquinas's image [as an Augustinian] cannot but profoundly impact the way Protestants relate to his thought. The Reformation was indeed an Augustinian movement, but the Augustinian treasure was widely disseminated in the later Middle Ages and Aquinas can safely be regarded as an important representative of that tradition.' See Manfred Svensson and David VanDrunen, 'Introduction: The Reception, Critique, and Use of Aquinas in Protestant Thought,' in *Aquinas among the Protestants*, by Manfred Svenson and David VanDrunen, eds. (Oxford: Wiley Blackwell, 2018), 6.

15. Arthur Hyman et al., eds., *Philosophy in the Middle Ages: The Christian, Islamic, and Jewish Traditions*, 3rd ed. (Indianapolis: Hackett Publishing Company, 2010), 539. The editors write, 'When one learns that several of [Thomas's] positions were condemned shortly after his death, it may well be wondered whether the reputation of Aquinas as the master voice of the golden age of scholastic philosophy may not owe more to modern intellectual politics than to authentic history. But when one looks to authentic history, it is clear that Thomas Aquinas was an important thinker in his own day and was controversial just because of that' (Hyman et al., 447). Paul Tyson goes so far as to label the condemnation of 1277 as one of the precursors of modernity, which led to the downfall of Christian Platonism. See Paul Tyson, *Returning to Reality: Christian Platonism for Our Times* (Eugene: Cascade Books, 2014), 150.

to Nicholas Healy, a fellow Dominican named Robert Kilwardy wrote a condemnation against Thomas in 1277, and yet another was created 'by a Franciscan, William de la Mare, who in 1279 wrote a *Correctorium fratris Thomae,* a "correction" of over one hundred supposedly erroneous propositions draw from Thomas.'[16] Even though the condemnation of 1277 and the following disputes are sometimes referred to as a 'brutal victory for Augustinianism over Aristotelianism,' the latter continued to flourish in European universities.[17] For Thomas, however, the divisions between Aristotelianism, Neoplatonism, and Augustinianism were not as clear as the secondary literature sometimes make them appear. Rather, as will be shown below, Thomas is often portrayed as a great synthesizer of classical Greek, patristic, and biblical thought. Being sure, however, that extra biblical thought was modified when needed to best align with biblical teaching.

Thomas died around the age of forty-nine in 1274 after undergoing an unusual experience that put an end to his writing career. According to Kerr:

> On 6 December 1273, the Feast of Saint Nicholas, something happened during the celebration of Mass. The result was that he decided to write no more: 'Everything I have written seems to me as straw in comparison with what I have seen.' Presumably he had some kind of mystical experience. According to recent commentators, he perhaps suffered a stroke, likely enough after years of overwork.[18]

It is difficult to separate history from legend when discussing this mystical experience near the end of Thomas's life. While some scholars suggest Thomas experienced a stroke, others suggest that he witnessed a glimpse of the beatific vision or of the eternal life to come.[19] Regardless, Thomas's health began to decline, and he died shortly after suffering

---

16. Healy, 10. Geisler notes, 'Some of Aquinas's students even stood up in his class and read pamphlets against him' (Geisler, 33).

17. Hyman et al., 540.

18. Kerr, 19.

19. For a brief summary of a few supernatural occurrences in Thomas's life, including his potential glimpse of the beatific vision, see McInerny, 26 and Tugwell, 259-67. Tugwell's account of Thomas's debilitating vision is particularly helpful. For a summary of Thomas's life that rejects much of the legendary aspects within tradition, see Geisler, 25-35.

a head injury on route to the Second Council of Lyons.[20] He was canonized as a saint fifty years after his death and declared a doctor of the church in 1567.[21] According to Brian Davies, 'His influence on Christian thinking is second only to writers like St Paul and St Augustine.'[22] It is, of course, unsurprising that Thomas's thought has shaped Roman Catholic doctrine and practice. It may be surprising to some, however, that Thomistic thought has helped shape the trajectory of Protestantism as well.

The Influence of Thomistic Thought on Protestantism

Some scholars deny the claim that this Dominican friar greatly influenced Protestant thought in any positive way, and thus the historical precedence for Reformed Thomism as a legitimate historical movement is questioned. Rather than acknowledging the critical reception of Thomas in the works of Protestant thinkers, some scholars reject Thomas's influence outright. In this view, Protestant thinkers cannot be properly identified as Thomists since it was primarily the Catholic theology of Thomas that Protestant reformers opposed. To these thinkers, to be Protestant demands rejection of Thomism.[23]

Additionally, a popular scholarly movement known as 'Calvin against the Calvinists' promotes the idea that the philosophical leanings of the later Reformed Orthodox, many of which are cited as evidence of the influence of Thomas, are opposed to the biblical commitments of John Calvin and represent a deviation from Reformed thought rather than a development of it. Carl Trueman describes this movement as obtaining a 'near-canonical status and is apparently considered so self-

---

20. Feser, *Aquinas*, 6; Healy, 7; Tugwell, 234. Tugwell's account examines Thomas's last days under the care of the monks of Fossanova. The monks grew especially attached to Thomas and, after his passing, became nervous that the 'Dominicans would obtain possession of the precious corpse, so they removed and hid Thomas' head' (Tugwell, 235).

21. Nevitt and Davies, xxviii.

22. Davies, *The Thought of Thomas Aquinas*, vii.

23. See, for instance, Jeffrey Johnson, *The Failure of Natural Theology: A Critical Appraisal of the Philosophical Theology of Thomas Aquinas* (Conway: Free Grace Press, 2021). See also the many caricatures that Arvin Vos addresses within Arvin Vos, *Aquinas, Calvin, and Contemporary Protestant Thought: A Critique of Protestant Views on the Thought of Thomas Aquinas* (Grand Rapids: Eerdmans, 1986).

evident that it is cited in textbooks without any defense of its accuracy or even a reference to its origin.'[24] For supporters of the 'Calvin against the Calvinists' theory, any trace of Thomism in the Reformed Scholastics is a theological landmine to be removed, defused, and replaced with Calvin's more biblically consistent theological conclusions.[25]

Other historians, however, see a dramatic, albeit eclectic, influence of Thomas on the work of the Reformers, Reformed Orthodox, Puritans, and contemporary evangelicals.[26] Fortunately, contemporary scholarship is moving away from the 'Calvin against the Calvinists' theory and is embracing a more nuanced appreciation for the critical use of Thomas by the Reformers and post-Reformation theologians. These historians see a continuity of thought and method between medieval Scholasticism, the Reformation, the post-Reformation Scholastics, and beyond.[27]

The Influence of Thomistic Thought on the Reformers

Thomas's influence can be seen from the very onset of Protestantism. It is, admittedly, easy to read Martin Luther's hostility toward Thomas

---

24. Carl R. Trueman, 'A Small Step Towards Rationalism: The Impact of the Metaphysics of Tommaso Campanella on the Theology of Richard Baxter,' in *Protestant Scholasticism: Essays in Reassessment*, by Carl R. Trueman and R. Scott Clark, eds., Studies in Christian History and Thought (Eugene: Wipf & Stock, 2006), 181.

25. This theory was named after the influential essay by Basil Hall. See Basil Hall, 'Calvin against the Calvinists,' in *John Calvin*, by Gervase Duffield, ed. (Grand Rapids: Eerdmans, 1966), 12-37. The most prominent proponents of the 'Calvin against the Calvinists' movement were Brian Armstrong and R. T. Kendall. See Brian Armstrong, *Calvinism and the Amyraut Heresy* (Madison: University of Wisconsin Press, 1969); R. T. Kendall, *Calvin and English Calvinism to 1649* (Oxford: Oxford University Press, 1979).

26. For instance, see Richard A. Muller, *Post-Reformation Reformed Dogmatics*, four volumes (Grand Rapids: Baker, 2003); Willem van Asselt and Eef Dekker, eds., *Reformation and Scholasticism: An Ecumenical Enterprise* (Grand Rapids: Baker, 2001); Manfred Svensson and David VanDrunen, eds., *Aquinas among the Protestants* (Hoboken: Wiley & Sons, 2018); Norman Geisler, *Thomas Aquinas: An Evangelical Appraisal* (Eugene: Wipf and Stock Publishers, 2003).

27. Willem J. van Asselt and Eef Dekker provide an overview of the discontinuity theory, the negative continuity theory, and the positive continuity theory in Willem J. van Asselt and Eef Dekker, 'Introduction,' in *Reformation and Scholasticism: An Ecumenical Enterprise*, by Willem van Asselt and Eef Dekker, eds. (Grand Rapids: Baker, 2001); Jordan J. Ballor, 'Deformation and Reformation: Thomas Aquinas and the Rise of Protestant Scholasticism,' in *Aquinas among the Protestants*, by Manfred Svensson and David VanDrunen, eds. (Hoboken: Wiley & Sons, 2018), 28-38.

into the thought of other Reformers, and Thomas's reception was varied among the early Protestants.[28] It is not unusual, in fact, for historians to cite William of Ockham's nominalism or John Duns Scotus's univocity of being as the theological impetus of early Protestant thought.[29] Some scholars, however, believe that the relationship between Protestant Reformers and Thomistic thought reflect a genuine appreciation, albeit an appreciation that was both complicated and critical.[30] Some Protestants, such as Paul Helm, have argued that even John Calvin was significantly influenced by Thomas.[31] Others focus their attention on reformational thought beyond Calvin and Luther in the works of such authors as Peter Martyr Vermigli and Jerome Zanchi.[32] Regardless, good reasons exist to believe that many Reformers desired to show their partial continuity with Thomas rather than a total rejection of his thought. As Carl Trueman and R. Scott Clark point out, 'Since the early 1960s ... the academic world has become increasingly aware of the significant points of continuity between medieval philosophy, theology, and exegesis, and the theologies of the Reformation.'[33] This continuity can be shown in a few ways.

---

28. Martin Luther famously described Thomas as 'the source and foundation of all heresy, error, and obliteration of the Gospel.' See Martin Luther, *Widder den Newen Abgott*, in *Werke Kritische Gesamtausgabe* (Weimar, Ger: H. Böhlau, 1899), 15:184, 2.32f. Originally cited in Manfred Svensson and David VanDrunen, 'Introduction: The Reception, Critique, and Use of Aquinas in Protestant Thought,' in *Aquinas among the Protestants*, ed. Manfred Svensson and David VanDrunen (Oxford: Wiley Blackwell, 2018), 1. See also Ballor, 'Deformation and Reformation,' 43.

29. See, for instance, Michael Allen Gillespie, *The Theological Origins of Modernity* (Chicago: University of Chicago Press, 2008), 19-44, 101-28.

30. Ballor, 'Deformation and Reformation,' 29.

31. See Paul Helm, *John Calvin's Ideas* (Oxford: Oxford University Press, 2004). Specifically, Helm draws a strong connection between Thomas's and Calvin's distinction between God *in se* and God *quoad nos*. In another article, Helm identifies more Protestant thinkers influenced by Thomas, including Peter Martyr Vermigli, Franciscus Junius, Francis Turretin, and John Owen. See Paul Helm, 'Nature and Grace,' in *Aquinas among the Protestants*, by Manfred Svensson and David VanDrunen, eds. (Hoboken: Wiley & Sons, 2018), 232-37.

32. David Systma, 'Thomas Aquinas and Reformed Biblical Interpretation: The Contribution of William Whitaker,' in *Aquinas among the Protestants*, by Manfred Svensson and David VanDrunen, eds. (Oxford: Wiley Blackwell, 2018), 67.

33. Carl R. Trueman and R. Scott Clark, 'Introduction,' in *Protestant Scholasticism: Essays in Reassessment*, edited by Carl R. Trueman and R. Scott Clark, Studies in Christian History and Thought (Eugene: Wipf & Stock, 2006), xi-xix. Obviously, this

First, it should be recognized that reformational disputes with Rome often overlooked the doctrine of God and focused more on ecclesiological and soteriological matters. The Reformers did not significantly depart from their Catholic predecessors on the nature or attributes of God. Classical theism and Nicene Trinitarianism were not relics of the Catholic Church jettisoned by Protestantism. Rather, the Reformation's retention of a classical theology proper demonstrates continuity between the Reformers and the prior 1,500 years of church history. This continuity partially explains why topics such as divine omniscience are frequently left unaddressed in reformational works, as there was simply an absence of debate, unlike the era of the Reformed Orthodox, which encountered both variant strains of Molinism and Socinianism.[34] As Scott Swain writes, 'In terms of doctrinal development, therefore, the Reformation did not witness substantive revision to the doctrine of God confessed by the church catholic in previous centuries.'[35] Therefore, Reformers did not champion a rebellion against the model of God articulated within the first forty-three questions of Thomas's *Summa Theologiæ*.

Furthermore, due to the popular 'Calvin against the Calvinists' theory, it was common for scholars to find a sharp break in philosophical thought between medieval Scholastics, Reformers, and the Reformed Scholastics. Within this theory of discontinuity, the biblically minded Reformers are pitted against the overtly philosophical emphasis of the Reformed Scholastics. The influence of this theory is waning, and as Christopher Cleveland writes, 'Rather than seeing the reformers as biblical and their successors as Aristotelian, the reassessment has brought a clearer picture of the role of Aristotelianism in the Renaissance and the Reformation.'[36] This development is opposed to the divisions seen in earlier works wherein 'Calvinism is considered to be a positive influence, and Thomism is considered to be a

---

statement is meant to reference influences beyond that of Thomas but certainly does not exclude Thomas.

34. Muller, *PRRD* 3:392.

35. Scott R. Swain, 'The Being and Attributes of God,' in *Reformation Theology: A Systematic Summary*, edited by Matthew Barrett (Wheaton: Crossway, 2017), 221. Swain continues, 'Drawing on resources from across classical philosophical and theological traditions, Protestant theologians expounded with great learning and conviction the doctrine of God as historically confessed by catholic Christians' (ibid., 237).

36. Christopher Cleveland, *Thomism in John Owen* (New York: Routledge, 2013), 11.

negative influence.'[37] Rather, the mixture of acceptance, such as it concerned Thomas's doctrine of God and modified Aristotelianism, and rejection, such as it concerned Thomas's ecclesiology, can now be better appreciated.

Second, the continuity between medieval Scholasticism and the Reformers can be seen in some of the specific claims by one of the Reformation's key figures, John Calvin.[38] Calvin's work on predestination, for instance, greatly resembles the conclusions of Thomas and other Scholastics such as Scotus.[39] It is also significant to note, as Frank A. James III has, that although Calvin is not usually grouped with the Scholastics, he 'nevertheless employed fourfold Aristotelian causality in his discussion of predestination in his Commentary on Ephesians.'[40] Calvin's use of Aristotelian metaphysics in this instance resembles Thomas much more than Scotus or other Scholastics such as Ockham. David Steinmetz repeats this Scholastic connection:

> Calvin's reconception of theology as a school theology for the church represents a democratization and expansion of the scholastic ideal. The time is therefore overdue for historians and theologians to acknowledge what they can no longer credibly deny, namely, that the phrase, 'the scholastic Calvin' is not an oxymoron.[41]

Furthermore, the Scholastic influence on Calvin's thought can be reasonably linked to Thomas more so than other strains of medieval Scholasticism, as '[a] recent study of the library of Calvin's academy at

---

37. ibid.

38. See Richard A. Muller, 'Scholasticism in Calvin: A Question of Relation and Disjunction,' in *The Unaccommodated Calvin: Studies in the Foundation of a Theological Tradition* (Oxford: Oxford University Press, 2001), 39-61. See also Helm, *John Calvin's Ideas*, esp. 1-30.

39. John Calvin, *Institutes of the Christian Religion*, trans. by Henry Beveridge (Peabody, MA: Hendrickson Publishing, 2008), 626, 3.23.2. See David C. Steinmetz, *Calvin in Context* (Oxford: Oxford University Press, 2010), 40-52; David C. Steinmetz, 'The Scholastic Calvin,' in *Protestant Scholasticism: Essays in Reassessment*, ed. Carl R. Trueman and R. Scott Clark (Eugene: Wipf & Stock, 2005), 27.

40. Frank A. James III, 'Peter Martyr Vermigli: At the Crossroads of Late Medieval Scholasticism, Christian Humanism and Resurgent Augustinianism,' in *Protestant Scholasticism: Essays in Reassessment*, by Carl R. Trueman and R. Scott Clark, eds., Studies in Christian History and Thought (Eugene: Wipf & Stock, 2006), 71. Steinmetz adds, '[Calvin] employed a causal scheme borrowed from Aristotle to set in order the causes of salvation, accepting as well a scholastic distinction between consequent necessity and necessity of the consequence' (Steinmetz, 'The Scholastic Calvin,' 25).

41. ibid., 30.

Geneva has stressed the possession of many works of the Thomist school and the total absence of nominalist works.[42] This is not to suggest that John Calvin should be described as a Thomist *per se*, as the Reformer was unafraid to reject significant Thomistic conclusions in favor of other medieval Scholastics.[43] Instead, it should simply be noted that recent scholarship highlights a more nuanced and complicated appraisal of Thomas within Calvin's work than had been previously assumed.[44]

Third, beyond Calvin and Luther there exists a strong Thomistic influence on other reformational thinkers. Indeed, it was this retrieval of Reformed thought from lesser-known Reformers that helped clarify the role of Thomas in Protestantism. Christopher Cleveland writes, 'Many of the reformers ... were trained as monks and priests and were therefore strongly influenced by the ideas in which they were trained. Luther was taught the theology of Occam, while Bucer and Vermigli received Thomistic training.'[45] Martin Bucer, for instance, was a Dominican friar whose library included many Thomistic works.[46] Regardless of works owned, however, Bucer's role as a Dominican should not be overlooked, since 'before the French Revolution, more than half the Thomists in each century were members of the Dominican Order ...'[47] Others, such as Jerome Zanchi, promoted Thomistic conclusions concerning analogical predication, the doctrine of divine simplicity, grace, predestination, and the Scholastic use of the Neoplatonic method known as the *Triplex Via*.[48]

---

42. John Patrick Donnelly, 'Calvinist Thomism,' *Viator* 7 (1976): 453.

43. When Scotus and Thomas disagreed on predestination, for instance, Calvin often followed Scotus. See Steinmetz, 'The Scholastic Calvin,' 27.

44. In a note regarding Zanchi's dogmatic theology, Donnelly writes, 'The first three tomes of his "summa" deal with the Trinity, the nature of God and creation. While their methodologies were very different, *Thomas and Calvin were largely in agreement on these subjects*' (Donnelly, 'Calvinist Thomism,' 451).

45. Cleveland, 11.

46. ibid., 12. Martin Greschat writes, 'About half his library, to be sure, as shown by 1518 inventory of his books, did consist of theological and philosophical works representing the thought of the great Dominican teacher Thomas Aquinas' (Martin Greschat, *Martin Bucer: A Reformer and His Times*, trans. Stephen E. Buckwalter [Louisville: Westminster John Knox Press, 2004], 18).

47. Romanus Cessario, *A Short History of Thomism*, English ed. (Washington, DC: The Catholic University of America Press, 2005), 21

48. Harm Goris, 'Thomism in Zanchi's Doctrine of God,' in van Asselt and Dekker, *Reformation and Scholasticism*, 122-33. Cleveland, 14. See also Donnelly, 'Calvinist Thomism,' 446.

Jerome Zanchi and Peter Martyr Vermigli are frequently cited as the most Thomistic of the Reformers.[49] Zanchi refers to Thomas as the 'purest among [the Scholastics]' and positively cites the *Summa Theologiæ, Summa Contra Gentiles, De Veritate* and Thomas's commentaries on *the Sentences, Physics, On Interpretation,* and *Metaphysics.*[50] As such, Stefan Lindholm concludes, 'Aquinas and Zanchi belong to a continuous academic community in which Aquinas was a reliable guide to truth, not least in the face of polemical debates.'[51] Specifically, Lindholm lists the doctrine of God, theological methodology, and the use of natural philosophy as key areas of Thomistic influence in the writings of Zanchi, and further notes that Zanchi was not afraid to make use of Aristotelian hylomorphism in his theological anthropology.[52] The Thomistic influence on Zanchi's understanding of the divine intellect is especially pertinent. As Donnelly explains:

> In those areas where there was no quarrel between Catholics and Calvinists, Zanchi follows Aquinas more closely. ... A good example of this is their treatment of divine knowledge. The sixteen articles devoted to God's knowledge make it the longest and most complex question in the *Prima pars* of the *Summa theologiae.* Zanchi's chapter has sixteen theses which repeat all the articles in the *Summa* except one that deals with propositional knowledge.[53]

Likewise, Vermigli has been called a 'pioneer of Calvinist Thomism.'[54] Vermigli received a Thomistic education at the University of Padua where he studied under two Dominican friars.[55] It is worth noting that

---

49. There is significant overlap concerning the Reformers and the Reformed Scholastics, especially in light of Scholasticism pertaining more to methodology than content. As such, Zanchi and Vermigli are sometimes listed among the Reformers and sometimes listed among the Reformed Scholastics.

50. Stefan Lindholm, 'Jerome Zanchi's Use of Thomas Aquinas,' in *Aquinas Among the Protestants,* by Manfred Svensson and David VanDrunen, eds. (Hoboken: Wiley & Sons, 2018), 76.

51. ibid.

52. Lindholm, 'Jerome Zanchi's Use of Thomas Aquinas,' 75, 85.

53. Donnelly, 'Calvinist Thomism,' 448.

54. James, 63. Joseph McLelland also refers to Vermigli as a 'Reformed Thomist' and 'Calvinist Aristotelian.' See Joseph C. McLelland, 'Calvinism Perfecting Thomism? Peter Martyr Vermigli's Question,' *Scottish Journal of Theology* 31, no. 6 (1978): 571, 576. Again, note that 'Calvinist Thomism' and 'Reformed Thomism' are used synonymously.

55. James, 63-64.

'Padua's "glory" was its instruction in Aristotle.'[56] Due to Vermigli's Aristotelian and Thomistic training, Donnelly comments, 'Martyr's career shows that a Protestant theology could rest on a Thomistic base.'[57] It is unsurprising that Brian Armstrong, one of the chief voices in the 'Calvin against the Calvinists' movement, included Peter Vermigli, along with Theodore Beza and Jerome Zanchi, in his 'villainous triumvirate' who 'cast an Aristotelian spell upon the Reformed tradition, resulting in the displacement of the essentially biblical vision of Calvin with a philosophical orientation and a reliance on speculative reason.'[58] This Thomistic training did not lead Vermigli to accept all of Thomas's conclusions, as Vermigli used Aristotelian language and argumentation to refute Roman Catholic doctrines such as transubstantiation.[59] Indeed, McLelland states that 'one could argue that Vermigli provides a case study in a variant form of Reform: "Calvinism" not destroying Thomism but perfecting it.'[60]

To conclude his survey on Thomas's influence on reformational thinkers, Jordan Ballor claims:

> Dominicans, Augustinians, Benedictines, secular clergy, and laypersons are all represented among the early generations of reformers. With some notable exceptions, particularly Luther, those with formal theological training were educated substantially in the *via antiqua*, in some cases with an explicit emphasis in the theology of Thomas Aquinas.[61]

---

56. McLelland, 573.

57. John Patrick Donnelly, *Calvinism and Scholasticism in Vermigli's Doctrine of Man and Grace* (Leiden: E. J. Brill, 1976), 27.

58. James, 65. See also Armstrong, 129. Donnelly agrees with Armstrong's classification, albeit in a more positive tone. Donnelly writes, 'Jerome Zanchi was the most thoroughgoing and influential in pioneering Calvinist scholasticism, Theodore Beza was the best known and most prolific, but Vermigli was the first and the inspiration of all who came after' (Donnelly, *Vermigli's Doctrine of Man and Grace*, 207).

59. James, 71. James cites Vermigli, *Defensio Doctrinae Veteris et Apostolicae de Sacrosancto Eucharistiae Sacramento ... adversus Stephani Gardineri ... librum* (Zurich: Froschauer, 1559), 235-59.

60. McLelland, 574.

61. Ballor, 38. Ballor continues, 'Contrary to accounts of the Reformation which assert a radical intellectual break effected by Luther's increasingly hostile criticisms of particular doctrines and figures, this broader perspective provides evidence for seeing a greater intellectual coherence and continuity from at least the Middle Ages and the time of Thomas Aquinas to the post-Reformation period (ca. mid-eighteenth century)' (Ballor, 43).

As stated above, the reception of Thomas was varied among the Reformers, but the critical use of medieval Scholasticism within Protestant works prohibits confessing a complete rejection of Thomistic belief by the Reformed. Rather, an eclectic Thomism existed in early Protestantism wherein Reformers grafted some of Thomas's conclusions into their philosophical and theological systems while rejecting other Thomistic ideas that did not cohere. Depending on how broadly one defines Thomism, then, one can make the case for the term to apply to men such as Peter Vermigli, Jerome Zanchi, Martin Bucer, Theodore Beza, and, perhaps even, John Calvin.

The Influence of Thomistic Thought on Reformed Scholasticism

While identifying a Protestant Reformer is relatively simple, the movement known as Protestant Scholasticism, Reformed Scholasticism, or Reformed Orthodoxy has been harder to define. When the 'Calvin against the Calvinists' theory was at its height in popularity, the Reformed Scholastics were defined primarily by their supposed emphasis on philosophy.[62] An increasing number of scholars, however, are now defining Reformed Scholasticism in terms of methodology rather than content. L. M. de Rijk, for instance, defines Scholasticism as 'an approach, which is characterized by the use, in both study and teaching, of a constantly recurring system of concepts, distinctions, definitions, proposition analyses, argumentative techniques and disputational methods.'[63] Notice that the preceding definition does not mention any specific premise or conclusion but rather focuses solely on methodology.

Likewise, Reformed Scholastic historian Richard A. Muller highlights four methodological qualifications for a work to be included among the Scholastics: the presentation of a thesis, the indication of the subjects to be discussed, the treatment of arguments or objections

---

62. See James, 65; Trueman, 'A Small Step toward Rationalism,' 181.

63. Cited in Willem J. van Asselt and Eef Dekker, eds., 'Introduction,' in *Reformation and Scholasticism: An Ecumenical Enterprise* (Grand Rapids: Baker Academic, 2001), 25; originally in L. M. de Rijk, *Middeleuwse Wijsbegeerte. Traditie en Vernieuwing*, 2nd ed. (Netherlands: Assen, 1982), 25, 111.

against the adopted position, and the formulation of an answer.[64] Specifically, Muller defines Reformed Scholasticism as

> [a] highly technical and logical approach to theological system, according to which each theological topic or *locus* was divided into its component parts, the parts analyzed and then defined in careful propositional form. In addition, this highly technical approach sought to achieve precise definition by debate with adversaries and *by use of the Christian tradition as a whole in arguing its doctrines*. The form of theological system was adapted to a didactical and polemical model that could move from biblical definition to traditional development of doctrine, to debate with doctrinal adversaries past and present, to theological resolution of the problem. This method is rightly called scholastic *both in view of its roots in medieval scholasticism and in view of its intention to provide an adequate technical theology for schools, seminaries and universities*. The goal of this method, the dogmatic or doctrinal intention of this theology, was to provide the church with 'right teaching,' literally 'orthodoxy.'[65]

Methodological and contextual emphases run through Muller's definition. As such, two Protestant Scholastics, such as Jacob Arminius and Francis Turretin, could reach radically different theological conclusions while maintaining the same Scholastic methodology.[66]

The Reformers were primarily focused on the pulpit, but the Reformed Scholastics were primarily focused on the lectern.[67] The Scholastics attempted to take the core tenets of Protestantism as outlined in the Reformation and trace the necessary dogmatic implications of such tenets into a full-fledged theological system to teach within

---

64. Richard A. Muller, 'Scholasticism and Orthodoxy in the Reformed Tradition: An Attempt at Definition' (inaugural address, Calvin Seminary Chapel, Grand Rapids, MI, September 7, 1995), 4-5. Cited in van Asselt and Dekker, 'Introduction,' 26.

65. Richard A. Muller, *Dictionary of Latin and Greek Terms* (Grand Rapids: Baker Academic, 1985), 8; emphasis added.

66. See Richard A. Muller, 'Arminius and the Scholastic Tradition,' *Calvin Theological Journal* 24, no. 2 (1989): 263-77. It's noteworthy that Muller specifically draws attention to the Thomistic influences in Arminius's work. See Muller, 'Arminius and the Scholastic Tradition,' 267-71.

67. Trueman and Clark write: 'Protestant scholasticism had a different locus to that of the earlier Reformation: the latter was largely, though not universally, ecclesial in nature, while the former was involved perhaps more centrally in theological and methodological reform of the classroom and university' (Trueman and Scott, xvii).

universities.[68] As Muller writes: '[Protestant Scholasticism] must be understood primarily as a method of theological discourse, suited to the classroom and altered in the light of changes in logic and rhetoric that belonged to the fifteenth and sixteenth centuries.'[69] The Scholastics were simultaneously churchmen and schoolmen. As previously mentioned, since such concepts as the Trinity, the doctrine of God, and Christology were often not addressed at length by the Reformers, the Reformed Scholastics had to research pre-Reformation resources, including medieval Scholastics, for the sake of their pedagogy. As Jack Kilcrease writes: 'Since the Reformers viewed these parts of the catholic tradition as accurate explications of the biblical material, there was no reason to reinvent the proverbial wheel.'[70] Due to this study of medieval Scholasticism, it is common to note at least some Thomistic influence on the thought of the Protestant Scholastics.

Reformed Orthodoxy may be divided into three stages of chronological development: early, high, and late orthodoxy.[71] Early orthodoxy, the time spanning the deaths of the Reformers to the Thirty Years War, 'was the era of the confessional solidification of Protestantism.'[72] High

---

68. Again, Trueman and Clark state: 'Scholasticism was the attempt to adapt the Reformation to the demands of the academy in terms of a precritical world-view' (ibid., xii). This codification led Muller to describe the work of the Reformed Scholastics as 'the form of theological system in and through which modern Protestantism has received most of its doctrinal principles and definitions' (Muller, *PRRD* 1:37). Indeed, 'The contemporary relevance of Protestant orthodox theology arises from the fact that it remains the basis for normative Protestant theology in the present' (Muller, *PRRD* 1:29).

69. Muller, *PRRD*, 1:39. Kilcrease adds: 'Muller considers it far more reasonable to interpret the emergence of the Protestant scholastic tradition as, among other things, a response to the pedagogical needs of the Reformation. The Reformers freshly appropriated scriptural insights into soteriology and ecclesiology. Such truths needed to be taught in universities in a systematic form that was intellectually defensible according to the standard theological methodology of the day (Muller 1987–2003, 1:27-84)' (Jack Kilcrease, 'Johann Gerhard's Reception of Thomas Aquinas's *Analogia Entis*,' in *Aquinas Among the Protestants*, by Manfred Svensson and David VanDrunen, eds. [Hoboken: Wiley & Sons, 2018], 111).

70. Kilcrease, 112. See Muller who wrote, 'We must not forget that the Reformers were trained in the late medieval scholastic system, and that their reformist enterprise was intended to restore Catholic orthodoxy' (Muller, PRRD 1:48).

71. Muller, *PRRD* 1:31-32. See also Ryan M. McGraw, *Reformed Scholasticism: Recovering the Tools of Reformed Theology*, paperback edition (New York, NY: T&T Clark, 2020). 96.

72. Muller, *PRRD* 1:31.

orthodoxy extended from 1640 to 1725, built upon the confessions of early orthodoxy, and featured a 'more explicit grasp of the tradition, particularly of the contribution of the Middle Ages.'[73] High orthodoxy also featured a greater emphasis upon internal debate. Finally, late orthodoxy, which nears the dawn of modernity, was 'less secure in its philosophical foundations,' and 'less certain of its grasp of the biblical standard.'[74] Due to the variability of late orthodoxy, we will focus on the thought and methodology of early and high orthodoxy.

The Protestant Scholastics of early and high orthodoxy practiced what has been called a 'critical-evangelical-catholicity of the church,' and this practice has been well documented.[75] One such example is the work of Johann Gerhard, who Jordan B. Cooper referred to as 'the greatest thinker to arise from the entire Protestant theological tradition.'[76] According to Cooper, Gerhard 'formulated an extensive system of theology which incorporated the best insights of Thomas Aquinas (including a heavy use of Aristotle), Augustine, and Martin Luther.' These Thomistic insights include Gerhard's division of knowledge into two sources: natural and supernatural revelation. Cooper continued,

> Gerhard sets forth his own version of Aquinas's five proofs for God's existence, arguing that together they demonstrate the ontological necessity of God and several of the divine attributes. He positively cites pre-Christian Greek sources on topics such as divine simplicity and divine immutability, contending that the light of reason was able to reveal a significant amount of truth to the philosophers. Like Aquinas (and Luther), Gerhard contends that God's nature as triune and the facts of the gospel cannot be known by reason alone, but instead are only grasped by special revelation and God-granted faith.[77]

Still, Gerhard continued to demonstrate the critical reception of Thomas as displayed by earlier Protestant thinkers, as special revelation in Gerhard's system 'is not to be identified with church tradition as

---

73. ibid.

74. Muller, *PRRD* 1:32.

75. Kilcrease, 113. Specifically, Kilcrease is referring to the work of Melanchthon, but the phrase adequately summarizes Protestant Scholasticism as a whole.

76. Cooper, 33.

77. ibid., 33-34.

preserved by the magisterium (as was Aquinas's view) but is found solely in the text of the sacred Scripture.'[78]

In addition to what is mentioned above, Gerhard adopted several additional key Thomistic principles into his theological system. One of the most pertinent to the current discussion is Gerhard's use of the analogy of being, which, according to some, is 'the touchstone of the Thomistic tradition.'[79] Gerhard specifically rejects Scotus's understanding of the univocity of being in favor of a modified version of Thomas's *analogia entis*. Indeed, this conclusion was not unusual since '[w]hen forced to grapple more directly with the metaphysical issues raised by medieval theology, the Protestant scholastics widely (though not uniformly) accepted a version of Thomistic analogy and rejected Scotist univocity.'[80] Gerhard's use of Thomistic analogy should not be overstated, however, as it does differ significantly from contemporary interpretations of Thomas's doctrine, but, as Kilcrease states, 'Gerhard interprets analogy in terms of what has been called "analogy of proportion".' Within Gerhard's historical context, this makes a great deal of sense, since this was the popular interpretation of Aquinas in the early modern period. Specifically, Cardinal Thomas Cajetan advocated it.'[81] As such, it is fair to connect Gerhard's doctrine to Thomistic influence even if the understanding of Thomas has shifted over time.

Other Protestant Scholastics are worth briefly mentioning as they reference Thomas's work or doctrines frequently. Petrus van Mastricht, for instance, was educated in Thomistic thought and passed on some of Thomas's ideas through his teaching.[82] Adriaan C. Neele writes: 'Didactic-dogmatic theology, which included the *Summa theologica* of Thomas Aquinas, the *Synopsis purioris theologiae*, and the scholastic *disputationes* of Voetius's Saturday morning classes ... would contribute

---

78. Cooper, 34.

79. Kilcrease, 117. Kilcrease cites Erich Przywara, *Analogia Entis: Metaphysics: Original Structure and Universal Rhythm*, trans. John Betz and David Bentley Hart (Grand Rapids: Eerdmans, 2013); Thomas Joseph White, *The Analogy of Being: Invention of the Antichrist or Wisdom of God* (Grand Rapids: Eerdmans, 2010).

80. Kilcrease, 120.

81. Kilcrease, 121.

82. The inclusion of Mastricht as a Protestant Scholastic follows the distinction of Adriaan C. Neele, *Petrus van Mastricht (1630–1706): Reformed Orthodoxy: Method and Piety* (New York: Brill, 2009).

to Mastricht's theological formation.'[83] Mastricht positively cites Thomas and some of the previously mentioned Reformed Thomistic theologians throughout his *Theoretical-Practical Theology*.[84] He is even willing to include Aquinas's opinion, which Mastricht affirms, alongside the Reformers when it comes to man's ability to reason to the Trinity, again demonstrating the importance of theological continuity with pre-Reformation sources.[85] Likewise, Franciscus Junius reflects Thomistic thought in his major doctrinal contribution – archetypal and ectypal theology.[86] Additionally, Junius had to rely on the works of medieval Scholastics when it came to theological prolegomena, since these topics were frequently left undiscussed by the Reformers.[87]

The Influence of Thomistic Thought on the Puritans

Much like Reformed Scholasticism, Puritanism is difficult to define. Certain authors popularly labeled as Puritans could also be accurately classified as examples of Reformed Orthodoxy, such as John Owen and Thomas Goodwin. Puritanism, however, is not limited to the Reformed Orthodox. Ryan McGraw explains: 'Puritanism encompassed such diverse figures as the Arian-leaning John Milton, "antinomians" such as Richard Baxter and Thomas Jackson, [and] the Arminian John Goodwin. ...'[88] According to McGraw, the emphasis of piety alone

---

83. Adriaan C. Neele, 'Petrus van Mastricht (1630–1706): Life and Work,' in *Theoretical-Practical Theology*, vol. 1, *Prolegomena*, by Petrus Van Mastricht, ed. Joel R. Beeke, trans. Todd M. Rester (Grand Rapids: Reformation Heritage Books, 2018), xxvi.

84. Mastricht includes Thomas's *ST* as an example of the proper method and order of theology, Mastricht, *TPT* 1:68. At the same time, Mastricht was unafraid to disagree with Thomas, such as his analysis of transubstantiation as in Mastricht, *TPT* 1:85. Some of Mastricht's objections against Thomas, however, are clearly incorrect, such as the claim that Thomas placed the philosophers on equal footing as Scripture (Mastricht, *TPT* 1:85).

85. Mastricht, *TPT*, 2:517.

86. Willem J. van Asselt, 'Introduction,' in Franciscus Junius, *A Treatise on True Theology*, trans. David C. Noe (Grand Rapids: Reformation Heritage Books, 2014), xxvi, fn.39. See also Donald Sinnema, 'Reflections on the Nature and Method of Theology at the University of Leiden before the Synod of Dort' (MA thesis, Institute for Christian Studies, Toronto, 1975), 67-78.

87. van Asselt, xxxii.

88. Ryan M. McGraw, *Reformed Scholasticism: Recovering the Tools of Reformed Theology*, paperback edition (New York, NY: T&T Clark, 2020), 187.

is not enough to distinguish Puritans from other thinkers.[89] Rather, Puritanism is best defined by two central concerns: 'the desire to reform the worship of the Church of England, and the cultivation of personal holiness.'[90]

Considering the breadth of the movement, Thomistic influence within Puritanism will be variegated. Still, those Puritans that closely resemble the Reformed Orthodox demonstrate a willingness to use Thomistic principles. The most famous Puritan, John Owen, provides a great example of the critical reception of medieval thinkers that defines reformed Thomism.[91] In defining Thomistic influence on Owen, Christopher Cleveland lists a few categories of Thomistic thought in Owen's works, including direct quotations of Thomas or Thomists and the use of Thomistic theological concepts.[92]

Trueman lists several topics within Owen's theology that were affected by Thomas, including divine knowledge, providence, divine simplicity, election, causality, and sin.[93] Additionally, Trueman points out the Thomistic nature of Owen's theological education.[94] In terms of metaphysics, Trueman writes:

> Consistent with the approach of his tutor, Owen is also typical of the Reformed Orthodox tradition on this point, using the language and distinctions of medieval theology for his own particular theological

89. ibid., 188.

90. McGraw, 187.

91. Both of the men highlighted in this section, John Owen and William Ames, are listed as Puritans in the *Pocket Dictionary of the Reformed Tradition* and are frequently seen as test cases for Puritanism within the pertinent literature. See Kelly Kapic and Wesley Vander Lugt, eds., *Pocket Dictionary of the Reformed Tradition* (Downers Grove: IVP Academic, 2013), s.v. 'Ames, William,' 'Owen, John.'

92. Cleveland, 3.

93. Carl R. Trueman, *John Owen: Reformed Catholic, Renaissance Man*, Great Theologians (Burlington: Ashgate, 2007), 23. Gavin Ortlund also notes this list in Gavin Ortlund, *Theological Retrieval for Evangelicals: Why We Need Our Past to Have a Future* (Wheaton: Crossway, 2019), 42. See also Cleveland, 23.

94. Trueman writes: 'Some idea of the kind of bibliographical emphases to which an Oxford theology student of Owen's day would have been exposed is provided in the fascinating, and posthumously published, basic theological reading list of Thomas Barlow, Owen's tutor. ... Barlow stresses Aquinas, and commentators on Aquinas, as of particular use, indicating his own strong Thomistic instincts, many of which parallel concerns in Owen' (Trueman, *Owen*, 9).

purposes. In addition, he drew deeply upon the medieval metaphysical tradition, with a particular liking for the thought of Thomas Aquinas.[95]

Specifically, Trueman cites Owen's *A Display of Arminianism* as an example of his Reformed Thomistic tendencies, listing, for example, Owen's use of 'the common late medieval technical distinctions and definitions such as the divine knowledge of simple intelligence and the knowledge of vision, and also the will of the sign.'[96]

According to Trueman, however, Thomas's influence on Owen is not limited to one work. Trueman writes:

> Owen's Thomism is not restricted to the issue of anti-Pelagianism. In a later work, *A Dissertation on Divine Justice,* Owen uses Thomist approaches to theological language and natural theology in order to defend the idea that retributive justice is an essential part of God and that, once God decided to forgive sin, the incarnation and death of Christ became necessary, not just convenient; and he does this in explicit disagreement not simply with the Socinians but even with Reformed Orthodox writers such as Twisse and Rutherford who are more influenced in their doctrine of God by a kind of Scotist voluntarism, with all the theological and linguistic implications that contains.[97]

Even Owen's disagreements with Thomas should not be mistaken as a rejection of Thomistic thought. Trueman believes that the evidence should lead scholars to believe 'that, despite the anti-Roman rhetoric, his relationship to medieval theology, especially that of Thomas Aquinas, was far more nuanced if not generally positive than such rhetoric might have led us to suspect.'[98]

Cleveland lists three main areas of Thomistic influence on Owen: the concept of God as a pure act of being, the concept of infused habits of grace, and the Thomistic understanding of the hypostatic

---

95. Trueman, *Owen*, 22.

96. Trueman writes: 'This is evident even in his earliest extant work, *A Display of Arminianism*, where Aquinas is explicitly cited on a number of occasions, and where the Thomist tradition clearly stands in the background of much of his argumentation' (Trueman, *Owen*, 22).

97. ibid., 23.

98. Trueman, *Owen,* 23. Trueman also points out continuity between Owen and Thomas in 'his understanding of the nature of God, of God-talk, and of the analogy between human concepts of justice and the divine attributes' (ibid., 58).

union.[99] This influence does not mean that Owen merely repeated Thomistic belief, as he was unafraid to modify Thomas when needed. For instance, Owen applied the infused habits of grace to a believer's sanctification rather than justification and reprimanded Thomas for a misunderstanding of soteriology.[100] Still, Owen was even willing to utilize Aristotelian terminology when he deemed appropriate.[101]

Owen was not alone in his use of Thomas, and even Puritans who were oftentimes critical of Thomas invoked his teaching. William Ames, for instance, was much more indebted to Puritan fathers than medieval Scholasticism, referring to the latter as 'often without life.' Still, Ames spoke highly of Thomas's analytical thought and mirrored Thomistic arguments, sometimes almost verbatim, when it came to personal ethics, the use of wealth, the definition of money, and the perennial question, '[W]ho is my neighbor?'[102] Ames's positive interactions with Thomas is exceptionally important, as 'few men had as much influence over Reformed theology on either side of both the English Channel and Atlantic Ocean as Williams Ames.'[103] Indeed, concerning one of Ames's works that reflects numerous Thomistic ideas, Joel Beeke writes,

> The Marrow of Theology was most influential in New England, where it was generally regarded as the best summary of Calvinistic theology ever written. Both Marrow and Conscience were required reading at Harvard and Yale. ... Thomas Hooker and Increase Mather recommended the Marrow as the most important book beyond the Bible for making a sound theologian.[104]

If the Marrow endorses Thomistic ideals, then those ideas were spread throughout Protestantism in both Europe and North America.

---

99. Cleveland, 4.

100. John Owen, *Works* (Edinburgh: Banner of Truth, 2000), 5:12, 64. See also Cleveland, 5.

101. Cleveland, 9.

102. John Dykstra Eusden, 'Introduction,' in *The Marrow of Theology*, by William Ames, trans. John Dykstra Eusden (Grand Rapids: Baker Books, 1997), 15-17. See, for instance, Ames, *The Marrow of Theology*, 246-49.

103. Joel Beeke and Mark Jones, *A Puritan Theology: Doctrine for Life* (Grand Rapids: Reformation Heritage Books, 2012), 52.

104. ibid., 53.

Conclusion

Contemporary research and primary documentation agree – the Reformed have consistently used Thomas when deemed beneficial. It is important to note the modesty of this conclusion, however, as early Protestants were just as willing to distinguish themselves from Thomas as they were to join him. These Protestants did not canonize Thomas nor did they deem his entire theological system anathema. While it is true that men such as Martin Luther were outspoken in their disapproval of Thomas, the Reformation goes beyond the beliefs of any single individual. Once one takes a broad view of the Reformation and the subsequent years of Reformed theological development, it is clear to see that certain Thomistic principles were welcomed into Protestant systems. The eclectic Protestant use of Thomas does not eradicate the need, validity, or success of the Reformation, but rather provides a continuity of thought that connects Protestantism with church history – a history that belongs to Protestants! At this point, we may turn to specific Thomistic beliefs essential to a proper definition of Reformed Thomism.

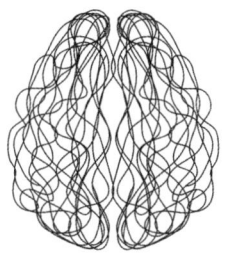

CHAPTER FOUR

Key Doctrines of Reformed Thomism

Early Protestant thinkers practiced a critical reception of Thomistic theology. Note the emphasis, however, on the *critical* nature of this Thomistic reception. A critical Protestant retrieval will necessarily lead to both affirmations and denials of Thomistic propositions. This careful treatment, however, in which some Thomistic principles are embraced while others are rejected, need not disqualify one from being counted among the Thomists, broadly defined. Separating the form of Thomism practiced by Protestants from the form adopted by Roman Catholics requires a distinction between the principles that must be affirmed and those that may, or in some cases must, be discarded.

While it is difficult to provide a strict definition of Thomism, the following points are a few key doctrinal affirmations that one must adopt if one wishes to be classified as a *Reformed* Thomist in any significant sense. After all, a rejection of certain load-bearing claims within any system of thought would necessarily lead to a rejection of the system itself. The following Thomistic principles have been selected due to their permeating influence on the entirety of Thomas's philosophical and theological works, their relevance pertaining to a correct understanding of Thomas's doctrine of God, and to their positive appearance within Protestant scholarship. Furthermore, a familiarity with these concepts will be necessary in order to properly understand Thomas's exposition of the divine intellect.

The Difficulty of Defining Thomism

Thomism is a notoriously broad movement that is even difficult to define within Catholicism. Some Thomists reflect Thomas's thought more than others. Indeed, at times it may seem that '[o]ver the course of history, almost every thesis essential to Thomas was either contested or ignored by one or another of the "Thomists".'[1] Things are complicated even more when one begins tracing Thomism through the eight hundred years of its historical development. A primitive Thomism is quite different than twentieth-century Neo-Thomism, which is different still than the Reformed Thomism discussed in this book.[2] For those interested in theological retrieval, rather than theological novelty, continuity of thought is obviously a significant goal. Therefore, a classification of essential tenets must be kept broad if one desires to maintain such continuity with earlier thought.

An emphasis on the broad parameters of Thomism is not unusual when it comes to the historical definitions of the movement. For instance, J. A. Weisheipl believes that, in a broad sense, a commitment to the use of Thomas's basic principles and conclusions in contemporary discussions was the only necessary characteristic of a Thomist.[3] Furthermore, the inclusion of what has been termed 'eclectic Thomism' allows for the integration of Thomas's thought into Protestantism. Romanus Cessario explains, 'What is distinctive about the efforts of eclectic Thomists is their willingness to import large portions of other philosophical and theological systems so that they are led to relativize the principles and conclusions that constitute the Thomism of Thomas Aquinas.'[4] The definition of Thomism has traditionally been kept so broad, in fact, that Cessario believes that a comprehensive history

---

1. Géry Prouvost, *Thomas d'Aquin et les Thomismes* (Paris: Le Cerf, 1996), 9. Originally cited in Cessario, 12. Cessario believes that Prouvost overstates the problem of discontinuity among the Thomists.

2. For a brief history of Thomism within Catholicism, see Healy, 8-22. Cessario notes that Thomism has been historically divided into early, or first Thomism, second Thomism, and Neo-Thomism. See Cessario, 28.

3. J. A. Weisheipl, 'Thomism,' in *Catholic Encyclopedia* (New York: Robert Appleton Company, 1912), 14:698. Cessario notes, 'Wide Thomism ... includes any author who gives the principle and conclusions of Thomas Aquinas a privileged place in the development of his own proper theological or philosophical reflections' (Cessario, 16).

4. ibid., 17-18.

of the movement would essentially compose 'a history, not of one school of thought, but of almost the entire Christian tradition from the late medieval to the contemporary period.'[5] As such, the presence of disagreements among self-identified Thomists, combined with the popularity of Thomas's ideas and the historical development of the movement, necessitates a 'big tent.'

Still, this ambiguous definition of Thomism does not prevent one from identifying some key parameters of the movement. Weisheipl, for instance, lists philosophical boundaries, including the distinction between form and matter, metaphysical realism, God as *actus purus*, and analogical predication, all of which are examined at length below.[6] Additionally, the Catholic Church has produced Twenty-Four Thomistic Theses that separate the philosophy of Thomas from other Scholastic and contemporary thinkers, and the theological presuppositions that provide the framework of Thomas's thought will necessarily separate Thomism from various streams of modern and postmodern theism.[7] These distinctions mean that while an eclectic Thomism may include many scholars from various philosophical and theological backgrounds, the term cannot be ubiquitous for all Christian thinkers. It is believed that the proceeding beliefs provide a broad enough base to include as many thinkers as possible without becoming too inclusive or unhelpful, while still providing enough exclusivity to separate these Reformed thinkers from the broader stream of Christian thought.

The following survey will be divided into two somewhat anachronistic portions. First, we will focus on the doctrinal and biblical claims necessary to Reformed Thomism. In Chapter 5, we will shift our focus to the metaphysical, Aristotelian, and broadly philosophical claims that characterize the movement. I refer to this distinction as anachronistic because Thomas would not concede metaphysics to a non-theological discipline. For Thomas, and for Reformed Thomism, Christian

---

5. ibid., 18.

6. Weisheipl, 127. This list is summarized in ibid., 22-24.

7. See W. H. Marshner, 'The Twenty-Four Thomistic Theses,' accessed September 22, 2021, https://marshner.christendom.edu/wp-content/uploads/2016/07/24-theses-webedit.pdf. The Thomistic Theses were ratified in 1916, so Marshner's translation is obviously not original, but the document includes helpful explanatory footnotes and is widely accessible.

philosophy is a mode of Christian theology and not a separate discipline. One cannot separate his doctrine of God from his metaphysics.

Theological Thomistic Commitments

Thomas was first and foremost a theologian and did not consider himself to be a philosopher, despite popular misconceptions. In fact, Thomas reserved the term 'philosopher' to describe pagan thinkers, such as Plato and Aristotle, and did not employ the term to describe the work of Christians.[8] 'Even when making distinctively philosophical arguments for the existence of God in *ST* I, q.2,' explains Thomas Joseph White, 'Aquinas is conducting what he takes to be an exercise in Catholic theological *sacra doctrina*.'[9] Thomas obviously made use of reason, logic, and argumentation, but he was investigating that which was received via revelation. In this sense, Thomas continued the classical mode of theology as faith seeking understanding. Indeed, Thomas believed that his 'philosophical' investigation was the outworking of biblical principles: 'For whatsoever is encountered in the other sciences which is incompatible with [Scripture's] truth should be completely condemned as false: accordingly the second epistle to the Corinthians alludes to the pulling down of ramparts, destroying counsels, and every height that rears itself against the knowledge of God' (Aquinas, *ST* 1.1.6 ad 2).

Even though Thomas reserved the term 'philosopher' for pagan thinkers, strong 'philosophical' concepts, terms, and arguments were a hallmark of medieval theology. Indeed, 'During the Middle Ages practically all the philosophers were monks, priests, or at least simple clerics' so it's not surprising that we recognize the theological aspects of

---

8. Davies writes, 'Some have argued that Aquinas was not really a philosopher since his thinking is always theological, and this position is defensible for a number of reasons. Aquinas never formally taught philosophy and never describes himself as a philosopher. He would have understood the word 'philosopher' to signify a pagan thinker, not a Christian, and certainly not someone functioning as a Master of Theology or a teacher of Dominicans.' See Brian Davies, *Thomas Aquinas's Summa Contra Gentiles: A Guide and Commentary* (Oxford: Oxford University Press, 2016), 6.

9. Thomas Joseph White, *The Trinity: On the Nature and Mystery of the One God*, Thomistic Ressourcement Series 19 (Washington, DC: The Catholic University of America Press, 2022), 187. For more information concerning Thomas's understanding of *sacra doctrina*, see Bruce D. Marshall, '*Quod Scit una Uetula*: Aquinas on the Nature of Theology,' in *The Theology of Thomas Aquinas*, by Rik Van Nieuwenhove and Joseph Wawrykow, eds., paperback ed. (Notre Dame: University of Notre Dame Press, 2005), 1-35.

their philosophical arguments and vice versa. This overlap between the clergy and philosophy is far removed from the current scene in which 'modern philosophy has been created by laymen, not by churchmen, and to the ends of the natural cities of men, not to the end of the supernatural city of God.'[10] Wisdom, however, is only found where God exists, so a philosophy that accomplishes its goal must be practiced *coram deo*.

Since Thomistic philosophy is an outworking of Thomas's theology, then, it is appropriate to begin a definition of Reformed Thomism with the necessary theological commitments, especially those pertaining to the doctrine of God, before we address the metaphysical commitments. As discussed in Chapters 1 and 2, when alternative forms of theism set themselves against the classical model, it was frequently Thomas's doctrine of God that was in view. Considering this close association between classical theism in general and Thomas's doctrine of God in particular, it is not surprising that an emphasis on the classical doctrine of God is a major component of Carter's definition of Reformed Thomism. Carter writes:

> Reformed Thomism is a form of Augustinian theology developed during the Protestant Reformation that views *the doctrine of God outlined by Thomas Aquinas in the first forty-three questions of the Summa Theologica* as an exemplary expression of the trinitarian classical theism at the heart of classic Nicene orthodoxy.[11]

Considering that, for Thomas, God is the proper object of theology, it would seem impossible for alternative forms of theism to qualify as Thomistic. The doctrine of God is the starting point and end goal for Thomas's entire system of thought. In theology as in history, God is both the alpha and omega (Rev 1:8; 22:13).

Indeed, apart from the theological premises of classical theism, it is difficult to consistently accept Thomistic conclusions and equally difficult to explain why a non-classical theist would want to, since the doctrine of God provides the foundation for most of Thomas's overarching arguments. For Thomas, Christian theology is the study of God and all things in relation to God, and the pursuit of divine knowledge is the

---

10. Gilson, *God and Philosophy*, 74.

11. Craig Carter, *Contemplating God with the Great Tradition: Recovering Trinitarian Classical Theism* (Grand Rapids: Baker Academic, 2021), 7; emphasis added.

core of wisdom. Thomas writes, 'That person, therefore, who considers maturely and without qualification the *first and final cause* of the entire universe, namely God, is to be called supremely wise ...' (Aquinas, *ST* 1.1.6). The interconnectedness between all created things due to their corporate relation to God is the reason why one cannot separate Thomas's philosophy from his theology. As Norman Geisler explains, 'Aquinas's view of God is an integral part of his view of reality (metaphysics) ...' This doctrine of God that shaped Thomas's philosophy was not novel, as 'Aquinas's view of God falls within the classical tradition of Augustine and Anselm.' Yet, 'Aquinas is the greatest classical theist ever to write extensively on the topic.'[12] Thomas's doctrine of God included a commitment to and defense of the teaching that he had received from the doctors of the church who preceded him. This teaching includes the classical view of divine attributes such as immutability, eternity, simplicity, and infinity. In fact, Thomas's articulation of doctrines such as simplicity have even become the common designation of such doctrine, despite the existence of diverse definitions.[13] This continuity with previous thought combined with Thomas's detailed and thorough exposition of Christian doctrine has led many to conclude that Thomas's doctrine of God is the premier example of classical theism.

The Doctrinal Structure of the *Summa Theologiæ*

It is fitting to focus on Thomas's doctrine of God because the structure of his magnum opus, the *Summa Theologiæ*, reflects the God-centered nature of reality. Every part, question, and article of the *ST* points readers to God in some fashion. Thomas divided the *ST* into three parts by treating 'first, of God, secondly, of the journey to God of reasoning creatures, thirdly of Christ, who, as man, is our road to God' (Aquinas, *ST* 1.2, Introduction).[14] For Thomas, God is the beginning and end of all things, and without Him, reality loses all meaning.[15] Indeed, 'Now all things are dealt with in holy teaching in terms of God, either

---

12. Geisler, *Aquinas*, 103.

13. For a broad overview of patristic and medieval perspectives of divine simplicity, see Ortlund, 117-40.

14. cf. Davies, *The Thought of Thomas Aquinas*, 21

15. Rudi te Velde, *Aquinas on God: The 'Divine Science' of the Summa Theologiae*, Ashgate Studies in the History of Philosophical Theology 4 (New York: Routledge, 2016), 11.

because they are God himself or because they are relative to him as their origin and end' (Aquinas, *ST* 1.1.7). The purpose of sacred doctrine, the subject Thomas intends to explain in his *Summa*, is to 'communicate knowledge of God,' which means that 'the whole of the *Summa* is, in this sense, *sermo de Deo*.'[16] Disagreeing with Thomas on matters of ecclesiology or soteriology does not render the entirety of his theological system useless, but if someone were to reject Thomas's understanding of theology proper, then the entire project, indeed all of reality in Thomas's estimation, has lost its meaning.

Divine Transcendence

A commitment to Thomas's doctrine of God will necessarily include the 'profound thrust toward the transcendent [present] in medieval theology.'[17] Thomas's apophatic theology, his use of analogical predication, and his understanding of the divine perfections are all closely related to God's transcendence, a category that popular theologians progressively diminished throughout the twentieth century. While it may, at times, feel as if Thomas is splitting metaphysical hairs, all his arguments are made with the Creator-creature distinction in mind, and he is careful to uphold this distinction in all of his doctrinal conclusions. Concepts such as the distinction of act and potency or divine simplicity are not arbitrary philosophical or theological inclusions in the *ST* but are employed to explain Thomas's understanding of divine transcendence.

This transcendence is intertwined with divine independence, and the doctrine stands at odds against all forms of theistic mutualism. This belief enabled Thomas to write, 'Since God is outside the whole created order and every creature is ordered to him, but the contrary is not true, so it is clear that there is a real relation of creatures to God. There is, however, no real relation of God to creatures, but only a rational one, in so far as creatures are referred to him' (Aquinas, *ST* 1.13.7).[18] This statement is obviously opposed to the give-and-take relationships that

---

16. te Velde, 11.

17. Rik Van Nieuwenhove, *An Introduction to Medieval Theology*, 2nd ed. (Cambridge: Cambridge University Press, 2022), 2. This emphasis of transcendence is one reason Nieuwenhove believes that the medieval theologians are prime candidates for theological retrieval.

18. On the distinction of various relations in Thomas's writing, see White, *The Trinity*, 426.

theistic mutualism seeks to defend. Even though theistic mutualists use the term 'transcendent' to describe their models of God, the meaning of the term within theistic mutualism differs wildly than what it means in a Thomistic system.[19]

Divine transcendence, of course, should be affirmed by all Bible-believing Christians. Isaiah affirms that there are no equal comparisons to God (Isa. 40:25-26) and Job's friends rightly extol the limitless depth of the divine (Job 11:7-10). His thoughts and ways are incomparable to man's (Isa. 55:8-9) and His will is not bound by human limitations (Ps. 115:3). Simply put, He is the great I AM – the source of all being that does not receive being from another (Ex. 3:14). It is no surprise that the Westminster Confession of Faith describes this God as the 'fountain of all being, of whom, through whom, and to whom are all things' (Rom. 11:36). Indeed, 'his knowledge is infinite, infallible, and *independent* upon the creature, so as nothing is to him contingent, or uncertain' (Rom. 11:33-34; Ps. 147:5).[20] The historical Reformed interpretation of Scripture affirms God's absolute transcendence and independence.

Actus Purus

Specifically, a Thomistic form of transcendence, and the Creator-creature distinction with which it is so closely aligned, finds its metaphysical grounding in the division of being into act and potency. A critical concept within Thomism is the understanding of God as *actus purus* – pure act (Aquinas, *ST* 1.4.2). *Actus purus* will be explained in greater detail below but, for now, it should be noted that the division of being into act and potency provides the metaphysical framework for several significant theological conclusions. Within the Thomistic framework, act is understood as the perfection of existence, in which a substance is fully actualized, lacks nothing, and stands complete.[21] In this sense, *actus purus* is a specific description of God's perfection.

---

19. For instance, compare how the term 'transcendent' functions within John C. Peckham's covenantal theism with Thomas's understanding of transcendence. See Peckham, *Divine Attributes*, 2, 23, 42n11.

20. WCF 2.2

21. Gilson, *God and Philosophy*, 82. Gilson is describing Descartes's view of God rather than Thomas's specific model, but the description is fitting nonetheless.

Potency, however, is understood as the capability of being acted upon by external forces and always suggests an imperfection or possibility of growth, change, or progression. To suggest that God is pure act, then, means that God is perfectly absolute and lacks the capability of being acted upon. Any passive potentiality would suggest movement either toward perfection (which God already exemplifies) or away from perfection (an impossibility for anything fitting the title of God).

For Thomas, God is immutable because He lacks potency; God is simple because He lacks potency; God is impassible because He lacks potency; If God has no potency then He must exist infinitely; in short, God is God *because* He lacks potency.[22] Absolute perfection, then, is a non-negotiable aspect of divinity. This lack of potency, however, does not mean that God is immovable or stagnant, as Thomas makes clear when he discusses such topics as God's governance of creation and God's imminent operations.[23] It does, however, mean that God's being – the divine essence itself – lacks anything that awaits fruition. As Cessario writes, 'God enjoys his own subsistent fullness of pure actual being and possesses no limitation of any kind, because nothing of potential is to be found in him.'[24] Brian Davies further explains:

> To cast things in the manner of negative theology, God must be perfect since he is in no way potential – since there is nothing which he could be but is not. Since God, for Aquinas, has no potentiality, he cannot be modified and cannot, therefore, be either improved or made worse. ... For

---

22. See, for instance, what Thomas writes concerning immutability: 'Our findings so far prove God to be altogether unchangeable. First, because we have proved that there must be some first existent, called God, sheerly actual and unalloyed with potentiality, since actuality, simply speaking, precedes potentiality. Now any changing thing, whatsoever the change, is somehow potential. So it clearly follows that God cannot change in any way' (Aquinas, *ST* 1.9.1 ad 1). See also Renard, 36.

23. The idea of immobility or stagnation within a Thomistic doctrine of God is incompatible with the way Thomists speak of God. For instance, Peter Kreeft writes, 'Thus God is always active, dynamic, and willing, yet not in process and time and potentiality. "Process theology" argues that God must be in time and process for Him to be dynamic and active and personal. St. Thomas would reply that a temporally active God may be more perfect than an eternally static God, but an eternally active God is the most perfect of all.' See Peter Kreeft, ed., *Summa of the Summa: The Essential Philosophical Passages of St. Thomas Aquinas' Summa Theologica Edited and Explained for Beginners* (San Francisco: Ignatius Press, 1990), 155n143.

24. Cessario, 23.

God to be, therefore, is for God to be as divine as it takes divinity to be. It is for God to be fully God and, therefore, perfectly God.[25]

It is easy to see why Thomas's commitment to *actus purus* prevents him from accepting any form of theistic mutualism. God cannot gain anything from creation, as that would be an admittance of potentiality within the divine essence, which would, in turn, eliminate God's divinity altogether. A God that can receive something from His creation has room for growth and is, therefore, not yet perfect. If there's more for God to learn, then He is ignorant of something, and ignorance has no home in divinity.

While the term *actus purus* does not appear in Scripture, the corresponding elements of God's perfection and self-sufficiency are frequently discussed. Contra the idols, God is not served by human hands and He does not reside in temples made by human hands (Acts 17:24-25). Indeed, God needs nothing and, instead, gives all life, breath, and being to His creation. The author of the Pentateuch declares, 'The Rock! [God's] work is perfect, For all his ways are just; A God of faithfulness and without injustice, Righteous and upright is he' (Deut. 32:4; cf. Ps. 19:7). God's knowledge is complete thus requiring no counselor (Rom. 11:33; Ps. 147:5; Isa. 40:13), God's love is complete thus requiring no emotional awakening (1 John 4:16), and God's power is complete thus requiring no assistance (Matt. 19:26; Job 42:2). He is the blessed one, great in power, majesty, victory, and glory (1 Chron. 29:10-13). Anselm was summarizing what he received from Scripture when he described God as 'something-than-which-nothing-greater-can-be-thought.'[26]

Nicene Trinitarianism

Thomas's affirmation of a transcendent, classical model of theism, in which God is understood as pure act, is incomplete without Nicene Trinitarianism. As Carter explains,

> [c]lassical theism without trinitarian theology gives us the god of the philosophers, that is, the remote and impersonal god of Deism, who does not speak or act and who, crucially cannot save us. But trinitarian theology

---

25. Davies, *The Thought of Thomas Aquinas*, 81.
26. Anselm, *Proslogion 2, Major Works*, 87.

without classical theism results in a God who is part of the cosmos with us, differing from creatures only by degree and not by nature.[27]

The doctrine of the Trinity prevents an embrace of a strictly 'unmoved Mover' in Thomas's system as '[t]he Trinity, the inner procession of persons in God, is thought to result from a divine *activity*, from an act of *generation* by which the Son and Holy Spirit proceed from the Father within the unity of the divine essence.'[28] Aristotle misunderstood God precisely because he did not know the *triune* God that Thomas learned about via special revelation.

Some theologians, however, have critiqued Thomas's analysis of the Trinity, claiming that the doctrine serves as an addendum in Thomas's system once everything important about God has already been said.[29] Again, Thomas's commitment to God's absoluteness helps clarify his doctrine at this point. Te Velde explains that the misconceptions surrounding Thomas's Trinitarianism stem from a misunderstanding of how transcendence functions in Thomas's doctrine of God. There are certain aspects of the divine essence that can be known through properly functioning human reasoning, including God's existence and divine perfections such as simplicity, immutability, eternity, etc. A transcendent God, however, is ultimately beyond human comprehension. As such, it is unsurprising to find that there are certain aspects of God that can only be known via special revelation and embraced in faith, such as the Trinity and the Incarnation of Christ.

Thomas works through the aspects of divinity knowable through reason, which in turn are those aspects common to the divine persons, before moving on to the articles of faith, specifically the Trinity. Te Velde writes: 'If we were in possession of an adequate concept of God, enabling us to understand what He is, we would grasp immediately the triune character of the divine essence. We would then understand that to be God necessarily means to be one-God-in-three-persons.'[30] Thomas,

---

27. Carter, *Contemplating God*, 29.

28. Te Velde, *Aquinas on God*, 69.

29. Pannenberg, Grenz, and Moltmann all lobbied similar claims about Thomas. See footnote 78 in Chapter 2. Additionally, see Karl Rahner, 'Remarks on the Dogmatic Treatise de Trinitate,' in *Theological Investigations* (London: Darton, Longman, Todd, 1966), 4:78; te Velde, *Aquinas on God*, 68.

30. Te Velde, *Aquinas on God*, 71.

therefore, always has the Trinity in mind when speaking of God. Even though Thomas admits that the Trinity transcends general revelation, he certainly does not discount the doctrine's importance. As Davies points out: 'For [Thomas], the heart of Christian teaching is the doctrine of the Trinity, which is the first *specifically Christian topic* he turns to in the *Summa theologiae*. ... Historically speaking, Aquinas is one of the most important writers on the doctrine of the Trinity.'[31] Everything Thomas wrote about God up to this point in the ST has specifically described the *triune* God of the Bible, and a proper Trinitarian confession is necessary in order to adopt Thomas's system.

The same classical models of God and the Trinity that Thomas affirms appear in numerous Reformed confessions. As stated in Chapter 1, this definition of God makes appearances in the Belgic Confession, the Thirty-Nine Articles of Religion, the Westminster Confession of Faith, and the Second London Confession of Faith.[32] In fact, the Westminster Confession follows a similar route as Thomas's *ST* by first describing the divine essence before discussing the divine persons. After God's immutability, eternality, infinity, aseity, and transcendence have all been affirmed, the authors write: 'In the unity of the Godhead there be three persons, of one substance, power and eternity: God the Father, God the Son, and God the Holy Ghost: the Father is of none, neither begotten, nor proceeding; the Son is eternally begotten of the Father; the Holy Ghost eternally proceeding from the Father and the Son.'[33] Thomas would, of course, affirm this statement in its entirety.

The Reformed simply did not find it necessary to edit the doctrines of God and the Trinity that were passed down to them. In particular, the Second London Confession of Faith testifies that God has all 'life, glory, goodness, blessedness, in and of Himself, is alone in and unto Himself all-sufficient, not standing in need of any creature which He hath made, nor deriving any glory from them.'[34] Furthermore, this commitment to God's transcendent absoluteness and independence can

---

31. Davies, *The Thought of Thomas Aquinas*, 185.

32. Dolezal, *All That Is in God*, 1.

33. WCF 2.3. The WCF cites a host of passages to support this Trinitarian point including Matt. 3:16-17; Matt. 28:19; 2 Cor. 13:14; Eph. 2:18; John 1:14, 18; Heb. 1:2-3; Col. 1:15; John 15:26, and Gal. 4:6.

34. LBCF 2.2.19.

be seen in Protestant theologians such as Petrus van Mastricht, Francis Turretin, Stephen Charnock, and countless others. Jack Kilcrease makes this continuity especially clear when he affirms Muller's analysis of the Thomistic influence of the Protestant Scholastics. Kilcrease writes:

> Muller correctly notes that although the Reformers sought to reform Western catholic teachings regarding soteriology and ecclesiology, they largely left the patristic and medieval teachings on the subjects of faith and reason, the divine essence and attributes, the nature of the Trinity, the hypostatic union, creation, and providence intact (Muller 1987–2003, 1:34). Therefore, in order to teach these subjects, the Protestant scholastics found it necessary to draw on the intellectual resources of the previous Christian tradition.[35]

In light of the Reformation's commitment to the classical doctrine of God and the Trinity, Swain writes, 'It is a lamentable situation, therefore, that many who consider themselves as heirs of Reformation theology have found themselves of late taking an increasingly ambivalent stance toward the doctrine of God that early Protestants confessed and proclaimed.'[36] Indeed, this ambivalence is one of the chief benefits of theological retrieval according to Gavin Ortlund. Ortlund cites the 2016 Trinity controversy that took place within evangelical circles as an example of theological ambivalence and specifically highlights a contemporary reformed Thomistic work, James Dolezal's *All That Is in God*, as a needed corrective.[37] Ortlund not only cites the underdevelopment of theology proper as a problem, but also the lack of knowledge concerning the significance of these doctrines. Ortlund writes, 'How else can we understand the casualness with which doctrines as important and mainstream throughout church history as, say, the eternal generation of the Son, or divine simplicity, are often jettisoned by evangelicals today?'[38] In many theological ressourcement projects, a proper understanding of the divine nature, attributes, and persons is the primary concern. Thomas would, no doubt, emphasize the necessity of this undertaking.

---

35. Kilcrease, 111.

36. Swain, 'The Being and Attributes of God,' 237.

37. Ortlund, 54.

38. ibid., 56.

Special Consideration: The Doctrine of Divine Simplicity

Out of all the divine perfections pertinent to a Thomistic doctrine of God, special attention should be dedicated to the doctrine of divine simplicity (DDS). All the classical divine perfections are debated by one source or another in contemporary theological discourse, but DDS may be the most controversial claim classical theists have to offer.[39] Contemporary theologians and philosophers alike seem increasingly comfortable dismissing DDS for supposed less-problematic formulations of God's unity. DDS – specifically what it entails for the relationship between God's knowledge and the divine essence – will play a significant role in our argument, so it is wise to articulate what the doctrine does and does not entail. Indeed, Davies suggests, 'If you take Aquinas to be wrong in what he says about divine simplicity, you will think that there is little of value in SCG I, 44–71 [Thomas's exposition of the divine intellect]. That is because so many of its arguments presuppose that God is simple in the way that Aquinas takes him to be in SCG I, 16–25.'[40] Again, this idea will be investigated in greater depth during the discussions regarding Thomistic metaphysics, Thomas's exposition of the divine intellect, and the proper definition of truth, but a general overview is necessary, nonetheless.

A Thomistic version of DDS claims that God is free from all modes of possible division; all that is in God, is God.[41] Specifically, Thomas dismisses any composition in God concerning bodily parts, form and matter, substance and accidents, essence and existence, and act and potency (Aquinas, *ST* 1.3.1–8). Potentially, the most controversial implication of this doctrine is that the divine attributes, while distinct

---

39. Ed Feser calls Thomas's treatment of divine simplicity 'perhaps the most controversial aspect of his teaching on the divine attributes' (Feser, *Aquinas*, 126). He then adds: 'Though the idea of divine simplicity might seem odd or eccentric to some contemporary readers, it is historically speaking the mainstream view of God's nature within the classical theistic tradition, being defended not only by Aquinas, but by thinkers as diverse as St. Athanasius, St. Augustine, St. Anselm, Maimonides, Aviceena, and Averroes, to name just a few' (Feser, *Aquinas*, 129). Impassibility may be a close second in terms of controversy.

40. Davies, *Summa Contra Gentiles*, 112.

41. ibid., 104.

and diverse in the minds of creatures, are one and the same in God.[42] God's love is the same as God's power, which is the same as God's justice, which is the same as God's mercy.[43] Thomas explains:

> To this diversity which belongs to reason, there corresponds the plurality of predicate and subject; the intellect signifies the identity of the thing through the very fact of uniting them (*per ipsam compositionem*). However, God considered in himself is entirely one and simple; but our intellect knows him by differing concepts; this is because it is not able to see him as he is in himself. *Yet, although it understands him under diverse conceptions, it actually knows that to all these notions there corresponds one and the same object simply.* This plurality, therefore, which is according to reason, it represents through the plurality of predicate and subject; the unity however intellect manifests by composing them unto unity (Aquinas, *ST* 1.13.12).

Human knowledge of the divine perfections is filtered through the creaturely effects from the divine cause. Still, since act precedes potency and the perfections in God precede the imitated perfections in creatures, humanity may receive true knowledge of the cause from the effects, albeit in analogical fashion. Hankey summarizes this point well:

> God can be named from creatures and substantially. The names signify him properly; indeed, 'they more properly belong to God than to creatures.' They are not mere synonyms; their variety and plurality make them more adequate for speaking of him than the contrary. They are not stated of him univocally but analogically, in the way a principle is related to inferior causes; thus, 'as far as what is signified through the name is concerned they are more primarily predicates of God than of creatures.' God is not really related to creatures but rather they to him.[44]

---

42. White writes: 'Aquinas … affirms, as we have seen above, that the various "names of God" attributed to God in virtue of his divine essence are identical in reality, in God himself. … God in his pure actuality is not formally composite or complex, so while we do not know immediately or intuitively "what" God is in himself, we do know that the names we ascribe to the divine essence are somehow co-extensive, united, and indeed identical in the very being of God' (White, *Trinity*, 383).

43. Thomas speaks of the attributes in this manner. For instance, Thomas writes: 'God's power is his goodness; hence he can only use his power in a good way' (Aquinas, *ST* 1–2.2.4 ad 1). This quote was originally discovered in Josef Pieper, *The Human Wisdom of St. Thomas: A Breviary of Philosophy from the Works of St. Thomas Aquinas*, trans. Drostan Maclaren, repr. ed. (San Francisco: Ignatius Press, 2002), 71.

44. W. J. Hankey, *God in Himself: Aquinas' Doctrine of God as Expounded in the Summa Theologiae*, Oxford Theological Monographs (Oxford: Oxford University Press,

Readers will notice that the Neoplatonic *Triplex Via* is in full effect. The *Triplex Via*, most commonly associated with the thought of Pseudo-Dionysius, is the 'threefold way of knowing' God from the study of His creatures.[45] The *Triplex Via* consists of the threefold path of causality, negation, and eminence. Any perfection that exists within creation must be caused by God, exist in God perfectly apart from any creaturely imperfections, and exist in God in a transcendent and more glorious mode of being. Scott Swain writes, 'Taken together, the threefold way of divine naming teaches us that God's fatherly goodness is the source of all creaturely goods and that it radically transcends the vicissitudes of creaturely being.'[46] The reason that creatures can demonstrate creaturely goodness is because goodness first exists in God without limits, imperfections, and potentiality.

Creaturely perfections are limited but genuine reflections of perfections that first and primarily exist in God. What is demonstrated through diversity and multiplicity in creation, however, exists simply as the eternal principle of all creaturely being – the divine essence.[47] Creaturely minds exist compositely and are thus incapable of comprehending true simplicity. As a result, composite minds experience a variety of attributes as they contemplate the 'absolute simplicity of infinite Being in God.'[48] The supposed division of attributes, then, exist in human minds rather than in the divine essence itself, which is perfectly simple.

A popular caricature of the Thomistic model of divine simplicity is found in those who suggest that Thomas denies any and all distinctions pertaining to God. 'This is clearly false,' White teaches, 'since [Thomas] thinks there is a real distinction of persons in God. In fact, Aquinas's

---

1987), 89. Notice that this explanation is opposed to theistic mutualism. Likewise, White writes, 'The divine simplicity likewise excludes certain conclusions of process metaphysics – as one finds in the philosophy of Albert North Whitehead, or in the theories of Open Theism – in which God is undergoing continual change in relation with and reaction to the world, in an inward historical time within God's own nature, like a kind of duration of consciousness' (White, *Trinity*, 256).

45. Scott Swain demonstrates that the *Triplex Via* is not limited to natural theology but is also present in revealed theology in Swain, 'On Divine Naming.'

46. Swain, 'On Divine Naming,' 213.

47. According to Thomas: 'Perfections found in creatures in a state of division and multiplicity exist in God without division and in unity ...' (Aquinas, *ST* 1.14.1 ad 2).

48. Thomas Gornall, 'Introduction,' in *Summa Theologiæ: Knowledge in God*, by Thomas Aquinas, trans. Thomas Gornall (Cambridge: Cambridge University Press, 2006), xxi.

doctrine of "non-composition" is restricted to a very limited set of ontological topics: form and matter, individual and essence, existence and essence, and substance and accidents ...'[49] As one can see, while Thomas does deny all forms of bodily/material composition in the Godhead, most of the categories pertaining to Thomas's understanding of divine simplicity are metaphysical. Specifically, any metaphysical category that would lead to any form of divine dependence upon His creatures is excluded from divinity.[50] Yet, Thomas's understanding of DDS does not pertain to the eternal relations of origin that truly distinguish the triune persons from one another. The Thomistic version of DDS is specifically a triune simplicity.

DDS is often portrayed as a relic of a bygone era, unnecessary now that humanity has progressed beyond medieval metaphysics.[51] Some consider classical theism's commitment to such an unreasonable doctrine as a major hindrance to the movement's larger theological goals. Critics claim that modifying the doctrine significantly, or dropping the concept altogether, is the only way forward in a post-Kantian world where metaphysical presuppositions are met with significant suspicion.

---

49. White, *The Trinity*, 243.

50. Michael Bergmann and Jeffrey Brower write: 'The appeal of this doctrine is that it makes it completely clear that God does not depend on things in any way at all, not even in the way that wholes depend on their proper parts or that things depend on their properties (in order to exemplify them).' See Michael Bergmann and Jeffrey Brower, 'A Theistic Argument against Platonism (and in Support of Truthmakers and Divine Simplicity),' in *Oxford Studies in Metaphysics* (Oxford: Oxford University Press, 2006), 2:357.

51. Indeed, medieval discussions concerning simplicity are typically full of metaphysical argumentation. For example, Boethius's groundwork for divine simplicity and participation can seem far removed from biblical language and imagery. Boethius explains: 'Being and that-which-is are diverse. For being itself as yet is not. That-which-is however, once the form of being has been taken on, is and stands together. What-is can participate in something, but being itself in no way participates in anything. For participation occurs when something already is. Something is, however, when it has received being. That-which-is can possess something other than what it itself is. Being itself, however, has nothing else outside itself as an admixture. ... Everything that is participates in that which is being with the result that it be. It participates in something else with the result that it be something. And through this, that-which-is participates in that which is being with the result that it be. ... In every composite, being is other than the item itself. Every simple item possesses its being and that-which-is as one.' See Thomas Aquinas, *An Exposition of the 'On the Hebdomads' of Boethius*, trans. Janice L. Schultz and Edward A. Synan, Thomas Aquinas in Translation (Washington, DC: The Catholic University of America Press, 2001), 15.

Even those theologians who wish to identify with the major claims of classical theism are sometimes willing to depart from their predecessors when it involves DDS.

Yet, a retrieval of Thomistic simplicity is a significant identifier of Reformed Thomism, especially in its contemporary advocates. James Dolezal's *All That Is in God*, Matthew Barrett's *Simply Trinity*, and Steven Duby's *Divine Simplicity: A Dogmatic Account* are all attempts to defend the doctrine against its opponents and demonstrate the necessity of simplicity when articulating other classical doctrines – such as Nicene Trinitarianism. If one wished to identify a single divine perfection that most divided Thomists from non-Thomists, then we should look no further than the doctrine of divine simplicity.

Qualifications of Reformed Thomism

Even though concepts such as divine simplicity are often articulated in metaphysical terms, philosophy – Aristotelian, Platonic, or otherwise – is not the methodological foundation for Reformed Thomism. That privilege is reserved for inspired Scripture alone. Those who oppose the Protestant use of Thomas often suggest that Thomas's thought was built on secular philosophy rather than on the biblical text. As such, these scholars claim that the use of Thomas compromises the Reformed commitment to *Sola Scriptura* and should be abandoned by Protestants. According to this opposition, Thomas did not believe that Scripture sufficiently describes the revealed God, and men thus need the help of philosophers to fill in the gaps left by Scripture. It should be noted, however, that Thomas was heralded as a biblical expert long before he was seen as a theological expert, and Thomas's commitment to Scripture continues to be demonstrated by the Protestant scholars whom he influenced.

As Sytsma points out, 'Before he began composing his famous *Summa Theologiae* around 1265, Aquinas had already lectured on the Bible for over a decade, first at Cologne prior to 1252 (Isaiah, Jeremiah, and Lamentations), and then from 1256 as *magister in sacra pagina*.'[52] Indeed, as McInerny writes, 'When a Master of Arts became a student in theology, eight years lay between him and the baccalaureate. At that

---

52. Sytsma, 'Thomas Aquinas and Reformed Biblical Interpretation,' 49.

point, he was a biblical bachelor who for at least a year was required to lecture on Scripture under the direction of the master to whom he was assigned.'[53] Thomas's theological work was preceded by years of exegetical training. It is possible, of course, to disagree with his interpretation of Scripture (as all Protestants will do at some point), but to suggest that Thomas neglected, ignored, or felt his Bible was insufficient for the task at hand stems from a misunderstanding of his life's work.

As Steinmetz explains, exegetical work was an important component to the Scholastic method of theology. He writes:

> Medieval theologians did not draw a sharp distinction, as we would, between biblical exegesis and dogmatic theology. The words 'theology' and 'sacred page' could be used interchangeably since biblical interpretation was by definition theological and dogmatic theology exegetical.[54]

Steinmetz goes on to specifically cite Thomas, writing, 'Thomas Aquinas was not more scholastic when he presided at disputations concerning the nature of truth than when he lectured on the literal sense of Job.'[55] Again, one may also consider a Reformed Thomist such as Vermigli who held a 'life-long vocation as a biblical exegete and commentator.'[56] Vermigli's entire body of scholarly work was an 'attempt to derive his theology directly from the Scriptures.' He published commentaries on 1 Corinthians, Romans, and Judges during his lifetime, and further works on Genesis, Lamentations, 1 and 2 Samuel, and 1 and 2 Kings were published posthumously.[57] The best examples of Reformed Thomism have always been exegetical movements.

It would have been difficult for Thomas and his contemporaries to articulate the division of theology and exegesis or biblical commentary. As Healy writes, 'Scripture itself is theology or *sacra doctrina* ... and

---

53. McInerny, 17.

54. Steinmetz, 'The Scholastic Calvin,' 21. Indeed, Thomas himself made such an argument: 'What is peculiar to this science's knowledge is that it is about truth which comes through revelation, not through natural reasoning.... For whatsoever is encountered in the other sciences which is incompatible with its truth should be completely condemned as false: accordingly the second epistle to the Corinthians alludes to the pulling down of ramparts, destroying counsels, and every height that rears itself against the knowledge of God' (*ST* 1.1.6 ad 2).

55. Steinmetz, 'The Scholastic Calvin,' 23.

56. James, 68.

57. James, 68-69.

so theology is largely the explication of Scripture.'[58] Thomas's responsibilities as a master of the sacred pages would have included the regular preaching of the biblical text, the analysis of the biblical text through the writing of commentaries, and regular participation in public debates, or disputations, concerning the proper interpretation and implications of the biblical text.[59] His daily profession revolved around the exposition of Scripture.

Reformed thinkers, such as William Whitaker, have made much of Thomas's biblical exegesis and have even pointed to him as an example worth following. According to Sytsma,'[Whitaker] cited many commentaries of Aquinas on the nature of Scripture to make the case that Aquinas, although problematically dependent on the Vulgate in his exegesis, was not far removed from Protestant beliefs regarding the authority of Scripture.'[60] Furthermore:

> [Whitaker] argues that significant continuity exists between Aquinas's hermeneutics and the Reformed understanding of the clarity of Scripture and reception of traditional fourfold exegesis (*quadriga*). Second, he uses Aquinas's exegesis to illustrate sound means for the interpretation of Scripture.[61]

Indeed, Thomas's system expressly invests final authority of the Bible. In volume 1 of the *Summa*, Thomas addresses the basis of his theological method – the canonical and inspired books of Scripture. Indeed, the Christian faith only rests on the revelation made to prophets and apostles, and it would not even include revelation made to other learned men. While it is proper to learn from the doctors of the Church, their arguments cannot be certain and are only a matter of probability. It is divine revelation as it is transmitted through an inspired and inerrant canon that is the standard by which all thought is judged.[62]

---

58. Healy, 2-3.

59. ibid., 3.

60. Sytsma, 'Thomas Aquinas and Reformed Biblical Interpretation,' 52. Notice the distinction between Thomas's commitment to exegesis and his practice of exegesis. One can note that Thomas reached erroneous conclusions without making him an opponent of biblical exposition.

61. ibid., 62.

62. Thomas writes, 'And so holy teaching makes use also of the authority of philosophers in matters where they were able to know the truth through natural reason, in the way that Paul quotes a saying of Aratus in Acts (17:28), "As some also of your own poets said, 'we are God's offspring'."' Nevertheless, holy teaching makes use

Fritz Bauerschmidt reaffirms this view and claims that Thomas ranked three levels of authority. First, 'Thomas grants the views of pagan thinkers a certain authority, but of the lowest sort. Having Aristotle on your side adds rhetorical force to your argument. But as Thomas sees things, it does not prove anything (though the rational cogency of one of Aristotle's arguments might).'[63] Second, the next level of author lies with the views of 'the "doctors" – those Christian teachers (doctores) whose views have been widely accepted by the church.'[64] Still, the authority of doctors can only establish *probability* and cannot serve as the ultimate authority. Finally, 'the authority of Scripture, which is supreme – resting, as it does, on the revelation given to the prophets and apostles. Arguments based on the authority of Scripture can attain a certainty that arguments based on the authority of philosophers and theologians cannot.'[65]

As such, a non-critical reception of Thomas, in which Thomas's authority was cited as the determinant of truth, would contradict Thomistic ideals. Furthermore, while Thomas no doubt respects Aristotle tremendously, he also makes it clear that pagan philosophers are at a stark disadvantage when compared to those who approach God in faith. Thomas writes, 'Despite all of their effort, none of the philosophers before the coming of Christ was able to know as much about God, and about what is necessary for life, as one old woman [*uetula*] knows by faith after Christ's coming.'[66]

---

of these authorities only as *inessential and probable arguments. But it properly uses the authority of the canonical Scriptures in making necessary arguments. The authority of other church teachers may properly be used in arguing, though only as probable.* For our faith rests upon the revelation made to the apostles and prophets who wrote the canonical books, and not on the revelations – if there are any – made to other teachers' (Aquinas, *ST* 1.1.8 ad 2).

63. Frederick Christian Bauerschmidt, *The Essential Summa Theologiae: A Reader and Commentary*, 2nd ed. (Grand Rapids: Baker Academic, 2021), 13n37.

64. Bauerschmidt, 13n37.

65. ibid.

66. Thomas Aquinas, *Collationes Credo in Deum* I, in *The Sermon-Conferences of St. Thomas Aquinas on the Apostles' Creed*, ed. Nicholas Ayo (Notre Dame: Notre Dame University Press, 1988), 20. Quote originally cited in Bruce D. Marshall, '*Quod Scit una Uetula*: Aquinas on the Nature of Theology,' in *The Theology of Thomas Aquinas*, by Rik Van Nieuwenhove and Joseph Wawrykow, eds., paperback ed. (Notre Dame: University of Notre Dame Press, 2005), 1.

Reformed Critiques of Thomas

As has been repeatedly affirmed, Reformed Thomism does not endorse an uncritical reception of Thomas. Reformed Christians will obviously note significant disagreements with Thomas when it comes to soteriology, ecclesiology, and sacramental theology. If not, the Reformed Thomists could not be *Reformed* Thomists, nor would they demonstrate a *Protestant* application of Thomistic thought. As such, Reformed Thomism is marked by an acceptance of Reformed confessions as well as the five solas of the Reformation.[67]

This Protestant distinction is essential to determine the boundaries of *Reformed* Thomism. Ortlund lists four potential dangers of theological retrieval: distortion, artificiality, repristination, and minimalism. Ortlund defines 'repristination' as 'the impression that classical sources represent some kind of grand, immovable, final verdict on all matters they address.' Ortlund continues: 'This kind of retrieval tends to leapfrog over the problems associated with modernity, as though premodernity offered us a way out of these challenges simply by preexisting them.'[68] In this inferior method of theological retrieval, theological construction becomes an act of commentary or translation rather than an advancement of theological discourse. The best versions of Reformed Thomism, then, acknowledge the points of significant disagreement with Thomas when they occur and refuse to compromise Protestant convictions established by the proper interpretation of Scripture.

As noted, theological retrieval is not simply the work of translating classical works into twenty-first-century terminology but is rather a critical appropriation of truth into the contemporary historical context. The goal of Reformed Thomism is not to graft the Protestant Church back into Rome but to embrace the Protestant Church's theological inheritance. As Fred Sanders notes, 'The whole point of actual Protestantism (when it's not having a new meaning forced on it as a

---

67. Carter, *Contemplating God*, 7.

68. Ortlund, 74. This idea is closely related to Ortlund's fourth danger, minimalism. Ortlund writes: 'We must remember that cause of genuine unity is better served by respectfully engaging our differences within the body of Christ than by ignoring or suppressing them' (Ortlund, 75).

term of abuse) is to claim the full heritage of the church while making necessary adjustments in recent deviations.'[69] Likewise, none other than Herman Bavinck wrote: 'Men like Irenaeus, Augustine and Thomas do not belong exclusively to Rome. They are *patres* and *doctores* to whom the entire church owes a great debt.'[70]

This robust Protestantism is exactly what Reformed Thomists hope to promote. Reformed Thomists seek to claim the full heritage of the Church, including the works of the Angelic Doctor, by using thoughts of his which are congruent with Scripture, while discarding his errors. Concerning the retrieval and application of Platonic thought in contemporary philosophy, Davison quips, 'For my part, I am more interested in "what can be thought with the help of Plato" than I am with sticking to "what Plato thought".'[71] In the same vein, Reformed Thomists do not wish to discover Thomas's thought to become Roman Catholic but rather to become better Protestants. When other medieval Scholastics, such as John Duns Scotus or William of Ockham, explained truth better than Thomas, then thoughtful Protestants have always been willing to promote the best argument. The ultimate goal in retrieval is not the promotion of an individual but the promotion of truth, wherever it might be found.

It has been said numerous times before, but nothing inherent to a broad definition of Thomism eliminates the possibility of Protestant adherents. While it is true that Reformed Thomism must be an eclectic Thomism, one which adopts ideals that cohere with its larger theological or philosophical framework while dismissing contradictory ideals, this is a perfectly legitimate form of Thomism. Indeed, while Thomas is traditionally referred to as the Angelic Doctor, he also has another title that is pertinent to the current conversation. Cessario writes:

> The universal compass of [Thomas's] scholarly achievements explains the custom whereby the Church even today venerates Thomas Aquinas as her 'Common Doctor,' a title that confirms the pervasiveness of his influence, at

---

69. See Fred Sanders, 'Does Protestantism Need to Die?,' *Christianity Today* (Nov 2016), 70-71. cf. Ortlund, 60.

70. Bavinck, *RD* 1:3.

71. Davison, *Love of Wisdom*, 30.

least in the West, on the received theology and philosophy that is practiced in Christian schools and used to illuminate authentic Church teaching.[72]

Thomas is called the Common Doctor because he has influenced all Western denominations and is, therefore, for all Christians. Thomas's home may be in Rome, but he can be felt alive and well in Christian centers from Canterbury to Nashville. Readers may follow Joseph de Maistre in balancing the reception of past theologians by abiding by two rules:

> 1) Not to believe that the ancients, even the most celebrated, were oracles: for they said some very stupid things. 2) Not to reject brusquely their observations under the pretext that they conflict with some of our current ideas; this would be another error perhaps more dangerous than the first.[73]

Protestants afraid to affirm Thomistic truth due to their Reformed heritage may sadly miss out on both.

Conclusion

Thomism is an emphatically theological system and requires more than mere philosophical commitments. A transcendent, absolute, self-sufficient, triune God stands at the center of everything Thomas describes. Furthermore, this God is not the 'god of philosophers' wherein divinity is the result of logical syllogisms but is rather the God explicitly described in Scripture. If Thomas and the Reformed thinkers who carried on Thomistic conclusions believed that the God of the Bible differed from the transcendent, self-sufficient, and triune God described above, then there is reason to believe that they would have adapted their theological systems accordingly. Rather, it was specifically their commitment to the God of the Bible that fueled further theological and philosophical investigations. While someone may qualify for many camps without heralding the God described by classical theism, he certainly cannot be described as a Thomist. The doctrine of God stands as the primary commitment in any Thomistic system, Reformed or otherwise. With this bedrock foundation in place, we may now address Thomas's metaphysical claims.

---

72. Cessario, 2.

73. Joseph de Maistre, 'Philosophie C' (unpublished reading notes, 1807), MS, Maistre Archives, Archives Departementales de Savoie, Chambery, 19. Retrieved from Morello, 9.

CHAPTER FIVE

Modified Aristotelian Metaphysics

Although Thomas is first and foremost a theologian, an examination of Thomism would be incomplete apart from a survey of the philosophical ideas that frequently placed him in the midst of controversy, namely, his 'judicious use of Aristotelianism in Theology.'[1] Indeed, the use of a modified Aristotelianism is what originally separated Thomas and early Thomists from their Scholastic contemporaries. Furthermore, 'It has been said that without Thomas, Aristotle would be mute; it can equally well be said that without Aristotle, Thomas would be unintelligible.'[2] For this reason, it is critical for Reformed Thomists to wrestle with Aristotelian claims, but there is a risk of overstating Aristotle's influence of Thomas. Thomas did not simply add biblical justification to Aristotle's ideas but practiced good philosophical retrieval – adopting that which was helpful and rejecting that which was not.

Thomism: Platonic, Aristotelian, or Something New?

While scholarship from the recent past frequently pitted Thomas's Aristotelianism against Platonism, as if these two classical systems were independent from one another, contemporary works suggest a

---

1. Cessario, 22.
2. McInerny, 30.

more complicated relationship between Thomas and the Greeks.[3] In short, it is not entirely accurate to portray Thomas as a strict Platonist or a strict Aristotelian.[4] Rather, Thomas is a Thomist, and Thomism was an entirely new system of thought, progressing the broader Platonic movement while making use of both Platonic and distinct Aristotelian ideas when appropriate. Thomas neither uncritically accepts Plato and Aristotle nor entirely rejects all their philosophical claims. The conclusions of both thinkers needed to be modified, as neither Plato nor Aristotle adequately aligned with the Christian understanding of reality that Thomas sought to articulate. Consider, for instance, Thomas's exposition of John 1:1-2 in which he writes: 'If one considers these four propositions [John 1:1-2] well, he will find that they clearly destroy all the errors of the heretics and of the philosophers.'[5] He then proceeds to show specifically how a proper reading of John 1 would correct the mistakes of both Plato and Aristotle.[6]

---

3. For examples of scholars who make too much of Thomas's Aristotelianism at the expense of his other philosophical influences, see Sebastian Morello, *The World as God's Icon: Creator and Creation in the Platonic Thought of Thomas Aquinas* (Brooklyn: Angelico Press, 2020), 13-23. Morello includes prominent names such as Ed Feser and G. K. Chesterton in his survey.

4. Richard Muller wrote: 'Aquinas did draw on Aristotle as the primary source of epistemological and ontological categories for his "synthesis" of theology and philosophy, but his use of Aristotle was critical and selective and was significantly modified by Platonic and Augustinian understandings. To read Aquinas as strictly Aristotelian or as an uncritical reader of Aristotle is to misrepresent his thought' (Richard A. Muller, 'Reading Aquinas from a Reformed Perspective: A Review Essay,' *Calvin Theological Journal* 53, no. 2 (January 1, 2018): 257).

5. Thomas Aquinas, *Commentary on the Gospel of John*, vol. 1, *Chapters 1–5*, trans. Fabian Larcher and James A. Weisheipl, 3 vols., Thomas Aquinas in Translation (Washington, DC: The Catholic University of America Press, 2010), 28.

6. Thomas Aquinas, *Commentary on John*, 29–30. Thomas writes: 'Plato, however, thought that the Ideas of all the things that were made were subsistent, i.e., existing separately in their own natures; and material things exist by participating in these. For example, he thought men existed through the separated Idea of man, which he called Man *per se*. So lest you supposed, as did Plato, that this Idea through which all things were made be Ideas separated from God, the Evangelist adds, *and the Word was with God* ... Aristotle, however, thought that the ideas of all things are in God, and that in God, the intellect, the one understanding, and what is understood, are the same. Nevertheless, he thought that the world is coeternal with him. Against this the Evangelist says, *He*, the Word alone, *was in the beginning with God*, in such a way that *He* does not exclude another person, but only another coeternal nature.'

Rather than accepting one classical model, many Thomists describe Thomas as a synthesizer of Platonic and Aristotelian philosophy. Indeed, as W. Norris Clarke writes, 'We find ourselves forced to the conclusion that it is no longer possible without the most serious qualifications to evaluate the philosophical contribution of St. Thomas ... as a decisive option for Aristotle against Platonism.'[7] Rather, at least as far as metaphysics is concerned, Thomas has woven together the thoughts of Plato and Aristotle to the point that 'the metaphysical system of the Angelic Doctor can legitimately be described ... either as an Aristotelianism specified by Neoplatonism, or as a Neoplatonism specified by Aristotelianism.'[8] The pursuit of truth sometimes requires us to transcend the limits of any singular philosophical boundary. Still, if a theologian is committed to truth, then he cannot pick-and-choose philosophical conclusions based on preferences but must synthesize proper conclusions into a consistent system of thought.

The description of Thomas as a great synthesizer is not to suggest that Platonic and Aristotelian thought are opposed to one another or inherently contradictory. Rather, philosophers such as Lloyd P. Gerson have shown that Aristotle represents and progresses Platonic thought.[9] Instead, Thomas harmoniously combines ideas unique to both thinkers. Specifically, Thomas makes use of Platonic participation, an idea largely absent in Aristotle's work, and the division of being into act and potency, an idea absent in Plato.[10] This synthetic use of Plato and Aristotle can

---

7. W. Norris Clarke, 'The Limitation of Act by Potency in St. Thomas: Aristotelianism or Neoplatonism?' In *Explorations in Metaphysics: Being, God, Person* (Notre Dame: University of Notre Dame Press, 1994), 82. Morello echoes this sentiment as he writes, 'There still dominates, among philosophers and readers of philosophy, a perception that Aquinas's system is essentially that of Aristotle, only adjusted to accommodate the ideas of medieval Christianity. This perception is much to be regretted, for it distorts Aquinas's philosophy to its disadvantage' (Morello, 2). See also Boersma, *Heavenly Participation*, 36.

8. Clarke, 'The Limitation of Act by Potency in St. Thomas,' 82.

9. See Lloyd P. Gerson, *Aristotle and Other Platonists* (Ithaca: Cornell University Press, 2005).

10. W. Norris Clarke wrote: 'The achievement of St. Thomas was to recognize that the strength of each doctrine [Aristotelian act/potency and Neoplatonic participation/limitation] remedied precisely the weakness of the other and to fuse them into a single highly original synthesis, condensed in the apparently simple yet extremely rich and complex formula: Act is not limited except by reception in a distinct potency' (W. Norris Clarke, 'The Limitation of Act by Potency in St. Thomas: Aristotelianism or

be seen throughout Thomas's system, but it intersects with Thomas's understanding of the divine intellect through his discussion of the doctrines of participation and the divine Ideas. Cooper writes:

> Christian Platonists (and Jewish ones) identified the [Platonic] forms with ideas in the mind of God. Aristotle's view is often identified as moderate realism, and it was this view that entered into scholasticism by means of Thomas Aquinas. ... [I]t should be noted that Aquinas's notion of divine ideas was not strictly identical with Aristotle's, as Aquinas spoke of divine ideas as exemplar causes of created things, *thus articulating something of a mediating position between Plato and Aristotle.*[11]

This willingness to reject, adapt, and mediate between philosophical positions means that Thomas did not adopt Aristotelianism in toto. As McInerny writes, 'Thomas was not so much interested in what Aristotle taught as in what he could be made to say that would be in agreement with Christian faith.'[12] Thomas critically reviews Aristotle's work, adopting what could be beneficial to Christian doctrine, and abandoning that which contradicted truth. 'Thomas was not so loyal to the opinions of Aristotle,' explains Steinmetz, 'that he did not abandon them when what he regarded as better opinions could be found elsewhere. ... Philosophy was the scholastic theologian's tool, not his principle subject matter. The tune to which he danced was played by a different piper.'[13] Indeed, even outside the thought of Thomas, the pluriform nature of Aristotelianism as it was passed on and received through the Middle Ages prevented a blanket acceptance of some ideal 'Aristotle.' As Trueman writes,

> Renaissance thinkers did not simply preserve Aristotle's thought in academic formaldehyde, but subjected it to constant revision and modification in the light of their own views on rhetoric, grammar, etc. ... . The pluriformity of Renaissance Aristotelian systems is such that the classification of any given thinker as 'Aristotelian' allows us to draw few, if any, conclusions about the content of his thought prior to a detailed engagement with the relevant primary texts.[14]

Neoplatonism?,' in *Explorations in Metaphysics: Being, God, Person* (Notre Dame, IN: University of Notre Dame Press, 1994), 79-80).

11. Cooper, 38; emphasis added.

12. McInerny, 24.

13. Steinmetz, 'The Scholastic Calvin,' 23.

14. Trueman, 'Baxter,' 183.

Similar to Thomism, Aristotelianism exists in many forms with many different emphases. The specific philosophical concepts adopted by a thinker greatly outweigh the Aristotelian title.

Furthermore, it is ironic that Thomas's relationship with Aristotle has led some to discount him as a theologian due to his supposed philosophical baggage, yet his critical modification of Aristotle based on his Christian presuppositions led Thomas to be denounced as a philosopher by such men as Bertrand Russell.[15] The same sun that melts the wax will harden the clay. Nonetheless, there are additional metaphysical principles, indeed one may say Aristotelian principles once the proper caveats are provided, that must be accepted if one wishes to be a consistent Thomist. These principles include the following: metaphysical realism, the distinction between act and potency, and fourfold causation. While other principles may be necessitated by some, these three will be highlighted due to their importance within Thomas's doctrines of God and creation.[16]

Metaphysical Realism

While qualifications and distinctions are necessary, Thomas can be grouped with Plato and Aristotle as they are all, like most great premodern thinkers, metaphysical realists. This category of thinkers all believed in the existence of universals – those properties that transcend any singular representative and can exist in multiple entities. For example, while goodness may be demonstrated by many individuals, there is a universal Form of goodness by which all other examples of goodness are weighed and measured. Indeed, 'Thomism remains the noblest and paradigmatic articulation of metaphysical realism.'[17] One reason that Thomas is typically portrayed as an Aristotelian in secondary literature is that Thomas aligns with Aristotle's articulation of metaphysical realism more so

---

15. Russell wrote this concerning Thomas: 'The finding of arguments for a conclusion given in advance is not philosophy, but special pleading.' See Bertrand Russell, *History of Western Philosophy* (New York, 1945), 463. This source was also cited in Timothy McDermott's introduction to Thomas Aquinas, *Aquinas: Selected Philosophical Writings* (Oxford: Oxford University Press, 1993), xi.

16. See Feser, *Aquinas*, 8-30; Edward Feser, *Scholastic Metaphysics: A Contemporary Introduction* (Piscataway: Transaction Books, 2014).

17. Cessario, 23.

than Plato's. For Thomas, the Forms or Ideas did not exist in a third realm independent from a divine maker as they did in Plato's works. Rather, for Thomas, the realm of Forms are present in the divine mind, and universals are concretized in individuals. According to Doolan, citing Vivian Boland as evidence, Thomas's understanding of universals was one of his biggest departures from Plato:

> As he explains in the *De veritate*, individual things have being (*esse*) more truly than do universals, for universals subsist only *in* individuals. As a result, individuals have a greater need for ideas. As Boland observes, 'No clearer statement of his acceptance of radical aristotelian ontology is possible. The *quid est* is the concrete and in following Aristotle in this way Saint Thomas' account of the divine ideas is characterised by what has been called 'the radical intelligibility of the singular.'[18]

Yet, as is becoming increasingly apparent in contemporary scholarship, Thomas's 'radical aristotelian ontology' cannot be separated from a Platonic understanding of participation and exemplarism, as will be discussed below. For now, it is enough to recognize that Thomas's system is 'an innovative synthesis of Platonic and Aristotelian ideas whose insight and originality merit its fame and reproach its neglect.'[19] Once again, it should be noted that Aristotle's and Plato's models of universals should not be understood as two distinct schools of thought. Instead, Aristotle modified his Platonic training, which Thomas would modify further still. These Platonic influences are most clearly seen when Thomas discusses the divine Ideas and are specifically noticeable in Thomas's 'Fourth Way.'[20] So, while the details of Thomas's metaphysical realism may be debated, there is no denying that consistent Thomists must adopt some form of metaphysical realism.

The most significant opponent to realism in all its forms, and the most popular model in contemporary culture, is the school of thought known as 'nominalism.' The very term 'modernity' is related to the *via moderna*, the school of thought positioned against the *via antiqua*,

---

18. Gregory T. Doolan, *Aquinas on the Divine Ideas as Exemplar Causes* (Washington, DC: The Catholic University of America Press, 2014), 144. Doolan cites Vivian Boland, *Ideas in God According to Saint Thomas Aquinas: Sources and Synthesis*, Studies in the History of Christian Thought 69, (New York: E. J. Brill, 1996), 226.

19. Morello, 2.

20. Doolan, 69. Thomas's Fourth Way will be discussed at greater length in Chapter 5.

the older realist path. In this sense, to be modern is to be nominalistic in some regard.[21] Nominalists deny the existence of universals by suggesting that any appearance of universality is only linguistic, and the movement has gained widespread acceptance in the West since the late medieval era.[22] It is not unusual, in fact, for contemporary literature to place the conception of nominalism's popularity at the feet of the quintessential Protestant Reformer, Martin Luther.[23] Luther was trained in Ockhamistic nominalism, and, according to Donnelly, 'It is a commonplace that Luther's theology is at once an outgrowth of and reaction against this nominalist training. … There can be no doubt that Luther's nominalist training played an important role in his personal development.'[24] In fact, Roman Catholic historians and apologists

> have been at pains to link Luther's theology (especially his view of God and justification by faith alone) with a nominalist theology no longer authentically Catholic. Luther's theology then becomes the bad fruit of a bad tree. Nominalism and Protestantism become intrinsically linked.[25]

Their efforts, however, are misguided, as Donnelly concludes: 'Protestant fruit grows quite well on the Thomist tree, even better than on the bad nominalist tree.'[26] Protestantism is not dependent on nominalism, nor is it the cause of nominalism as the concept preceded Luther's birth. Indeed, due to the agreement between the Westminster Confession of Faith, Reformed Orthodoxy, and certain Thomistic conclusions, those who distinguish themselves from metaphysical realism 'at best stand at

---

21. Gillespie, 4. Gillespie writes: 'Originally, this was not a historical but a philosophical distinction between two different positions on universals, connected to two different ways of reading Aristotle' (ibid.).

22. Kreeft writes: 'Nominalism, the doctrine that universality is *only* linguistic, not real; that only names (*nomina*), not forms, are universal' (Kreeft, *Summa*, 258). For more information on how Ockham's nominalism has risen in popularity and negatively affected philosophical thought, see Richard M. Weaver, *Ideas Have Consequences,* expanded edition (Chicago: University of Chicago Press, 2013).

23. Gillespie, 101-28. Paul Tyson writes: '[N]ominalism became the dominant intellectual stance in the philosophy and theology characteristic of the proto-modern era. Nominalism is, for example, largely assumed by the Reformers of the sixteenth century' (Tyson, *Returning to Reality,* 73). This interpretation of the Reformation, however, is questioned by others. See, for instance, Connelly, 'Calvinistic Thomism.'

24. Donnelly, 'Calvinist Thomism,' 453.

25. ibid.

26. ibid., 454.

the margin of what can be called Reformed and, at worst, create a kind of sectarian theology and philosophy that is out of accord with the older Reformed tradition and its confessions.'[27] The link between nominalism and the Reformation, then, can be taken too far.[28] Elsewhere Donnelly writes: 'The striking thing about the rise of Reformed scholasticism is that its roots in medieval scholasticism run heavily to Thomism, hardly at all to nominalism.'[29] The Reformed tradition, then, offers a defense of Thomistic realism against the objections of nominalism, despite the claims of some Roman Catholics.

As opposed to Thomism and the Reformed tradition, however, some have rightly suggested that the alternative models of God that grew in popularity throughout the twentieth century did come from nominalistic soil. As Gilliespie writes: 'Since Plato, being had been understood as timeless, unchanging presence. Change was always a falling away from being, degeneration. Nominalism called this notion into question with its assertion that God himself was not only subject to change but was perhaps even change itself.'[30] This emphasis on change, of course, is reminiscent of such theistic mutualists as the process theologians we discussed in previous chapters. Not only can nominalism be seen as an impetus for alternative models of theism, but, as Feser points out, nominalism is a consistent presupposition by the movement known as the new atheists.[31] This influence on new atheists and theistic mutualists suggests that nominalism, while capable of producing new and various theological movements, ultimately requires a rejection, or at least a modification, of classical theism. Feser believed the effects of nominalism

---

27. Richard A. Muller, 'Reading Aquinas from a Reformed Perspective: A Review Essay,' *Calvin Theological Journal* 53, no. 2 [January 1, 2018]: 288.

28. Hans Boersma is one evangelical scholar who falls into this error. At times, Boersma sounds as if he believed the Reformation to be a mistake due to the effect it had on the 'sacramental tapestry.' For instance, Boersma writes: 'After all, the Reformation did not escape the general trend toward a nominalist view of the cosmos. By depicting the Reformation as a tragic (no matter how understandable) outcome of the disintegration of the Platonist-Christian mindset, I am obviously calling for a reevaluation of the Reformation and of the way in which evangelicalism should proceed theologically' (Boersma, *Heavenly Participation*, 104). See also Boersma, *Heavenly Participation*, 87, 99.

29. Donnelly, *Vermigli Doctrine of Man*, 205.

30. Gillespie, 36.

31. Edward Feser, *The Last Superstition: A Refutation of the New Atheism* (South Bend: St. Augustine Press, 2008).

to be so dangerous that he wrote, 'Abandoning Aristotelianism, as the founders of modern philosophy did, was the single greatest mistake ever made in the entire history of Western thought.'[32] Likewise, Peter Kreeft believes that nominalism is 'perhaps the most pervasive and destructive error in modern philosophy.'[33]

The late medieval shift from realism to nominalism provided the philosophical impetus for separating metaphysics and epistemology.[34] If nominalism is correct, then one's subjective internal experience need not correspond to objective reality in any way. In a realist framework, human words and ideas truly represent that which exists objectively in reality, but this confidence in language and knowledge is shattered under nominalism. As such, '[T]ruth is internalized, and knowledge of the external world is doubted (Hume) or only partially known by way of sense-experience (Kant).'[35] White's summarization of the dangers presented by nominalism is worth quoting in full:

> Nominalism is the *fourteenth century movement* associated with the English
> Franciscan, William of Ockham, which gave rise to widespread intellectual

---

32. Feser, *The Last Superstition*, 51. Remember that Feser closely aligns Thomism with Aristotelianism. Additionally, Feser elsewhere suggests that Aristotelianism and Scholastic Realism are nearly synonymous. He reiterates the cited claim when he writes, 'The fact is that a myriad of philosophical problems – indeed, many problems that have misleadingly come to be regarded as "perennial" or "traditional" problems of philosophy – arose only after and because of the early modern philosophers' abandonment of key Aristotelian and Scholastic notions' (Feser, *Aquinas,* 42).

33. Kreeft, *Summa*, 28.

34. Cooper calls Peter Abelard the father of nominalism: 'Peter Abelard is often considered the founder of this ideology [nominalism], and it fits rather well with his general attitude of skepticism and the challenging of assumed truths. ... The primary idea in Abelard related to essences and signification was his conception of a linguistic sign. He argued that the dominant realist approach as taught in popular medieval figures like Boethius – along with earlier thinkers – was incoherent. Universals, Abelard argued, were not real at all, but were mere linguistic significations (or *nomina,* as he called them)' (Cooper, 38-39).

35. Cooper, 59. Cooper calls Hume the 'ultimate nominalist' (ibid., 47). Boersma echoes Cooper's concern: 'Sympathetic to the earlier Platonist-Christian synthesis, they [contemporary historians, theologians, and philosophers; Radical Orthodoxy] point to two factors as contributing to the loss of a sacramental ontology and the origin of the autonomous natural realm of modernity: the rise of univocity and nominalism ...' Boersma calls 'univocity' and 'nominalism' the 'two blades of a pair of scissors that cut the tapestry by severing the participatory link between earthly sacrament (*sacramentum*) and heavenly reality (*res*)' (Boersma, *Heavenly Participation*, 68-69).

skepticism regarding the powers of the mind to know the metaphysical structures of reality. For instance, nominalists would come to argue that we cannot truly identify common natures that are present in multiple individuals, nor grasp the existence of singulars (their being as such), rather than their mere facticity. They also questioned our capacity to understand the existence of causality in realities we experience, such that we might affirm that things change or come to be as a result of their intrinsic properties (natural form), through the effects of others (efficient causality), and that they tend toward final ends (teleology or final causality). Here the philosophy of transcendentals (being, unity, truth, goodness) breaks down, because the notions appear unduly subjective. Nominalism led in turn to increased skepticism regarding our natural capacity to know God or to speak coherently about him, since theological depictions of God in classical scholasticism often appealed to causal dependencies and transcendental features of being in order to identify what we mean when we speak of God and to identify the divine attributes or 'names of God,' such as goodness, eternity, infinity, and so forth.[36]

If one wishes to answer contemporary philosophical and theological problems via the retrieval of premodern sources, such as Thomas, then this difference between realism and nominalism cannot be overlooked. It could even be said that the rise of nominalism is what necessitates theological retrieval in the first place. For our current purposes, we must recognize that the concept of truth loses its ontological force within a nominalistic framework, and the understanding of God as Truth becomes little more than rhetorical flourish. As such, a Reformed Thomist will hold to metaphysical realism, even if the specifics of such a viewpoint may differ slightly among the group.

Act and Potency

The distinction between act and potency is listed as the first of the Twenty-Four Thomistic Theses promoted by the Catholic Church and as the central metaphysical theme that holds several Thomistic concepts together.[37] The first thesis reads, 'Act and potency divide the set of beings in such a way that anything which "is" has to be either (1) pure act or else (2) a combination of potency and act, having these as the

---

36. White, *Trinity*, 34.
37. Feser, *Aquinas*, 7.

primordial factors within it.'[38] Thomas's metaphysical commitment to act and potency forms the foundation of many arguments concerning the doctrine of God, including his belief in divine simplicity, perfection, immutability, analogical predication, and the famous Thomistic dictum *actus essendi*. For instance, Thomas gives this argument for divine simplicity from the division of being into act and potency:

> In the first existent thing everything must be actual; there can be no potentiality whatsoever. For although, when we consider things coming to exist, potential existence precedes actual existence in those particular things; nevertheless, absolutely speaking, actual existence takes precedence of potential existence. For what is able to exist is brought into existence only by what already exists. Now we have seen that the first existent is God. In God then there can be no potentiality. In bodies, however, there is always potentiality, for the extended as such is potential of division. God, therefore, cannot be a body. (Aquinas, *ST* 1.3.1 ad 2)[39]

In favor of immutability, he argued:

> Our findings so far prove God to be altogether unchangeable. First, because we have proved that there must be some first existent, called God, sheerly actual and unalloyed with potentiality, since actuality, simply speaking, precedes potentiality. Now any changing thing, whatsoever the change, is somehow potential. So it clearly follows that God cannot change in any way. (Aquinas, *ST* 1.9.1 ad 1)

Indeed, Thomas references act and potency when discussing the attribute most pertinent to this project, omniscience: 'Knowledge in God is not a quality nor an habitual capacity, but substance and pure actuality' (Aquinas, *ST* 1.14.1 ad 1). While a theologian can defend classical attributes without referencing the division of act and potency, they would lose one of the driving forces behind Thomas's conclusions.

As Clarke makes clear, Thomas's explanation of act and potency is quite different than Aristotle's. Following a growing number of

---

38. See Marshner, 'The Twenty-Four Thomistic Theses.' The first three theses are all dedicated to the idea of God as *actus purus*.

39. Notice the subtle parameters of the divine attributes that are often overlooked. God is simple not only because He is not divided, but because He *cannot* be divided. Anything that *could* be divided, therefore, is absent in God. This also applies to attributes such as immutability. It is true that God does not change, but it is also true that God *cannot* change.

Thomistic voices, Clarke suggests that the Neoplatonic concept of participation shifts the fundamental structure of Thomas's metaphysics. 'This view of Thomism,' Clarke writes, 'with participation as the center doctrine would make that system primarily radically revised Platonism expressed in Aristotelian notions of potency and act with an extension of the meaning of these latter notions which is not found in Aristotle but is original with St. Thomas.'[40] Again, Clarke speaks of Thomism as an impressive synthesis of Platonism and Aristotelianism combined with the original thought of Thomas.

For Aristotle, act and potency can be used to explain the existence of change. If a being can change, then it must possess potency to receive new act. Pure act, then, would be synonymous with 'immutability, self-sufficiency, and incorruptibility which for Aristotle is the primary characteristic of the "divine" and the perfect.'[41] Thomas, of course, uses this Aristotelian argument for divine immutability, but he also progresses the argument in ways Aristotle did not. Thomas adapted the Aristotelian concepts of act and potency by placing them upon a Platonic foundation of participation. Unlike anything that can be found in Aristotle's writings, Thomas believes that act is *limited* by potency, and without such boundaries, act would exist in an unlimited fashion – as it does in God.[42] Renard explains: 'An act is called *pure act if* it is an absolute perfection. In such an act there is no potentiality, no capacity for further perfection, no limitation. There is simply actual infinite perfection.'[43] *Pure* act, therefore, receives priority and any composite being must receive its being from this divine source. This dependence of creaturely being on divine being is traditionally labeled as 'participation' within Christian theology.[44] If creatures are to exist, then God must

---

40. Clarke, 'The Limitation of Act by Potency in St. Thomas,' 65.

41. ibid., 74.

42. Morello writes: 'More specifically, Aquinas's Neoplatonic metaphysics of participation is expressed in terms of these Aristotelian principles of act and potency, or more precisely, the limitation of act by potency, relating to each other as esse to essentia. This has misled scholars to believe the doctrine itself is Aristotle's; however, Aristotle specifically rejects any notion of metaphysical participation in perfect transcendental forms' (Morello, 19).

43. Renard, 28.

44. This definition follows Cornelio Fabro who writes, 'In the Platonic tradition, the term "participation" signifies the fundamental relationship of both structure and dependence in the dialectic of the many in relation to the One and of the different in

'share' His being with His creation, albeit in a deficient and creaturely manner. Fabro further explains:

> [I]n an attempt to solve crucial issues of the constitutive relation between God and creatures, between the Infinite and the finite – such as those concerning total dependence (creation and divine motion), radical structure (composition of *essentia* and *esse*) and fundamental semantics (analogy) – St. Thomas had placed the Platonic notion of participation at the very foundation of the Aristotelian couplet of act and potency.[45]

For some, this combination of Aristotelian act and potency with a modified Platonic doctrine of participation is the defining and distinguishing attribute of Thomism.[46] This combination of ideas demonstrates a progression of broadly Platonic thought and is why Thomas cannot be accurately portrayed as a strict Platonist or Aristotelian. Readers must consider Thomism a distinct school of thought standing in continuity with classical philosophy. Thomism, then, does not destroy Platonism but perfects it.[47] This progression of thought is also why a Thomistic model of metaphysical realism better fits with the Christian doctrine of God than the models of Aristotle or Plato. Since this synthesis of Platonic and Aristotelian thought is such a distinguishing characteristic, and because it pertains so closely to Thomas's doctrines of God and creation, it would seem that a consistent Thomist would need to embrace Thomas's understanding of act and potency as defined by metaphysical participation. This concept will be further addressed in the following chapters.

We have already mentioned some aspects of *actus purus* taught in Scripture, such as God's perfection and self-sufficiency. Additionally, the biblical doctrine of immutability adds credence to the concept of act and potency. Broad change in general and specific examples of change are

---

relation to the Identical, whereas in Christian philosophy it signifies the total dependence of the creature on its Creator.' See Cornelio Fabro, 'The Intensive Hermeneutics of Thomistic Philosophy: The Notion of Participation,' trans. B. M. Bonansea, in *The Review of Metaphysics* 27, no. 3 (March 1974): 449.

45. Fabro, 450.

46. See Clarke, 'The Limitation of Act by Potency,' 65-68, 79-80.

47. Likewise, Donnelly progresses the argument further by suggesting that Calvinism perfects Thomism. See Donnelly, 'Calvinist Thomism.' Of course, both statements reference the idea that 'grace perfects nature.'

both excluded from the divine life (Mal. 3:6; Num. 23:19). Long after the created world fades away, God will remain the same (Ps. 102:25-27). Like all divine attributes, immutability applies to the divine Son who is 'the same yesterday, today, and forever' (Heb. 13:8). Indeed, the divine nature denies all hints of change as God is free from 'variation or shadow due to change' (James 1:17). *Actus Purus* provides significant explanatory value to these passages and makes it clear that God's lack of change is not due to His good choices, as if He could change if He desired, but due to His good nature – Goodness itself. While many modern authors are willing to accept that God's character does not change, the classical claim is much stronger. God *cannot* change because He lacks the passive potency required to do so.

Fourfold Causation

Additionally, fourfold Aristotelian causation is a cornerstone of Thomistic philosophy and Thomas's theology of divine omniscience. As is true for the previously mentioned philosophical categories, the reason that Aristotelian causation is included as a prerequisite for Thomism is not to promote a broad philosophical system *per se* but because of how Thomas employs causation when discussing his doctrine of God. Classical theism teaches that God is, of course, the cause of all created being. One can further specify, however, how God is creation's ultimate cause. For Thomas, God is not only the efficient cause of all creation but also the exemplar and final cause.

Thomas preferred to use the term 'exemplar cause' rather than 'final cause' to emphasize God's distinction from His creatures. Thomas writes: 'Now all these contain manifest untruth; since it is not possible for God to enter into the composition of anything, either as a formal or a material principle' (Aquinas, ST 1.3.8). It will be shown below, however, there exists a great continuity between exemplar and formal causation, and according to Gregory Doolan, an exemplar cause necessarily includes formal causation. Aristotle defines these four causes as such:

> Evidently we have to acquire knowledge of the original causes (for we say we know each thing only when we think we recognize its first cause), and causes are spoken of in four senses. In one of these we mean the substance [formal cause], i.e. the essence (for the 'why' is referred finally to the formula [*logos*], and the ultimate 'why' is a cause and principle); in

another the matter or substratum [material cause], in a third the source of the change [efficient cause], and in a fourth ... that for the sake of which and the good (for this is the end of all generation and change) [final cause].[48]

Genuine knowledge of an object requires knowledge of the object's causes.[49] Once the material, formal, efficient, and final cause of an object is identified, then the essence (including both form and matter in the Thomistic sense), source, and purpose of that object is understood.

Thomas, however, differs from the Aristotelian understanding of causation, as Andrew Davison explains. Even though Aristotle provides philosophers with the language to describe creaturely relations, 'Aristotle had remarkably little to offer by way of overarching metaphysical structure at the grandest level. He has no answer for why the world is the way it is: it just is.'[50] Grounding causation in God, as Thomas does, follows a more Platonic example. 'Plato,' continues Davison, 'was concerned above all with the overarching structure: the origins of the universe and how it comes to be that anything exists, or is beautiful, or good. Plato was a theorist of the relation of the world to that which transcends it.'[51] Thomas, then, may have made use of Aristotelian

---

48. Aristotle, *Metaphysics*, in *The Complete Works of Aristotle*, ed. by Jonathan Barnes (Princeton, NJ: Princeton University Press, 1984), 1.3.983a24-31, 1555. Feser illustrates these causes through the production of a rubber ball: 'Return yet again to the rubber ball of our example. The *material cause* or underlying stuff the ball is made out of is rubber, its *formal cause*, or the form, pattern, or structure it exhibits, comprises such features as its sphericity, solidity, and bounciness. In other words, the material and formal causes of a thing are just its matter and form, considered as two aspects of a complete explanation of it. Next we have the *efficient cause*, that which actualizes a potency and thereby brings something into being. In this case that would be the actions of the workers and/or machines in the factory in which the ball was made, as they molded the rubber into the ball. Lastly we have the *final cause* or the end, goal, or purpose of a thing, which in the case of the ball might be to provide amusement to a child. In combination, these causes provide a complete explanation of a thing' (Feser, *Aquinas*, 16).

49. Andrew Davison explains: 'Aristotle proposed *four causes*. ... Ever since Aristotle, philosophers have explored them using the example of a statue. The four causes are the four answers we can give to the question "why is there a statue?"' See Andrew Davison, *The Love of Wisdom: An Introduction to Philosophy for Theologians* (London: SCM Press, 2013), 35. For Davison's analysis of each type of cause, see Davison, *The Love of Wisdom*, 35-38.

50. Davison, *The Love of Wisdom*, 124.

51. ibid.

language 'to describe the detail,' but Thomistic metaphysics 'finds its natural expression in Platonic language.'[52]

Still, it should be noticed that God was previously identified as the exemplar, efficient, and final cause of all creatures, but Thomas is quite clear that God is not the material cause of creation since creatures are not made *up of* God.[53] In other words, if God was the material cause of creation, then the divine essence would be the 'building blocks' of creatures. The Creator and the creature would then be intermingled. Thomas's rejection of divine material causation is how a Thomistic understanding of omniscience and the divine Ideas can avoid claims of pantheism or panentheism, despite the close relationship between Creator and creature via the doctrine of participation.[54]

Thomas's understanding of omniscience and the divine Ideas helps us to further explain how God serves as the ultimate cause of creation. The divine Ideas serve as the prerequisite for all creaturely essences. To demonstrate how the divine Ideas relate to the doctrine of creation, Thomas describes the relationship between a builder and his blueprints. When a builder wishes to create, then he must start with an idea of his creation in his mind. The human creator then makes his art based upon his idea of the desired finished product. Similarly, God creates using the 'blueprints' of the divine Ideas. These ideas, then, serve as the source of all creaturely forms. In this way, we may specifically pinpoint the intellect of God as the exemplar cause of all created being.

It should be noted, however, that not all divine Ideas function as exemplar causes. Gregory Doolan explains:

---

52. ibid.

53. Thomas writes: 'God cannot have a relation to us that is not one of being our origin. While there are four causes, God is not our material cause. Rather, God has towards us the sense of efficient, final, and formal exemplary [causation].' The translation is the work of Davison. See Andrew Davison, *Participation in God: A Study in Christian Doctrine and Metaphysics* (New York: Cambridge University Press, 2020), 47. See also Aquinas, *ST* 1.44.4 ad 4.

54. Davison further explains: 'Aristotle provided resources to be deployed but Christians knew that they would have to go far beyond him in talking about God and creation. To God as efficient and final cause, found in Aristotle, they added God as the formal cause of all things, since the essence of everything stands as a participation in God. Although God is not the material cause of creation, the idea of creation out of nothing makes the revolutionary claim that God is the cause of matter' (Davison, *The Love of Wisdom*, 47).

For Thomas, the term [exemplar] is properly defined as 'a form that something imitates because of the intention of an agent who predetermines the end for himself.'... Following Thomas's mature use of the term 'exemplar,' we saw that only actually practical ideas should be called 'exemplars.'[55]

God knows all the diverse ways in which His essence may be imitated in creaturely forms, but He does not actualize all possible imitations. Strictly speaking, then, only the divine Ideas that are imitated within creation may serve as exemplars. From this point, readers can see how Thomas's doctrine of creation differs from Plato's understanding.

Thomas does not believe that God is obligated to create every being represented by the divine Ideas. Rather, God is free to choose through the means of the divine will which divine Ideas will be exemplar causes and which ones will not. It is the 'intention of an agent' that separates the speculative divine Ideas from the practical divine Ideas that serve as exemplars. Creation via necessary emanation, in which God does not choose to create but does so out of necessity, is an impossibility. Doolan continues:

> It is important to recognize this role of God's will in determining the divine ideas to act because it reveals the contingency of their exemplarism: unlike the Platonists whom he criticizes, Thomas rejects the theory of a necessary emanation. ... Indeed, Thomas insists that those who do maintain a doctrine of necessary emanation cannot truly admit of divine ideas, for things that act from a necessity of nature do not predetermine the end of their effects for themselves.[56]

While the divine Ideas are the exemplar cause of all created beings, they cannot be the efficient cause without divine intent. If the divine intellect and ideas function as the exemplar cause, then the divine will, working through the divine Ideas, functions as the efficient cause. Thomas thus summarizes the preceding argument as such:

> God's knowledge is the cause of things. For God's knowledge stands to all created things as the artist's to his products. But the artist's knowledge is the cause of his products, because he works through his intellect; and so the form in his intellect must be the principle of his activity ... (Aquinas, *ST* 1.14.8).

---

55. Doolan, 43.
56. Doolan, 158.

The divine Ideas, then, serve a crucial role in divine causation. The forms concretized within individuals first exist within the divine intellect as the divine Ideas. Anthropomorphically speaking, God works through these ideas when He creates, much like a carpenter follows a mental picture of a house when constructing his home. Thomas continued:

> But we may note that a natural form, merely as the form remaining in the thing to which it gives existence, does not indicate a principle of activity; it does so only in so far as it has an inclination towards producing an effect. And similarly an intelligible form does not indicate a principle of activity merely as it is in the knower unless it is accompanied by an inclination towards producing an effect; this is supplied by the will. (Aquinas, *ST* 1.14.8)

Unless God willed for a specific creature to exist, the divine Ideas would remain aspects of God's theoretical knowledge. Not every divine Idea is concretized in creation. God does not will for all divine Ideas to serve as exemplar causes but freely chooses which divine Ideas to work through in creation. The necessity of the divine will in causation leads Thomas to conclude that '[God's] knowledge, therefore, must be the cause of things when regarded in conjunction with his will' (Aquinas, *ST* 1.14.8). The divine Ideas, then, would serve as the exemplar cause of all creatures, whereas the divine will would serve as the efficient cause.

Analogical Prediction

The fourth Thomistic thesis states: 'A "being" is what a thing is called from its act of being. But "is a being" is not a description applied univocally to God and to creatures; neither is it applied just equivocally; rather, it is applied analogously, by both analogy of attribution and analogy of proportionality.'[57] Thomistic theology cannot function apart from analogical thought, and if one were to ignore the doctrine of analogy,

---

57. Marshner, 1. Davison is helpful in explaining the 'act of being.' Davison writes: 'We get close to the heart of his metaphysics when we note that, for Aquinas, being naturally overflows into doing, or what Aquinas would call *action* or *act*. ... Being is acting, so even a book, for example, is acting: it is performing the first and foundational act of any existing thing, which is be-ing, and being in its own particular, bookish, way. This remarkable and somewhat counterintuitive position makes sense for Aquinas on the basis that the being of any particular creature, books included, is its own particular trace of its creator. Its being is an imprint of God's being, and God for Aquinas is *all action* or *pure act* (an idea we encountered in the chapter on Aristotle). At the heart of every creature, therefore, is its first and deepest of actions, which is simply to be' (Davison, *The Love of Wisdom*, 135-36).

a misunderstanding of Thomas's theological arguments would result.[58]
The doctrine of analogy is so significant that Carter lists analogical
predication as the twelfth thesis of classical theism. Carter writes:

> The only way our language about God can be meaningful without reducing
> God to the level of a creature, then, is if it is *analogical*. In analogical
> language, one or more than one specific point or points of comparison
> between God and creaturely reality are valid, but there are always far more
> differences than similarities.[59]

The doctrine of analogy has come to be seen as a fixture of the
Thomistic tradition.[60]

Analogical predication first appears within the *Summa Theologiæ*
when Thomas addresses the names of God. Titles applied to God must
be analogical as 'univocal predication is impossible between God and
creatures' (Aquinas, *ST* 1.13.5). Whereas univocal predication assumes
that a single term can be used in the same sense to describe two different
subjects, equivocal predication assumes that a single term cannot describe
any true likeness between two subjects. Thomas, however, opts for a third
view of religious language. Analogical predication holds that a term can be
used literally in reference to two different subjects, in this sense God and
man, but the term cannot possess the same univocal meaning when applied
to the two distinct subjects respectively.[61] This difference in meaning,
however, does not suggest a complete dissimilarity between subjects, as

---

58. 'Any attempt to understand the analogy of being in Aquinas has to come to terms
with the simple fact that the topic of analogy is present from the very first moment of
Thomas's written work. At the danger of overstating the matter, there is simply no instance
in Thomas's work where analogy is not tacitly presupposed or being treated without being
named or simply being silently at work in the exercise of *sacra doctrina* itself' (Reinhard
Hütter, 'Attending to the Wisdom of God, from Effect to Cause, from Creation to God:
A "Relecture" of the Analogy of Being According to Thomas Aquinas,' in *The Analogy
of Being: Invention of the Antichrist or the Wisdom of God?* By Thomas Joseph White, ed.
[Grand Rapids: William B. Eerdmans Publishing Company, 2011], 214).

59. Carter, *Contemplating God*, 69.

60. Kilcrease, 70.

61. 'Thomists would admit ... in some significant sense there must be some common
core of meaning in all analogous predications of the same term, for otherwise it could not
function as one term and concept. But they insist, on the other hand, that this common
core of meaning is not therefore univocal, but remains analogous, similar-in-difference,
or diversely similar' (W. Norris Clarke, 'Analogy and the Meaningfulness of Language
about God,' in *Explorations in Metaphysics: Being, God, Person* [Notre Dame: University
of Notre Dame Press, 1994], 126).

equivocal predication assumes. Rather, a genuine similarity between the two subjects exists, but this similarity is placed in the foreground of a greater dissimilarity. Thus, as Carter explains, religious language can communicate literal truth about God, but the words used to convey this truth are inadequate to fully comprehend the truth as it exists in God.[62]

Davies summarized the theory of analogical predication as such:

> All it fundamentally maintains is that (1) that terms applied to God and to things in the world are never applied univocally (because creatures are composite and God is simple), but (2) that we need not equivocate when we apply a term to God and a creature (in saying, for example, 'I am good' and 'God is good' we use a word in the same sense to state what is true both of men and of God).[63]

As Thomas explains:

> Whatever is said of God and creatures, is said according to the relation of a Creature to God as its principle and cause, wherein all perfections of things pre-exist excellently. Now this mode of community of idea is a mean between pure equivocation and simple univocation. For in analogies the idea is not, as it is in univocals, one and the same, yet it is not totally diverse as in equivocals; but a term which is thus used in a multiple sense signifies various proportions to some one thing: thus *healthy* applied to urine signifies the sign of animal health, and applied to medicine signifies the cause of the same health. (Aquinas, *ST* 1.4.3 ad 3)

Thomas continues: 'Creatures are said to resemble God, not by sharing a form of the same specific or generic type, but only analogically, inasmuch as God exists by nature, and other things partake existence' (Aquinas, *ST* 1.4.3 ad 3). Clearly, Thomas rejects both univocal and equivocal predication when applied to religious language, partly due to the doctrine of divine simplicity, as Davies alludes to above. Thomas writes:

> An effect that does not receive a form specifically the same as that through which the agent acts cannot receive according to a univocal predication the

---

62. Mark McIntosh draws attention to how analogical language functions through our understanding of the divine Ideas. McIntosh wrote: '… *of course* our language about the divine Ideas is only a placeholder, a way of gesturing inadequately but in the right direction towards a divine reality that wonderfully exceeds our conceptual grasp – even while we attempt to speak.' See McIntosh, *The Divine Ideas Tradition in Christian Mystical Theology*, 16.

63. Davies, *Thought of Thomas Aquinas*, 70.

name arising from that form. … Now, the forms of the things God has made do not measure up to a specific likeness of the divine power; for the things that God has made receive in a divided and particular way that which in Him is found in a simple and universal way. (Aquinas, *SCG* 1.32.2)

According to te Velde, 'Analogy is the key term in Thomas's solution to the problem of how the infinite and transcendent God can be named by names which are originally at home in the finite and immanent sphere of the human world.'[64]

Thomas provides two characteristics in which terms are used analogously. 'First,' writes te Velde, 'things that are named analogously are related in such a way that the one is named from the other.' Secondly, 'a name, used in its proper meaning within the range of the same genus, is used analogously to designate something that belongs to a different genus.'[65] Indeed, 'analogy is a mode of predication in which the limits of a determinate genus are transcended towards something that lies outside that genus.'[66] Analogy, then, allows humans to establish a linguistic bridge across genera without compromising the differences between the two groups discussed.[67] The use of analogical language in God-talk, then, is a matter of 'transgeneric predication.'[68] Creatures do not share a genus with the Creator, hence the Creator-creature distinction, and language that adequately describes creaturely reality cannot apply univocally outside of creation.[69] Thus, analogical predication is the linguistic implications of divine transcendence.

It should be recognized that analogical predication deals with the literal sense of the terms in question. In other words, analogical predication is not metaphorical predication, as the words applied both to God and man are used literally. For instance, when Thomas

---

64. Te Velde, *Aquinas on God*, 97.

65. ibid., 111.

66. ibid.

67. ibid., 97.

68. Te Velde, *Aquinas on God*, 112.

69. Univocal language simply cannot make the trip: 'Between finite below and infinite above we draw a line which may not be crossed by univocal thought' (Thomas Gornall, 'Introduction,' in *Summa Theologiæ*, vol. 4, *Knowledge in God*, by Thomas Aquinas, trans. Thomas Gornall, Cambridge paperback, 62 vols. [Cambridge: Cambridge University Press, 2006], 1a.14–18, xxvi).

described both God and Solomon as wise, 'for him, that is because both Solomon and God really are wise.'[70] Contrary to Pannenberg's metaphorical discourse, analogical predication is different from Scripture's use of metaphors when discussing God. God is not literally a mother eagle, but He is literally good, even though that term does not apply to God and man in the same way. Goodness exists in God as an eminent, simple cause for all divided and derivative goodness present in creation.

Analogical predication finds its metaphysical grounding in the analogy of being, in which God and creature do not share the same type of being. Thus, the univocity of being present in the thought of Scotus has become a primary interlocutor for contemporary Thomists, Protestant and Catholic alike. Indeed, the works of Scotus and Ockham forced Thomists to clarify some of their thoughts regarding analogical language resulting in a 'second Thomism.'[71] Thomas's understanding of creaturely existence via participation can prove helpful when demonstrating the need for the analogy of being.

For Thomas, creaturely existence is received existence in which creatures participate in the ultimate source of all being, God. For Thomas, to 'participate' means that creatures receive in a limited and analogous fashion those perfections that exist primarily and eminently in God. Every perfection exists within an individual in one of two ways: substantially or via participation.[72] The divine perfections, however, only exist substantially within the divine essence; therefore God receives nothing via participation. Thomas explains,

> But that alone will be truly simple which does not participate in 'to be,' not inhering, in fact, but subsisting. This, however, can be but one. For if to be itself has nothing else admixed other than that which is to be, as has been said, it is impossible that this To Be Itself be multiplied through anything diversifying It, and because It has nothing outside Itself conjoined, it follows that It is susceptible of no accident. This – Simple, One, and Sublime – is God Himself.[73]

---

70. Davies, *The Thought of Thomas Aquinas*, 71.

71. Healy, 12.

72. Aquinas, *'On the Hebdomads,'* 33.

73. ibid., 27.

Creatures, however, are not simple, are thus not their own substantial existence. Therefore they must receive being from another. If creatures and the Creator possess univocal being, two possibilities would arise, both of which are unacceptable in Thomas's system. Either (1) both creatures and Creator have their existence substantially, which would require creatures to possess true simplicity; or (2) the Creator must participate in a higher source of being than Himself from which He receives His existence. When understood in this sense, univocal predication has been said to be a form of idolatry. Consider, for instance, the words of Boersma:

> [A] 'double idolatry' is involved in this move from analogy to univocity. … First, univocity means a reduction of God: God is subordinated to a higher concept, namely, that of being. … Second – and this point is particularly important in connection with the origin of an autonomous, desacramentalized realm of nature – univocity in effect renders the created order independent from God. We can now say of the created order that it exists just as much as we can say of God that he exists. No longer does created existence have being by participation *only*. Instead, the created order claims radical independence; it turns into a 'discrete, secular order.'[74]

Or readers could consider the analysis of Davison:

> To speak in the same way about God and creatures – for a participatory-minded person – might also imply some common participation in a yet-more-fundamental source, from which God and the creature share, or that God and creatures fall in common under a shared category, epistemologically prior to both. … That is a sort of blasphemy.[75]

For Thomas, God is not a being among beings. Rather, He is the source of all that participates in 'to be.' Again, the doctrine of participation and analogical predication will be revisited during the discussion of the divine intellect and participatory truth; but, for now, it should be clear that Thomas's understanding of analogy is a significant piece of his overall system of thought.

Conclusion

Protestants have been making use of Thomistic conclusions from the very beginning. The Reformers, Reformed Scholastics, and Puritans all

---

74. Boersma, *Heavenly Participation*, 75-76.
75. Davison, *Participation in God*, 177.

had a working knowledge of Thomas's theology and utilized his system of thought when it was deemed useful. This appreciation of Thomistic thought does not mean that Thomas was received without critique or modification, and at times Protestant thinkers preferred the conclusions of different medieval thinkers, but the existence of Thomistic conclusions within Protestant theology is irrefutable. The question is not whether it is appropriate to retrieve some of Thomas's conclusions, as that has been done for centuries, but rather, 'Which doctrines should be retrieved in the current era?'

After emphasizing the Thomistic conclusions present in Protestant works, the key elements of Thomism were identified. These attributes do not exhaustively describe all that could be said about Thomism, but they represent some of the key ideas that must be accepted in order to understand Thomas's theological and philosophical arguments, especially as they pertain to the divine intellect. These philosophical ideas include the division of being into act and potency, fourfold causation, and analogical predication.

Furthermore, in order to qualify as a Reformed Thomist, further qualifications are necessary. First, the commitment to Scripture present in Thomas's works must be emphasized. The retrieval of Thomas has very little to do with Thomas as an individual and more to do with the belief that his conclusions reflect biblical teaching. Second, the entire system must be safeguarded by a primary epistemic commitment to the boundaries provided by the Reformed confessions. It is believed that the Reformed tradition is a better representation of Scripture than Thomas, so the confessions are intentionally chosen to emphasize when we must depart from Thomas on theological matters. As such, a Reformed Thomist will separate himself from Thomas on matters of soteriology – unless significantly modified, as in the case of John Owen – and ecclesiology. The next chapter will now turn to those components fit to be retrieved from Thomas's doctrine of God, namely, his belief in a transcendent and independent divine intellect.

SECTION THREE:

Truth, Omniscience, and Participation

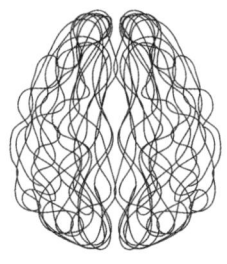

CHAPTER SIX

Truth Ad Intra:
A Transcendent Model of
Divine Omniscience

The preceding chapters have equipped readers to grasp the task at hand – a retrieval of Thomas Aquinas's (Thomas's) understanding of the divine intellect. Chapter 1 introduced the divinity–truth connection, while Chapter 2 highlighted some key differences between classical theism and theistic mutualism, especially how each articulates divine omniscience. Chapter 3 demonstrated the validity of a Protestant retrieval of Thomas and identified some of the key philosophical and theological beliefs necessary to understand the Thomistic arguments pertaining to the divine intellect. The focus now shifts to those particular beliefs that this work seeks to retrieve from Thomas, specifically what will be called a 'participatory theory of truth' and a 'transcendent model of divine omniscience.'

The participatory theory of truth emphasized in Chapter 5 necessitates an understanding of divine omniscience as transcendent and independent. To that end, this chapter will focus on the divine intellect as it stands apart from the contribution of creatures. The claim embedded in this argument, then, is that truth must exist fully and independently within God before it may exist external to God in creaturely, and thus contingent, fashion. In this sense, the content of this chapter provides the foundation for all creaturely truth. Concerning the divine operations and religious truth, Norman Geisler wrote:

Protestant theology, whether Calvinistic or Arminian, is dependent on Aquinas's view that God is all-powerful and omniscient. Without these attributes there is no predestination, whether based on foreknowledge (as Arminians claim) or not (as Calvinists hold). In fact, if the basic metaphysical attributes of God, as articulated by Aquinas, are not preserved, then all of orthodox Catholic and Protestant theology collapses.[1]

Indeed, without God's transcendent omniscience, truth itself disappears.

Yet, the classical Thomistic presentation of the divine intellect may seem strange and foreign to modern readers. It was so foundational for Thomas, however, that references to the content of divine knowledge or the divine operations are woven throughout the entirety of his *Summa Theologiæ* (*Summa*; *ST*). Thomas references the matter when discussing a wide array of topics including but not limited to the doctrines of eternal generation, predestination, the concept of truth, divine simplicity, and human psychology. Without God's comprehensive and independent self-knowledge, Thomas's entire system becomes unintelligible. This chapter will focus on the exposition of Thomas's understanding of the divine intellect. It will be shown that Thomas considers the divine intellect to exist perfectly without contribution from His creatures. Additionally, this independent and transcendent intellect means that the first Truth itself exists in pure *a se* actuality.

A Reformed Thomistic Model of the Divine Intellect

Contrary to the mutualistic models previously discussed, the Reformed Thomistic view focuses on God's *a se* (and thus independent) omniscience without compromising the distinction between God's natural knowledge and His knowledge of vision affirmed in Reformed theology. Within this model, God is not omniscient because He correctly interprets data external to Himself but because He is the perfect knowledge of Himself. The following survey will highlight some of Thomas's key points before demonstrating the continuity of thought between Thomas and early Protestants.

The Divine Intellect Within the *Summa Theologiæ*

Thomas's explanation of the divine operations follows his expositions of sacred doctrine (Aquinas, *ST* 1.1), the existence and nature of God

---

1. Norman Geisler, *Thomas Aquinas: An Evangelical Appraisal* (Eugene: Wipf & Stock, 2003), 117.

(Aquinas, *ST* 1.2–12), and his overview of analogical predication as it pertains to the divine names (Aquinas, *ST* 1.13). Many of the arguments that Thomas has made concerning divine knowledge and will are dependent upon conclusions already reached in the previous thirteen questions. Without a grasp of act and potency, analogical as opposed to univocal and equivocal predication, and the divine attributes – particularly simplicity – readers may miss the progression of Thomas's arguments and misunderstand conclusions concerning divine omniscience. Additionally, readers who assume strict continuity between Thomas and Aristotle – and therefore base their understanding of Thomas on preconceived philosophical assumptions – will miss a major departure from Aristotle's Unmoved Mover within question 14 of the *Summa*. This chapter will now journey through Thomas's exposition of divine knowledge starting with God's immateriality.

Divine Immateriality

The first article under the banner of question 14 addresses whether knowledge, specifically *scientia*, exists in God; and to affirm such a position, Thomas cites God's immateriality.[2] This starting point may be strange to readers steeped in Kantian epistemology or modern and postmodern anti-realism, but Thomas's starting point is dependent upon a specific understanding of creaturely composition and epistemic abstraction. In Thomas's understanding, all creatures exist as a composition of form and matter. A human's knowledge of an object occurs when the form of the object is mentally abstracted from its matter. For instance, when zoologists study the habits of elephants, they mentally separate what is true of all elephants universally from what is true of any particular elephant. In this way, the zoologist may move beyond any singular elephant to 'elephantness' itself, at which point the form of the elephant is comprehended in the mind of the knower.

---

2. *Scientia* refers to knowledge in the broadest sense. It is sometimes used to describe the 'knowledge acquired by demonstration and resting on self-evident first principles' (Richard A. Muller, *Dictionary of Latin and Greek Theological Terms: Drawn Principally from Protestant Scholastic Theology* [Grand Rapids: Baker Academic, 2017], s.v. '*scientia*.' In the restricted sense, *scientia* cannot apply to God but is rather used to describe man's theological systems. *Scientia* in the broad sense, however, is the topic that Thomas is tackling in Aquinas, *ST* 1.14.

This abstraction, however, occurs at an ontological level and is not the result of the knower imposing a fabricated mental image onto reality or creating a new concept within his mind.[3] Rather, the form of the known object (in this case 'elephantness') truly resides in the mind of the knower. The form that existed in the particular elephant now *also* exists within the zoologist, each proportionate to its appropriate mode of being.[4] The form exists as a sensitive soul combined with matter in the elephant, and the form exists as an intellectually abstracted form within the mind of the knower. This act of mental abstraction leads Peter Kreeft to suggest, '[W]hen we actually know a thing (truly), the same form that makes the thing what it is informs our intellect. St. Thomas (and Aristotle) held an *identity* theory of truth, not a *correspondence* theory of truth.'[5] This mental abstraction also means that the knower can possess a multitude of forms, an ability separating humanity from lesser creatures and providing the essential element of a rational soul.[6]

---

3. Contrast this realist interpretation with the nominalistic view. Jordan B. Cooper explains: 'For Ockham, people observe particular objects in the world, and from those objects, they abstract universal ideas that are then identified with particular linguistic signs. This abstraction from the particular to the general is in accord with Plato and Aristotle's way of explaining universals. However, Ockham differed from the Greeks in arguing that this process of universalizing is not the discovery of something real (as in Plato's allegory of the cave), but is creating something intellectual and then linguistic. Ockham's nominalism is not absolute, as he does argue that universals exist in a sense, but only within the human mind and soul. This form of nominalism is sometimes called "conceptualism," as universals exist as concepts.' (Jordan B. Cooper, *In Defense of the True, the Good, and the Beautiful: On the Loss of Transcendence and the Decline of the West* [Ithaca: Just and Sinner, 2021], 40-41).

4. Andrew Davison explains: 'In this way, one does not simply know a stone as an "object" of knowledge, "out there"; it presses its form into one's mind. Silvestri's caveat was only that the stone is in the mind "in an intelligible way", and not in the physical way in which a stone is physically stone. What…we called the *modus* principle is very much at work here: the intellect which knows a stone and to the mind that knows the stone is the "form": the stone's essence or nature. (Knowledge, in turn, provides a useful angle on what we mean by a thing's form in the first place: it is its intelligibility, and what is known when it is known truly.) The difference is between the form instantiated in matter and the form present in the mind' (Andrew Davison, *Participation in God: A Study in Christian Doctrine and Metaphysics*, paperback ed. [New York: Cambridge University Press, 2020], 306-07).

5. Peter Kreeft, ed., *Summa of the Summa: The Essential Philosophical Passages of St. Thomas Aquinas' Summa Theologica Edited and Explained for Beginners* (San Francisco: Ignatius Press, 1990), 277n24. This 'identity' aspect of truth is part of what I have called the 'participatory theory of truth.' The participatory theory is not less than Kreeft's identity theory, but more.

6. Renard, 14.

Indeed, this potency for the rational collecting of forms is that which defines humans as humans. According to Thomas, not even angels, the creatures seemingly the closest to humans in terms of rationality, think the way humans think. The process of abstraction, then, would seem to be the only way in which the physical world was aware of itself.[7]

Now, using the principles of the *Triplex Via*, specifically that of divine eminence, one can see why God's immateriality is the metaphysical basis for divine knowledge.[8] All perfections that exist in creatures must first exist in God in a higher and more perfect fashion. The ability to abstract an object's form from its matter is an immaterial process, and creatures unable to partake in immaterial cognition are incapable of the rational abstraction of forms. Thus, the human perfection of abstraction is due to the human's ability to transcend material limitations through immaterial rational thought.[9] With this understanding of mental abstraction in mind, we can comprehend Thomas's argument:

> In God there exists the most perfect knowledge. To prove this, we must
> note that intelligent beings are distinguished from non-intelligent beings

---

7. See Gilson, *God and Philosophy*, 20-21. Gilson further explains the intimate relationship between truth and man's knowledge on pages 58-59. Gilson writes: '[Augustine's] God is the intelligible sun whose light shines upon human reason and enables it to know truth; he is the inner master who teaches man from within; his eternal and unchangeable ideas are the supreme rules whose influence submits our reason to the necessity of divine truth.'

8. For more information on the *Triplex Via* and the role it plays in Thomas's theological system, see Scott Swain, 'On Divine Naming,' in *Aquinas among the Protestants*, by Manfred Svenson and David VanDrunen, eds. (Oxford: Wiley Blackwell, 2018), 207-28. Stephen Charnock's exposition of the divine intellect is also indebted to the *Triplex Via*. Charnock writes: 'As to what this knowledge is, if we know what knowledge is in man, we may apprehend what it is in God, removing all imperfection from it, and ascribing to him the most eminent way of understanding...' (Stephen Charnock, *The Existence and Attributes of God* [Grand Rapids: Baker Books, 2000], 410-11).

9. See Thomas Joseph White: 'Now, any perfection existing in creatures that is not intrinsically limited can be attributed to God, albeit in a higher and infinitely perfect way. ... If there are grounds for the attribution of a given perfection to God due to his causality of this perfection in creatures, and if a perfection is *capable* of being attributed to God properly by analogy, then we may rightly attribute it to God in a highly qualified sense. Following this line of reasoning, we can conclude that, since God is the cause of immaterial knowledge in creatures, and the effects must in some way resemble the cause, and since the notion of immaterial knowledge of itself implies no imperfection, so we can ascribe immaterial knowledge to God by analogy' (Thomas Joseph White, *The Trinity: On the Nature and Mystery of the One God*, Thomistic Ressourcement Series 19 [Washington, DC: The Catholic University of America Press, 2022], 324).

in that *the latter possess only their own form; whereas the intelligent being is naturally adapted to have also the form of some other thing; for the idea of the thing known is in the knower.* Hence it is manifest that the nature of a non-intelligent being is more contracted and limited; whereas the nature of intelligent beings has a greater amplitude and extension; therefore the Philosopher says (*De Anima* iii) that *the soul is in a sense all things.* Now the contraction of the form comes from the matter. Hence, as we have said above (Q.7, A.I) forms according as they are the more immaterial, approach more nearly to a kind of infinity. *Therefore it is clear that the immateriality of a thing is the reason why it is cognitive; and according to the mode of immateriality is the mode of knowledge.* … Since therefore God is in the highest degree of immateriality as stated above (Q. 7, A. I), it follows that He occupies the highest place in knowledge … (Aquinas, *ST* 1.14.1)

Due to the principle of eminence, one may argue that the perfection of abstraction as demonstrated in creatures exists in a more perfect fashion within God. Furthermore, using the principle of negation, one may remove any shortcomings of abstraction present in creatures – in this case, the limitation of forms due to their composition with matter. God, who is complete metaphysical simplicity, is not composed of form and matter and thus exists without material limitations and can contain all creaturely forms in His infinite immateriality.[10] Thus, using an Aristotelian form of epistemology and hylomorphism, the *Triplex Via*, and divine simplicity, Thomas can establish a metaphysical ground for scientific divine knowledge.

Notice here the use of the modus principle. As Thomas believes, 'Whatever is received into something is received according to the condition of the recipient' (Aquinas, *ST* 1.75.5). Kreeft helps explain:

A concrete, individual *receiver* requires a concrete, individual *reception*; and a concrete, individual *reception* requires a concrete, individual *thing received*, like a guest received into a house or a sardine into a can. A can

---

10. Consider the eighteenth Thomistic thesis: 'Intellectuality follows necessarily from immateriality and does so in such a way that the more removed a thing is from matter, the higher its level of intellectuality. The object co-extensive with "thing understood" is "a being" in the general sense of "a being"; the object distinctive to the human intellect in its present state of union with the body is limited to quiddities abstracted from material conditions' (W. H. Marshner, 'The Twenty-Four Thomistic Theses,' accessed September 22, 2021, https://marshner.christendom.edu/wp-content/uploads/2016/07/24-theses-webedit.pdf).

could not receive the universal form 'sardineness,' or sardine nature; but an immaterial *mind* can.[11]

While it is true that God does not 'receive' His knowledge from others, which will be shown below, it can still be affirmed that God's immateriality is the most proper mode of infinite knowledge.

Indeed, Thomas's epistemology and hylomorphism can help readers understand truth as a transcendental.[12] In the third article of question 16, Thomas addresses whether 'true' and 'being' are convertible terms. He answers that just as good is being related to the notion of desirability, truth is being related to the intellect. In fact, 'everything, in as far as it has being, so far is it knowable' (Aquinas, *ST* 1.16.3). This conclusion, however, does not mean that all being is knowable for any particular human knower. There may be many obstacles rendering any human knowledge of a certain object impossible. However, remembering Thomas's hylomorphism, any existent object that possesses being is composed of both form and matter, which means that all objects with being possess a form that is ready for intellectual abstraction by a knower. To summarize, if an object has being, then it has a form, and if an object has a form, then it is knowable; therefore all objects with being are knowable. As such, Thomas can conclude that God is not only capable of possessing knowledge but is capable of knowing all truth.

Of course, the same conclusion could easily be reached with a cursory glance at Scripture, as God is frequently depicted as a personal God possessing divine knowledge. Thomas is aware of this biblical data, of course, and cites Romans 11:33 before providing his answer to the question: 'O the depth of the riches of the wisdom and of the knowledge of God.' Thomas's goal here, however, is to demonstrate the rationality of biblical theism and to show how Christian theology is logically defensible. Divine knowledge, while an object of faith revealed

---

11. Kreeft, *Summa*, 248.

12. Frederick Christian Bauerschmidt writes: 'Like virtually all medieval thinkers, Thomas presumes what in technical language is called "the convertibility of the transcendentals," which refers to those perfections that necessarily accompany existence – such as goodness, truth, and unity – and therefore transcend the genera and species that divide beings into different kinds. So inasmuch as something exists, it is good, true, and one. And the more perfectly the existence of something is realized, the better, truer, and more unified it is' (Frederick Christian Bauerschmidt, *The Essential Summa Theologiae: A Reader and Commentary*, 2nd ed. [Grand Rapids: Baker Academic, 2021], 5n3).

to believers through Scripture, is also defensible from reason and is the proper conclusion of commonsense philosophical principles.

If Thomas were to stop here, however, theistic mutualism and classical theism would be indistinguishable. The best versions of theistic mutualism do not hesitate in affirming God's infinity and immateriality, and even pagan philosophers such as Aristotle posit that the first cause of the universe must be an intellectual being.[13] In classical theism, God's knowledge must be compatible not only with divine simplicity, immutability, and eternity, all of which Thomas has already committed himself to prior to question 14, but also with God's transcendence, which we have referred to as 'divine independence.' It is this synthesis of divine knowledge and classical attributes that separates Thomism from relational models of theism.

A Transcendent Intellect

Divine transcendence, aseity, and independence, properly understood, are hallmarks of classical theism and serve as the main point of departure between classical theists and theistic mutualists. Classical theists emphasize God's transcendent independence to protect His eternal divine perfections from the influence of creation, whereas theistic mutualists stress the need of mutual reciprocity for true loving relationships to exist between God and creatures. In addition to the supposed lack of true divine love within classical theism, some of the latter's opponents have also suggested that the classical model makes God too distant from creation – more akin to Aristotle's Unmoved Mover than the God of the Bible.[14] How can an independent God

---

13. Again, Cooper is helpful. Cooper writes: 'In arguing that the forms exist not in an ideal realm but within particular objects, Aristotle was not opting for a materialist view of the world as did the atomists. He viewed the essences (thus ideas) as not just a human invention but as something *real*. He simply thought that the divorce between the ideal and the physical as found in Plato's theory was inadequate. Aristotle's view of reality has been labeled hylomorphism, meaning that the world is a composite of both form and matter. The form of a thing is its essence, as Plato used the term; matter is that which a thing is composed of. ... However, what Aristotle recognized is that something immaterial and self-sufficient must exist beyond all contingent things in order for the world to make any sense. Truth, therefore, is not solely rooted in material reality' (Cooper, 20-21).

14. Eleonore Stump addresses a few of these objections in Eleonore Stump, *The God of the Bible and the God of the Philosophers*, *The Aquinas Lectures* 80 (Milwaukee: Marquette University Press, 2016), esp. 11-40.

initiate a covenant with His people, be grieved by His creatures, 'repent' of previous interactions with His creatures, or otherwise display the personal qualities demonstrated throughout the Bible?[15] Many such objections have been addressed repeatedly, but to articulate God's independent omniscience, readers must examine what Thomas means when he argues for God's essential independence.

Pure Act Necessitates Independence

Thomas does not merely assert God's independence but infers its necessity based on rigorous philosophical and theological argumentation. Still, although his philosophical argument will require the most attention at this point, it should be remembered that Thomas's entire theological system was dependent on God's revelation in sacred Scripture. Thomas defends his belief in divine transcendence and the Creator-creature distinction by writing, 'Holy teaching does not pronounce on God and creatures as though they were counterbalancing, but on God as principal and on creatures in relation to him, who is their origin and end' (Aquinas, *ST* 1.1.3 ad 1). It would be a mistake to conclude that Thomas's system depends entirely on philosophical presuppositions, as if he believes his position to be disconnected from the Bible. Rather, Thomas's philosophical argumentation is intended to expound the truth one finds in Scripture.

Thomas expounds this biblical imbalance between Creator and creature through the division of being into 'act' and 'potency.' There must be something between complete being and complete non-being, as certain abilities and attributes seem to be present in creatures without being actualized. Hence, they exist in potency, the midpoint between being and non-being.[16] The existence of potency, however, necessitates

---

15. Greg Boyd cites these and similar questions as the impetus of his journey into open theism. See Gregory A. Boyd, *God of the Possible: A Biblical Introduction to the Open View of God* (Grand Rapids: Baker Books, 2000).

16. Ed Feser explains potency by writing, 'Parmenides assumed that the only possible candidate for a source of change in a being is non-being or nothing, which (of course) is no source at all. Aristotle's reply was that this assumption is simply false. Take any object of our experience: a red rubber ball, for example. Among its features are the ways it actually is: solid, round, red, and bouncy. These are different aspects of its "being." ... But in addition to these features, we can distinguish the various ways the ball *potentially* is: blue (if you paint it), soft and gooey (if you melt it), and so forth. So, being and non-being are not the only relevant factors here; there are also a thing's potentialities' (Edward

composition and the ability to change. Indeed, change is simply the actualization of some potency.

The concepts of act and potency, as has been shown, were not original with Thomas but were common within medieval philosophy. The first existent, namely God, must be free from composition, change, or imperfections and, therefore, free from potency. Thomas follows Boethius on this point:

> Being itself … has nothing else outside itself as an admixture. … Everything that is participates in that which is being with the result that it be. It participates in something else with the result that it be something. And through this, that-which-is participates in that which is being with the result that it be. … In every composite, being is other than the item itself. Every simple item possesses its being and that-which-is as one.[17]

Being must exist in God purely and without admixture of potency since He is the first existent and simple entity. God's essence is His very act of being which, in turn, is everything that being itself could possibly be. Being is not something God possesses, gains, loses, or receives.[18] To put this concept in Thomistic language, God is pure act: *actus purus*. To suggest that God experiences any sort of passive potency is equivalent to positing a greater being standing behind God granting His actualization and serving as His efficient cause. The divine perfections or divine attributes, then, are human attempts to use finite language to express this simple pure act of being in a multiplicity of ways.[19] Thomas concludes:

Feser, *Aquinas: A Beginner's Guide*, Oneworld Beginner's Guides [2009; repr. London: Oneworld Publications, 2020], 10).

17. Thomas Aquinas, *An Exposition of the 'On the Hebdomads' of Boethius*, trans. Janice L. Schultz and Edward A. Synan (Washington, DC: The Catholic University of America Press, 2001), 15.

18. 'Our findings so far prove God to be altogether unchangeable. First, because we have proved that there must be some first existent, called God, sheerly actual and unalloyed with potentiality, since actuality, simply speaking, precedes potentiality. Now any changing thing, whatsoever the change, is somehow potential. So it clearly follows that God cannot change in any way' (Aquinas, *ST* 1.9.1 ad 1).

19. 'It ought to be said that we are not able to speak about simple things except through the mode of composition, by which we receive our knowledge. And therefore speaking about God we use concrete words in order to indicate the subsistence of a thing because with us things do not subsist except in composition; and we use abstract words to indicate their simplicity' (ibid., 1.3.3 ad 1).

For if to be itself has nothing else admixed other than that which is to be, as has been said, it is impossible that this To Be Itself be multiplied through anything diversifying It, and because It has nothing outside Itself conjoined, it follows that It is susceptible of no accident. This – Simple, One, and Sublime – is God Himself.[20]

One can see, then, why divine independence and *actus purus* are so closely connected. God is utterly complete within Himself in every way and lacks all potentiality. In the words of the second Thomistic thesis:

> Since anything's 'act' is a completion it has, act is limited only by a potency which is the thing's capacity for being completed. Hence, in any order of being where there is a 'pure act,' the pure act is unlimited and unique; but wherever an act is limited and has more than one instance, it is occurring in a genuine composition with potency.[21]

Being, as pure act, cannot be improved upon and is fully complete. For Thomas, everything that God is, or ever will be, is what God has always been within His eternal act of being. In a more devotional sense, for God to change in any way would be movement away from perfection to imperfection. Again, there is no sense in which potentiality could be applied to divinity without implying something greater behind God in which He participates. For Boethius, Thomas, and countless classical theists, this suggestion is an impossibility.

Likewise, the classical understanding of immutability is closely related to the distinction between act and potency. As Edward Feser summarizes, 'Change just is the realization of some potentiality; or as Aquinas puts it, "motion is the actuality of a being in potency" (*In Meta* IX.1.1770), where "motion" is to be understood here in the broad Aristotelian sense as including change in general and not just movement from one place to another.'[22] It should be noted that the medieval use of 'motion' as nearly synonymous with 'change' has caused confusion for certain Thomistic opponents. Jeffrey Johnson, for instance, accuses Thomas of assigning 'immobility' to God due to the lack of motion

---

20. Aquinas, *'On the Hebdomads,'* 27.

21. Marshner.

22. Feser, *Aquinas*, 10. See Thomas Aquinas, *Commentary on Metaphysics: Books 7–12* (Steubenville, OH: Emmaus Academic, 2020), 9.1.1770. Thomas is commenting on Aristotle, *Metaphysics*, in *The Complete Works of Aristotle*, ed. Jonathan Barnes (Princeton, NJ: Princeton University Press, 1984), 2:9.1.1045b27-1046a35, 1651-1652.

present in a God that exists as pure act.[23] This concern over immobility does not reflect an accurate evaluation of Thomas's argument or a proper understanding of the medieval use of certain philosophical terms. As will be shown below, God's pure act does not hinder His immanent or transitive operations in a Thomistic framework. Still, if change is the realization of some potency as Feser suggests, and God is pure act without any potency as Thomas suggests, then God is incapable of change. Furthermore, if God is incapable of change, then God cannot learn, forget, grow in knowledge, or decrease in knowledge.[24] Thus, God's purely actualized omniscience is independent of creaturely contributions.

This view of God – as pure act which is incapable of intellectual change – is obviously contrary to theistic mutualism as defined in previous chapters. As Brian Davies writes:

> One often finds it said, especially by those who favor the formula 'God is a person,' that God's knowledge of what is not divine arises by observation, by taking a look at things in some way. Such, however, is not Aquinas's view. When we know things by observing or looking at them we gain or acquire knowledge on the basis of sensory experience. So knowledge grounded in observation amounts to the actualizing of a potentiality and is caused in us by what is distinct from us.[25]

This interpretation seems to be an accurate summary of Thomas who suggested '[if] the divine intellect understood by an intelligible species

---

23. See, for instance, Jeffrey Johnson, *The Failure of Natural Theology: A Critical Appraisal of the Philosophical Theology of Thomas Aquinas* (Conway: Free Grace Press, 2021). See also Feser's responses to Johnson: Ed Feser, 'Doubting Thomas,' *First Things*, March 2022, accessed June 24, 2022, https://www.firstthings.com/article/2022/03/doubting-thomas; Ed Feser, 'The Failure of Johnson's Critique of Natural Theology,' accessed June 24, 2022, https://edwardfeser.blogspot.com/2022/02/the-failure-of-johnsons-critique-of.html.

24. 'Since God is unchangeable, it also follows that his knowledge is not discursive – i.e. (1) that God does not first know this and then know that, and (2) that he cannot pass from ignorance to knowledge' (Brian Davies, *The Thought of Thomas Aquinas* [Oxford: Clarendon Press, 1993], 131).

25. Brian Davies, *Thomas Aquinas's Summa Contra Gentiles: A Guide and Commentary* (Oxford: Oxford University Press, 2016), 106. Davies is not referring to those who highlight the personal nature of God demonstrated by intellect and will, which would obviously include Thomas. Rather, Davies is pushing back against theistic personalism, a group that is often compared to or considered synonymous with theistic mutualism.

other than the divine essence, something other would be added to the divine essence as principle and cause' (Aquinas, *SCG* 1.46). If, however, God does not learn from external observation, then two questions follow. First, what serves as the proper object of divine knowledge? Second, if the divine intellect is pure act and independent from creation, then how can such a God meaningfully interact with human beings?

Act, Potency, and the Object of Divine Knowledge

Elenore Stump wrote *The God of the Bible and the God of the Philosophers* to address these concerns. She argues that the God of classical theism can interact with His creation and, therefore, avoid contradicting the portrayal of God in Christian Scripture. To do so, Stump cites God's interaction with Jonah in which God responds to Jonah's disobedience, prayers, eventual obedience, and the repentance of the Ninevites all while maintaining His eternality, immutability, and simplicity. Specifically, it is the Thomistic model of God, and the Thomistic definitions of classical attributes, that Stump hopes to defend. Overall, Stump does an excellent job in explaining how God's immanence does not contradict His transcendence as the following summary of her case will indicate. As Stump correctly concludes,

> [T]here is nothing in the logic of the attributes of immutability, eternity, and simplicity, as Aquinas understands them, that rules out God's acting in time, responding to human beings, conversing with them, and altering his announced plans for them because of what they do. As Aquinas understands these divine attributes, the God of the story of Jonah, the God who is the indwelling Holy Spirit who brings love and joy, could also be truly immutable, truly eternal, and truly simple.[26]

This conclusion is to be applauded, but Thomas and the Reformed thinkers who followed his model would separate themselves from Stump as far as her understanding of the divine intellect is concerned.

For Stump, God's interaction with man requires a genuine *response* to man's free actions, although this response need not *follow* man's free action chronologically due to God's eternality. In other words, God's answer to prayers need not be willed *after* the prayer but must be willed *because*

---

26. Stump, 108-09.

of the prayer, where 'because' takes a causal definition.[27] In Stump's estimation, this response to the libertarian free actions of creatures does not introduce potentiality in God, even though His knowledge of the event is dependent on the action itself. The reason Stump can hold this position is that she believes that a Thomistic understanding of knowledge places the intellect under the category of act even when it receives information from an external source. Stump writes:

> On Aquinas's view, even a human intellect need not be acted upon when it knows something because that something is the case. For Aquinas, the human intellect is always active when it knows. That is, in the process of cognition the human intellect acts on the phantasms derived from sensory input to abstract the intelligible species enabling intellectual cognition; the phantasms do *not* act on the intellect. For Aquinas, there is in human beings an *active* or *agent* intellect. ... Similarly, God's intellect is not passive when God knows what Jonah does because Jonah does it, since God's intellect is active in the process of cognition just as much or more than human intellects are.[28]

Compare Stump's reading of Thomas with an alternative interpretation. Davies writes:

> [Thomas] thinks that human knowledge is, at least partly, a case of potentiality being actualized by virtue of causes outside the knower. God's knowledge, however, cannot be anything like this, he says. In his view, God is fully actual, and is the first cause of things being acted on. It follows, he concludes, that knowledge in God is not the actualization of a potentiality by virtue of something outside himself. It should rather be thought of on the model of self-knowledge.[29]

---

27. Stump explains: 'There are, however, some actions that seem to require that the action have an existence and location in time. So, for example, an answer to a prayer apparently needs to be given *after* the prayer. Consequently, someone might suppose that an eternal God cannot answer prayer. But in fact this supposition is mistaken. An answer to prayer needs to be given *because* of the prayer; it is this counterfactual condition that is essential to the action of answering prayer, not any temporal relation between the answer and the prayer' (Stump, 66).

28. Stump, 95-96.

29. Davies, *The Thought of Thomas Aquinas*, 131. Stump summarizes this view in her estimation of Réginald Garrigou-Lagrange's position. Stump writes: 'Garrigou-Lagrange goes so far as to apply this argument to God's knowledge. If God knows something because it exists or is the case, then there is passivity in "Intelligence itself," as Garrigou-Lagrange puts it. So, for Garrigou-Lagrange, even God's knowledge determines what

Now, Stump is correct when she claims that a Thomistic understanding of knowledge is not entirely passive. Thomas is quite clear that there are two powers of the intellect, active and passive, and both Stump and Davies agree that only the active powers of the intellect can be assigned to God.[30] How, then, do the powers of the intellect function in the divine mind?

First, it should be noted that Stump's analysis of human psychology does not rest on an entirely accurate portrayal of the Thomistic framework. Thomas does affirm an active power in human intellect, but there also exists a passive power of the intellect, and human beings cannot have one without the other.[31] Rather than two forms of intellect, it is best to articulate two powers of one intellect. As such, human intellect is both active and passive. Thomas teaches that passivity exists in three ways:

> Firstly, in its most strict sense, when from a thing is taken something which belongs to it by virtue either of its nature, or of its proper inclination: as when water loses coolness by heating, and as when a man becomes ill or sad. Secondly, less strictly, a thing is said to be passive, when something,

God knows in virtue of the fact that it is the cause of everything that God knows' (ibid., 23). Stump goes on to emphatically reject such a view of the divine intellect. It is unclear what Stump means, however, when she claims that Garrigou-Lagrange's viewpoint makes God's knowledge the cause of God's knowledge, as an object cannot cause its own existence, and Garrigou-Lagrange does not claim otherwise.

30. Concerning man's active intellect and its relationship to God's intellect, Thomas writes: 'The active intellect, of which the Philosopher speaks, is something in the soul. In order to make this evident, we must observe that above the intellectual soul of man we must needs suppose a superior intellect, from which the soul acquires the power of understanding. For what is such by participation, and what is mobile, and what is imperfect always requires the pre-existence of something essentially such, immovable and perfect. Now the human soul is called intellectual by reason of a participation in intellectual power; a sign of which is that it is not wholly intellectual but in part. Moreover it reaches to the understanding of truth by arguing, with a certain amount of reasoning and movement. Again it has an imperfect understanding; both because it does not understand everything, and because, in those things which it does understand, it passes from potentiality to act. Therefore there must needs be some higher intellect, by which the soul is helped to understand' (Aquinas, *ST* 1.79.4).

31. The Thomistic Theses draw attention to the active power of the human intellect. Thesis 19 reads: 'We get knowledge, then, from things available to the senses. But since being sensed is not the same as being actually understood, something else has to be admitted in the soul besides the intellect that is formally said to "do the understanding," namely, an active power which abstracts intelligible kinds from their sensible appearances' (Marshner).

whether suitable or unsuitable, is taken away from it. And in this way not only he who is ill is said to be passive, but also he who is healed; not only he that is sad, but also he that is joyful; or whatever way he may be altered or moved. Thirdly, in a wide sense a thing is said to be passive, from the very fact that what is in potentiality to something receives that to which it was in potentiality, without being deprived of anything. And accordingly, whatever passes from potentiality to act, may be said to be passive, even when it is perfected. *And thus with us to understand is to be passive.* (Aquinas, *ST* 1.79.2)

So, while it is true that the intellect is in act when separating forms from matter and thus rendering forms intelligible, the result of this act is a passive growth in understanding, an addition of forms to the human psyche that were not present before the act of the intellect occurred. Now, due to the principle of negation, one can surmise that however intellect operates within God, it is free of all creaturely imperfections. Therefore, the divine intellect must not be characterized by any of the three modes of passivity and potentiality mentioned above.

One is not left to wonder how Thomas handles this issue, however, as he makes his stance clear. Thomas distinguishes the human intellect as it operates its passive power and the divine intellect, which exists as pure act:

For the intellect, as we have seen above (Q. 78, A.1), has an operation extending to universal being. We may therefore see whether the intellect be in act or potentiality by observing first of all the nature of the relation of the intellect to universal being. For we find an intellect whose relation to universal being is that of the act of all being: and *such is the Divine intellect, which is the Essence of God, in which originally and virtually, all being pre-exists as in its first cause. And therefore the Divine intellect is not in potentiality, but is pure act.* But no created intellect can be an act in relation to the whole universal being; otherwise it would needs be an infinite being. Wherefore every created intellect is not the act of all things intelligible, by reason of its very existence; but is compared to these intelligible things as a potentiality to act. (Aquinas, *ST* 1.79.2)

Notice that Thomas specifically defends the lack of passivity and potentiality in the divine intellect by citing the divine essence as the source and cause of all being. So, as Stump suggests, Thomas removes all forms of passivity from the divine intellect, but not in the same manner as Stump. Rather, Thomas draws attention to the divine intellect's relation to universal being.

The distinction lies not in the power of the divine intellect, which without question must be an active power within a Thomistic system, but rather in the object of the divine intellect and the causation relative to the divine will. Indeed, the primary object of divine knowledge is the key difference between a classical Thomistic model of God's intellect and the theistic mutualistic models of God discussed in Chapter 2. While Stump suggests that the object of divine knowledge is external to God, namely, the free acts of creatures, Thomas is clear that God knows all things through His own self-knowledge, in which all being pre-exists.[32] 'The first important consequence of this identity between God's knowledge and his being,' writes White, 'is that his knowledge of realities other than himself, which is to say, of all creatures, can occur only through the medium of his own self-knowledge.'[33] Since God knows all things through His own self-knowledge, it is inappropriate to say that God learns from His consideration of creatures. An increase in divine knowledge based on creaturely events or decisions would mean that creatures contribute to the very being of divinity, and 'it would imply a composite and gradual form of developmental understanding in God, an anthropomorphic conception that ignores the mystery of

---

32. For instance, Stump writes: 'An eternal, immutable God is not changeable across times since he does not exist at any times. At each and every time ET-simultaneous with the one eternal *now*, God is one and the same. And so an eternal, immutable God cannot do anything *after* something happens in time. But such a God can certainly act *because* of something that happens in time. In one and the same eternal *now*, God can both will to introduce into time t[1] an announcement to the Ninevites of the destruction of their city within 40 days after t[1] and also will to introduce into time t[2] the retraction of the destruction of Ninevah *because* the people repented between t[1] and t[2]. In making this one simultaneous complex act of will, the plan of God is changing, but God is not changing' (Stump, 76).

33. White, *The Trinity*, 330. It should be noted that Stump does not go so far as to suggest that God learns, but rather suggests that the relationship between the divine intellect and the free acts of creatures has an eternal basis. Stump writes: 'On the doctrine of eternity, the logical dependence of God's knowledge of a temporal event at t[n] on that event does not rule out the causal dependence of that event at t[n] on God's acts with regard to times prior to t[n], and those divine acts are manifestly included in God's knowledge. What is there at a time t[n] for God to know is a function of what God does and knows that he does with regard to things prior to t[n]. And so, in this sense, temporal events are in fact dependent on God's knowledge' (Stump, 69-70). In this sense, Stump's view resembles the Molinist position.

God's transcendence and simplicity.'[34] The fact that Thomas posits the divine essence as the primary object of divine knowledge is unavoidable in light of the doctrine of divine simplicity (DDS).

Thomas believes that first and foremost, God has perfect comprehension of Himself. Thomas writes:

> God has completely comprehensive knowledge of himself. This is shown as follows. A thing is said to be known with comprehensive knowledge when knowledge of it can go no further, i.e. when it is known as completely as it is knowable. … Now it is evident that God knows himself as fully as he is fully knowable. But a thing is knowable in proportion to its actuality: as we read in the *Metaphysics*, a thing is known as being actual, not as being potential. But God's power to know is equal to his actuality in existence: for his power to know comes from his actuality, his freedom from all matter and potentiality, as has been shown. (Aquinas, *ST* 1.14.3)

This perfectly comprehensive self-knowledge is the logical implication of divine simplicity, *actus purus*, and divine immateriality. In God, there is no distinction between the knower, the act of knowing, and that which is known. To speak in terms of truth theories, there cannot be a greater correspondence between knower and knowledge than the correspondence found in divine self-knowledge.[35]

Even if one could argue, like Stump, that God's intellectual operation does not betray *actus purus*, one would still miss *why* Thomas posits the divine essence as the only proper object of the divine intellect. As shown, simplicity, transcendence, and immutability would all be compromised by a dependent divine intellect. Aquinas emphasizes that the divine intellect is the divine essence itself and that this same divine essence is the first cause of all creaturely being. For a creaturely act to contribute to God's knowledge, then, requires (1) that the divine essence be dependent upon creatures in some fashion and (2) that secondary creaturely causation somehow exists apart from primary divine causation.

---

34. White, *Trinity*, 330.

35. Hankey writes: 'On the other side, the divine side, God is fully known to himself because his immaterial simple being is a complete return upon itself and his names belong to his perfections' (W. J. Hankey, *God in Himself: Aquinas' Doctrine of God as Expounded in the Summa Theologiae*, Oxford Theological Monographs [Oxford: Oxford University Press, 1987], 91-92).

This emphasis on divine transcendence, however, does not necessarily involve rejecting human freedom. While a Thomistic understanding of free will is compatible with God's simplicity and providence, as will be discussed below, it is unclear how Stump's formulation adequately explains the relationship between these three concepts without applying dependence onto the divine intellect.

Indeed, Stump's description of the divine intellect seems to be indistinguishable from Thomas's description of the angelic intellect. Angels, according to Thomas, do not think discursively and possess 'truth simply and without mental discussion.'[36] But if there is no difference between angelic and divine intellect, then the *Triplex Via* proves ineffective for Stump, as any imperfections present in angelic intellect would exist in the divine intellect and the rules of eminence and negation would fail. A divine intellect free from creaturely imperfections would obviously exclude the creature's chief imperfection – dependence.

As shown, Thomas builds much of his argument concerning the divine intellect on the doctrine of divine simplicity. The doctrine of divine simplicity, however, not only grounds Thomas's explanation of the divine intellect, but it also creates some interesting theological dilemmas. For instance, it would seem that a simple God could not have a multiplicity of ideas without compromising the very simplicity on which Thomas has insisted thus far. This question leads readers to the chief distinction between Aristotle and Thomas regarding the divine intellect.

Transcendent Divine Knowledge and Divine Simplicity

Due to the doctrine of divine simplicity, Thomas believes that any contribution to divine knowledge by a creature would actualize a potentiality found in the divine essence – a possibility that Thomas repeatedly denies. One cannot separate what God knows from who

---

36. Thomas writes: 'Reason and intellect in man cannot be distinct powers. We shall understand this clearly if we consider their respective actions. For to understand is simply to [immediately] apprehend intelligible truth: and to reason is to advance from one thing understood to another, so as to know an intelligible truth [mediately]. And therefore angels who, according to their nature, possess perfect knowledge of intelligible truth, have no need to advance from one thing to another, but apprehend the truth simply and without mental discussion, as Dionysius says (*Div. Nom.* vii)' (Aquinas, *ST* 1.79.8). See also White, *Trinity*, 326.

God is.[37] In the fourth article under question 14, Thomas addresses whether or not God's intelligence is His substance, where substance is functionally synonymous with the divine essence. It is, of course, unsurprising in light of Thomas's understanding of divine simplicity that he responds with affirmation; God's intellect is indeed His substance. In fact, Thomas is quite specific: 'In God intellect and that which is known, and the knowledge-species, and the act of knowing, are entirely one and the same,' and '[s]ince his essence is his knowledge-species, as we have said, it necessarily follows that his act of knowing is his essence and his being' (Aquinas, *ST* 1.14.4). Again, Thomas reiterates the identity of the divine essence as the primary object of the divine intellect: 'For God's act of knowing, which is self-subsistent, is the knowing of itself, not a knowing of something else, which would involve proceeding *ad infinitum*' (Aquinas, *ST* 1.14.4 ad 2). It is true, of course, that God knows all creatures, but His knowledge of creatures is an extension of His own self-knowledge, as will be made clear when Thomas addresses the divine Ideas.[38]

Thomas's final point mentioned above is worth further exposition. In light of divine simplicity, transcendence, and God's pure act of being, the divine essence must serve as the primary object of divine knowledge. Thomas argues:

> For if [His act of understanding] were other than His substance, it would follow, as Aristotle says, that something other would be the actuation and completion of the divine substance, and we should have the altogether impossible conclusion that the divine substance would stand to it as potency to act: because the act of knowing is a completion and actuation of the knower. (Aquinas, *ST* 1.14.4)

According to Aristotle and Thomas, something external to God cannot determine the thoughts of the divine mind without actualizing a divine potency. Although both Thomas and Aristotle agree on this point, they address it in significantly different and conflicting ways.

---

37. Davies describes Thomas's view as such: '[Thomas's] idea is that God and what God knows are indistinguishable. He thinks that the subject and object of divine knowledge cannot be thought of as two different things and that God knows himself simply by being God' (Davies, *Summa Contra Gentiles*, 130).

38. See also Thomas Joseph White, *Wisdom in the Face of Modernity*, 278-79.

For Aristotle, the Unmoved Mover can avoid potentiality only if the object of his knowledge is exclusively his own mind. Here is Aristotle's explanation:

> The nature of the divine thought involves certain problems; for while thought is held to be the most divine of phenomena, the question what it must be in order to have that character involves difficulty. For if it thinks nothing, what is there here of dignity? It is just like one who sleeps. *And if it thinks, but this depends on something else, then (as that which is its substance is not the act of thinking, but a capacity) it cannot be the best substance;* for it is through thinking that its value belongs to it. Further, whether its substance is the faculty of thought or the act of thinking, what does it think? Either itself or something else; and if something else, either the same always or something different. Does it matter, then, or not, whether it thinks the good or any chance thing? Are there not some things about which it is incredible that it should think? *Evidently, then, it thinks that which is most divine and precious, and it does not change; for change would be change for the worse, and this would be already a movement.* First, then, if it is not the act of thinking but a capacity, it would be reasonable to suppose that the continuity of its thinking is wearisome to it. Secondly, there would evidently be something else more precious than thought, viz. that which is thought. For both thinking and the act of thought will belong even to one who has the worse of thoughts. Therefore if this ought to be avoided (and it ought, for there are even some things which it is better not to see than to see), the act of thinking cannot be the best of things. Therefore it must be itself that thought thinks (since it is the most excellent of things), and its thinking is a thinking on thinking.[39]

If this were Thomas's stance, then skeptics might have a case for believing the God of classical theism to be stagnant, disconnected, and uninterested with creation.[40] A God who is understood to be a mind

---

39. Aristotle, *Metaphysics*, 12.9.1074b15-35,1698; emphasis added. Aristotle goes on to write, 'A further question is left – whether the object of the thought is composite; for if it were, thought would change in passing from part to part of the whole. We answer that everything which has not matter is indivisible. As human thought, or rather the thought of composite objects, is in a certain period of time (for it does not possess the good at this moment or at that, but its best, being something *different* from it, is attained only in a whole period of time), so throughout eternity is the thought which has *itself* for its object' (Aristotle, *Metaphysics*, 1075a 5-10). A considerable overlap between Thomas and Aristotle's thought can be identified, which makes Thomas's departure from Aristotle more significant.

40. See Gilson, *God and Philosophy*, 82-83.

thinking only of its own thinking could not interact with creation like the personal God of the Bible. Richard Regan refers to Aristotle's model of God as 'a self-absorbed intelligence that had no providential design for the world or its human inhabitants ...'[41] Thomas, however, tackles this concern in article 5.

When discussing whether God knows things other than Himself, Thomas draws attention to two important objections that refer to Aristotle's argument. Both objections pertain to God's reception of possible perfection from external objects of knowledge, and it would seem at first glance that readers must affirm one or the other. First, if the object of knowledge is the perfection of the knower, then it stands to reason that God must not understand objects of knowledge other than Himself. This objection protects God's perfection from the contribution of creatures and is essentially Aristotle's view. Second, if God is both His intellect and His act of knowing, an idea that Thomas has already affirmed in article 4, and if God understands objects of knowledge other than Himself, then it seems as if the divine essence itself is determined and shaped by creatures. Again, since God is not composed of substance and accidents, anything that shapes God's knowledge must shape His very substance.[42] The second objection is reminiscent of the theistic mutualistic position, so readers may expect Thomas to follow the Aristotelian argument in order to protect divine independence, but Thomas will go on to show that Aristotle's stance would implicitly reduce God's perfection rather than protect it.

Although the primary object of divine knowledge within a Thomistic framework is the divine essence itself, much like Aristotle's articulation, this does not mean that God lacks knowledge of His creatures. Rather, God knows all things *through* His comprehensive knowledge of Himself. If God possesses comprehensive knowledge of Himself, then that knowledge must extend to the effects of His power that would

---

41. Richard Regan, 'Introduction,' in *Compendium of Theology*, by Thomas Aquinas, trans. Richard J. Regan (Oxford: Oxford, University Press, 2009), 4.

42. Davies writes, 'In *SCG* 1.46 Aquinas goes on to argue that God can only understand through his essence since there is no actualized potentiality in God and since there are no accidents in God. According to Aquinas, we *come* to know by means of intelligible species, which are *accidents* that arise in us, but there is no *coming about* in God, which means that God's understanding is, so to speak, a function of his essence, or that God's understanding is his essence' (Davies, *Summa Contra Gentiles*, 105).

necessarily include all created things (Aquinas, *ST* 1.14.5). God knows all that He could create and decree, and He knows what He has freely chosen to create and decree. Together, this knowledge encapsulates everything there is to know about the created order. As such, if one were to obtain perfect comprehension of the divine essence, then he would receive knowledge of all things.

Furthermore, divine knowledge is not limited to creatures in general but extends to each particular creature. In other words, God knows that which constitutes humanity, and God knows individual human beings. Indeed, 'To know something generically and not specifically is to know it imperfectly,' since even human beings with their limited capacity for knowledge can comprehend individual beings (Aquinas, *ST* 1.14.6; 1.14.11).[43] Even divine knowledge of individuals, however, does not compromise divine simplicity for 'all things are to be found first in God, not only in regards what they have in common but also as regards what they all have as distinct from one another' (Aquinas, *ST* 1.14.6). Thus, since the divine essence serves as the primary object of knowledge and the medium through which God knows individuals, one can affirm God's simple intellect and also God's knowledge of multiple specific individuals.[44] Thomas's explanation of this fact is critical for a participatory theory of truth and, as such, will be presented in full:

> Therefore, since the essence of God contains all that makes for perfection in the essence of every other thing, and more besides, God can know all things in himself with a knowledge of what is proper to each. For the nature proper to each thing consists in its *participation* in the divine perfection in some degree. But God would not know himself perfectly if he did not know all the ways in which his perfection can be participated by other things; nor would he know perfectly the nature of existence if he did not know all degrees of existence. Hence it is clear that God knows all things in what is proper to each and makes them different from one another. (Aquinas, *ST* 1.14.6)

43. Again, Thomas makes use of the *Triplex Via*: 'It has been shown above that all that makes for perfection in any creature is to be found first in God, and is contained in him in an eminent degree' (Aquinas, *ST* 1.14.6).

44. Thomas writes, 'Although we know universal and immaterial things by one faculty, individuals by another, God for his part knows both classes of object through his simple intellect' (Aquinas, *ST* 1.14.11).

There is no created perfection, whether it is found in a group as a whole or in various individual members of that group, which did not first exist in God in an eminent degree. Since God knows how the divine perfections may be *participated* in by creatures to various degrees, and since all things have their being through participation in the divine essence, then God's knowledge of Himself is the means through which God knows all things. Elsewhere, Thomas explains how God's knowledge of Himself as first cause extends to His knowledge of individual creatures: 'He knows things other than himself through his essence, in so far as it is the likeness of things as their productive principle; therefore his essence must be the sufficient principle for knowing all things that come into existence through him, not merely in their universal natures but in their individuality' (Aquinas, *ST* 1.14.11).[45] God is the eminent, transcendent, first cause in which all creatures receive their existence, perfections, and identity through their participation in the likeness of the divine essence.

Active vs. Passive Potency

At this point, it is helpful to draw attention to an important distinction that is frequently overlooked in contemporary discourse regarding active and passive potency. Opponents of classical theism exploit the connection between a God of pure act and Aristotle's Unmoved Mover. If God is entirely independent of creation, then how can God care for creation? If God is incapable of need, then what motivated God's decision to create in the first place? Most importantly, if God lacks potentiality, how can God create without undergoing change? To answer such questions, one may distinguish between active and passive potency.

The distinction between act and potency deals specifically with the lack of *passive* potency in the divine essence. 'Passive potency' is defined as the capacity to be acted on by an external agent, thus making the passive object capable of modification. Richard Muller writes: 'A distinction must be made between active or operative potency (*potentia operative*),

---

45. Davies writes, 'God knows himself not just as the cause of it being true that "X is a dog" is sometimes true. He also knows himself as cause of the fact that "X is a dog" is true for given values of X. ... If carpenters could plan, not just the look of their chairs, but also their matter (in Aquinas's sense of "matter"), they would know them through and through. By the same token, says Aquinas, God knows his creatures through and through, as material individuals and not just as things that can be described in general terms' (Davies, *The Thought of Thomas Aquinas*, 134).

namely, the capacity to effect something or of exercising and efficacy or efficiency in action; or passive potency (*potentia passiva*), in the sense of being capable of existing or of being acted upon.'[46] For instance, a piece of wood is said to contain passive potency since a carpenter may reduce its potency to act as he shapes it for his purposes. The wood could become many different things in the hands of the carpenter who adapts the wood to his will. It is, in the minds of Thomas and other medieval Scholastics, impossible to describe God in terms of passive potency. There is no external agent that may reduce God's potency to act since God is already fully actualized, perfect, and satisfied. The lack of passive potency in God is not a shortcoming but rather an implication of divine aseity.

This lack of passive potency does not mean, however, that God is devoid of *active* potency or the ability to act upon an external object. Active potency is, indeed, a perfection that God must possess in order to be the omnipotent God of the Bible. Again Muller comments: 'Passive potency is the inward foundation or basis of being acted upon by another. The divine power or *potentia*, usually identified as *omnipotentia* (q.v.), is therefore an active potency only. There is no passive potency in God.'[47] Thomas does not deny the active potency of God – he cannot if he wishes to affirm God's omnipotence and freedom to create. God, therefore, is free to create or not to create without compromising His own *actus purus* or immutability. The existence of active potency in God is also the concept on which Stump builds her argument for God's active intellect.

Yet, the question still remains: 'How does God act in creation without undergoing change?' It will be recalled that Aristotle, from whom Thomas inherited concepts such as act, potency, and *actus purus*, associated these terms with immutability. W. Norris Clark explained:

> Act, on the other hand, is always identified with the fully complete, the actually present. Pure act, therefore, is simply a correlative of the immutable, i.e., of pure actualized form, complete in all that is proper to it and incorruptible. It is this immutability, self-sufficiency, and

46. Muller, *Dictionary of Latin and Greek Theological Terms*, s.v. 'potentia.'

47. Muller, *Dictionary of Latin and Greek Theological Terms*, s.v. 'potentia activa/potentia passiva.' Likewise, Bernard Wuellner defines passive potency as 'the capacity to receive, to be acted on, or to be modified' (Bernard Wuellner, *Dictionary of Scholastic Philosophy* [Fitzwilliam, NH: Loreto Publications, 2012], s.v. 'passive potency.')

incorruptibility which for Aristotle is the primary characteristic of the 'divine' and the perfect.[48]

As such, the connection between immutability and *actus purus* is logically necessary.

Fortunately, readers are not left to wonder about Thomas's views, since he explains how one might balance these two seemingly contradictory points. When discussing relational terms that are used to describe God, Thomas writes:

> The names which import relation to creatures are applied to God temporally, and not from eternity. ... They are called relative, not forasmuch as they are related to other things, but as other are related to them. Likewise for instance, *on the right* is not applied to a column, unless it stands as regards an animal on the right side; which relation is not really in the column, but in the animal. Since therefore God is outside the whole order of creation, and all creatures are ordered to him, and not conversely, it is manifest that creatures are really related to God himself; whereas in God there is no real relation [relativity] to creatures, but a relation only in idea, inasmuch as creatures are referred to him. Thus there is nothing to prevent these names which import relation to the creature from being predicated of God temporally, not by reason of any change in him, but by reason of the change of the creature; as a column is on the right of an animal, without change in itself, but by change in the animal ... (Aquinas, *ST* 1.13.7)

As such, terms like 'creator' apply to God relationally and highlight a change in creatures rather than a change in God. The divine essence does not undergo change through the act of creation – everything true about God in the first thirteen questions of the *Summa* is still true about God. Kreeft offers a helpful illustration: 'We speak of the sun "coming out" or "shining again" when there was no change in the sun but only in our relation to it when a cloud has passed away; or of the sun "rising" when in fact it was the earth that moved relative to the sun rather than the sun relative to the earth.'[49] These relational changes between the sun

---

48. W. Norris Clarke, 'The Limitation of Act by Potency in St. Thomas: Aristotelianism or Neoplatonism?,' in *Explorations in Metaphysics: Being, God, Person* (Notre Dame, IN: University of Notre Dame Press, 1994), 74.

49. Kreeft, *Summa*, 129-30. Indeed, Aristotle used the sun as an illustration concerning motion and potency. Aristotle wrote: 'Nor, if there is anything eternally in motion, is it potentially in motion (except in respect of some starting-point or destination), and there is no reason why the matter of such a thing should not exist. Hence the sun and

and the earth do not affect the sun, regardless of what human language may suggest. Likewise, neither God's eternal and infinite active potency nor His free choice to create a world external to Himself entails a passive potency within the divine essence.[50]

As has been shown, Thomas Aquinas's model of God is not identical to Aristotle's Unmoved Mover, despite some similarities between the two. The Thomistic model can explain God's interaction with creatures without compromising God's pure actuality and can articulate God's knowledge of creatures better than Aristotle's model.

Omniscience and the Reality of Evil

At this point, readers may sense a problem with grounding God's knowledge of all things in their connection to and participation in the divine essence. If God is identified as the formal, efficient, and final cause of all things, then one must somehow account for the existence of evil without compromising His divine goodness. Alternatively, to suggest that God knows evil through means other than the divine essence compromises all that Thomas has claimed thus far. Thomas is obviously unwilling to deny God's goodness or to credit the existence of any creature to non-divine primary causes. The dilemma is further complicated when one recalls Thomas's articulation of divine simplicity. If all effects are somehow present within a cause, and God is the cause of all things, then it would seem that God's essence must contain some germ of evil. If this proposal is read in light of divine simplicity, however, then evil would not just be a part of God but would be the very essence of God. How does Thomas affirm God's absoluteness, His

stars and the whole visible heaven are always active, and there is no fear that they will ever stop. ...' (Aristotle, *Metaphysics*, IX.11.1050b 20-25). Aristotle considered the movement of the sun and stars to be an imperishable, necessary, and eternal reality. Thus, the movement of the celestial objects should not be considered a potency, as if their movement could cease to be.

50. This distinction between active and passive potency is frequently overlooked by critics of classical theism. When the difference between the two concepts is overlooked, then it is easy to make Thomas's arguments seem more extreme than they are in reality. As an example, see R. T. Mullins, 'Simply Impossible: A Case against Divine Simplicity,' *Journal of Reformed Theology* 7 (2013): 181-203. For a classical approach to God's immutability and relation to His creatures, see Steven J. Duby, 'Divine Immutability, Divine Action and the God-World Relation,' *International Journal of Systematic Theology* 19, no. 2 (April 2017): 144-62.

transcendent omniscience and identity as first cause, and the reality of evil in the created order?

For Thomas, much like the patristic thinkers that preceded him, evil was understood as a privation, or absence, of goodness.[51] Evil does not possess being *per se* but instead is the perversion of being in another. At the core of every evil act, then, is the reality of goodness. This definition of evil allows Thomas to affirm the goodness of all created being without denying the experiences of suffering and evil. Thomas writes:

> It must be said that every evil in some way has a cause. For evil is the absence of the good, which is natural and due to a thing. But that anything fail from its natural and due disposition, can come only from some cause drawing it out of its proper disposition. … But only good can be a cause; because nothing can be a cause except inasmuch as it is a being, and every being, as such, is good. … Now that good is the cause of evil by way of the material cause was shown above (Q.48, A.3). For it was shown that good is the subject of evil. But evil has no formal cause, rather is it a privation of form; likewise, neither has it a final cause, but rather is it a privation of order to the proper end; … Evil, however, has a cause by way of an agent [efficient cause] … (Aquinas, *ST* 1.49.1)

Evil is a corruption of good – the absence or perversion of what should be. Evil has no formal or final cause, and thus cannot be directly linked to the divine essence.[52] Furthermore, its material and efficient causes are secondary, meaning that it latches on to another but does not participate in causation *per se*. Indeed, the material and efficient causes that lead to evil are actually, in and of themselves, good.[53]

---

51. For instance, this definition of evil can be linked to the Neoplatonism found in Augustine's theology. 'Since everything that exists, no matter how tenuously, is derived from the One, evil is not itself a positive force in neoplatonism. It is not, strictly speaking, a being at all, but instead a kind of lack of being, an absence or deprivation of what ought to be present, as blindness is the lack of vision in the eyes' (Augustine, *On the Free Choice of the Will*, xiii).

52. 'God's knowledge relates to created things like artistry relates to works of art. Now, artistry not only knows about but also produces things made artfully, yet it only knows about mistakes made by deviating from the rules of art. Similarly, God's knowledge produces and knows about everything good, yet it only knows about evil or sin, which are deviations from God's eternal law; it does not cause them' (Marshall, *Quod* 5.1.1).

53. Kreeft writes: 'Though evil does not have a formal or final cause (for it is the deprivation of a being's form and end), it has a material cause, or subject, and an efficient cause, or agent, both of which must be ontologically good' (Kreeft, *Summa*, 214n39). It

God's knowledge, then, is mediated through His perfect comprehension of the good.[54] For God to know a good being is for God to know every way which that good can be corrupted, perverted, or fail. A perfect comprehension of marriage, then, includes a knowledge of adultery. This comprehensive knowledge of marriage does not mean that the evil of adultery is ontologically present in the mind of God, as if it possesses a certain level of being. Rather, it is similar to a doctor's knowledge of eyesight, which includes an understanding of blindness.[55] To know how eyes are designed to function is to know how they could fail to function properly. Furthermore, Thomas makes clear that God's knowledge of evil does not corrupt Him:

> In our own case the knowledge of evil is not considered blameworthy according to that which essentially belongs to knowledge, namely, the judgment that we have of evil things. But it is considered blameworthy by accident, in so far as through the consideration of evil one is sometimes inclined to evil things. This is not the case in God, because, as was shown above, He is immutable. (Aquinas, *SCG*, 1.71.9)

---

should be noted that some authors do not describe the efficient cause of evil but prefer to speak in terms of 'deficient causation.'

54. Gregory Doolan summarizes Thomas's position: 'In *In I Sent.*, he notes that evil, inasmuch as it is evil, is nothing since it is a certain privation. For this reason, there is no idea of evil in itself but only as it is a thing. Thus, God knows evil by means of knowing the opposed good, from which the thing that is subject to privation falls short. In other words, the only idea of evil is the idea that God has of the thing in which the evil is found' (Gregory T. Doolan, *Aquinas on the Divine Ideas as Exemplar Causes* [Washington, DC: The Catholic University of America Press, 2014], 137). Likewise, White writes: 'He knows evil in the creature through the medium of his eternal idea of the goodness of the creature, a goodness that he knows is diminished by the creature's moral evil' (White, *Trinity*, 335).

55. Thomas uses the example of blindness: 'Yet, other knowable things do not have an independent proper notion but, rather, one that depends on something else. This is the case with relations, privations, and negations, whose notion depends on their relationship to something else. The notion of blindness, for example, is not independent but, rather, dependent, because of its relationship to sight, of which blindness is the privation. Now God knows all things in their proper notions. ... But when things have a dependent proper notion with a relationship to other things, God knows them in their relationship to the things on which they depend. Now, the notion of evil is not independent but, rather, dependent, because of its opposition to created good. Therefore, God knows evil in its relationship to created good, viz. by means of its opposition to that good' (Marshall, *Quod* 11.2.1). To use another example Thomas employs, 'Since the nature of evil is the privation of good, God, through the very fact of knowing good, also knows evils; just as darkness is known through knowing light' (Aquinas, *ST* 1.14.10).

Just as a judge is not condemned when he considers the wickedness of a murder trial, God is blameless as He comprehends the wickedness of evil.

God, then, is the not the cause of evil, which is not in and of itself a thing, but He does have a perfect knowledge of all evil things.[56] His simplicity and omniscience are both protected with a proper understanding of evil. Furthermore, Thomas's line of reasoning has the additional benefit of affirming the goodness of creation. Evil, since it lacks being, cannot compromise the goodness of being, and evil will never outlast the good as it requires the good to function. In this way, evil is a parasite that would die along with its host if it were to prevail over the latter.

This paradigm of evil did not cause Thomas to downplay the significance of evil in creation. It is not as if Thomas may ignore personal experiences of evil because, philosophically speaking, evil does not possess being. In fact, Thomas only admits to two possible arguments against the existence of God, one of which is the reality of evil.[57] Indeed, it is understandable that the presence of evil in the world serves as a major impetus for various forms of theistic mutualism.[58] The goodness

---

56. 'God's knowledge is not the cause of evil; but it is the cause of good through which evil is known' (Aquinas, *ST* 1.14.10).

57. Note Kreeft's analysis: 'St. Thomas can find only two objections to the existence of God in the whole history of human thought! There are numerous alternative psychological explanations for belief in God (fear, folly, fallacy, or fantasy), and there are objections to each of the many arguments for the existence of God. But there are only two arguments that even claim to *disprove* the existence of God. And the second only claims to show that the existence of God is an unnecessary hypothesis, like the existence of leprechauns or Martians: disappearing Irish gold can be adequately explained without leprechauns, and the "canals" on Mars without Martians. The second Objection does not prove that God cannot possibly exist. Only the first Objection, the Problem of Evil, remains as an apparent *proof* of atheism' (Kreeft, *Summa*, 60n16). Indeed, in Craig Carter's analysis, 'Process theologians think that the omnipotence of God must be denied lest God be responsible for evil' (Craig A. Carter, *Contemplating God with the Great Tradition: Recovering Trinitarian Classical Theism* [Grand Rapids: Baker Academic, 2021], 17).

58. Consider, for instance, the open theist Richard Rice's analysis of Wolfhart Pannenberg's *Systematic Theology*: '[Eschatology] is also the only standpoint for responding to the problem of evil. Says Pannenberg, "There is no theodicy without eschatology" (2:173). It is a mistake to try to absolve God of responsibility for evil, he says. The attempt cannot succeed, and besides, the cross shows that God accepted responsibility for the world he created (2:166). Because he foresees and permits evil, responsibility for its entrance into the world inevitably falls on God. He risked sin and evil when he created human beings who were free. The important thing is that God cares for his creation and eventually overcomes its suffering' (Richard Rice, 'Wolfhart Pannenberg's

of creatures is truly corrupted, but this corruption does not eliminate the priority of goodness in the world. The lack of being found in evil actually says more about the maximal value of goodness then it does the minimization of evil.

Indeed, the participation of creatures in the divine essence is the cause of all goodness found in creation. As Andrew Davison writes: 'If something falls from full participation in God then, as to goodness, it becomes somewhat evil; as to truth, it becomes somewhat false; as to being, it becomes somewhat grey; as to beauty, it lacks effulgence.'[59] Especially pertaining to the topic at hand is the fact that when Thomas discusses the privation of goodness in a creature, he refers to it as evil, but when the discussion revolves around truth, then that same privation is referred to as falsity. More will be said on truth below, but for now, it should be noted that the doctrine of participation has much to say regarding the idea of evil. Davison continues:

> This 'relative' quality of evil also bears upon the important participatory point that there is no supreme evil, from which all evil proceeds in any parallel fashion to the way in which all good proceeds from God, as the supreme good. As Aquinas has it, 'Evil is not intensified by approach to a term [to some ultimate example or origin, or to some principle of evil], but by recession from a term: for as a thing is said to be evil as lacking in goodness.' All that various evils have in common is that they are failures or privations, but in very different respects, which demand to be understood in terms of the goods concerned.[60]

Crowning Achievement: A Review of His *Systematic Theology*,' *Andrews University Seminary Studies* 37, no. 1 [1998]: 61). This eschatological explanation of evil, much like many of Pannenberg's theological conclusions, follows Jurgen Moltmann. According to John Thiel, 'Whether this concern [of God's power over evil] arises in process theologies or in Moltmann's placing of the crucified Christ at the heart of the doctrine of God, modern theologies attempt to circumvent the divine aseity by imagining vulnerability and suffering in the very being of God' (John E. Thiel 'Sonderegger's Systematics: The Divine Attributes as the Divine Being,' in *International Journal of Systematic Theology* 19.2 (2017):195.

59. Davison, *Participation*, 241n7. Notice the emphasis of the transcendentals in this quote. Davison cites Thomas: Aquinas, *ST* 1.48.4 ad 2; 2-1.18.3; 2-1.85.1; Aquinas, *SCG* 3.7.1; Aristotle, *Metaphysics*, 4.2.1004a; 3.7.11; Aristotle, *On Evil*, 2.2, esp. *obj. 3 and ad 2*; and 2.12, esp. *ad 8*.

60. Davison, *Participation*, 244. Davison continues still: 'A thing's nature comes from its particular participation in God. It suffers evil, or exercises evil, to the extent that it fails to participate in God *in that way*.' ibid.

Since God knows how the divine essence may be imitated or participated in by creatures, He also knows how creatures may fail to imitate or participate in the divine essence. This knowledge of privation is what Thomas refers to as God's comprehension of evil.

God's Knowledge of Future Contingent Acts

Closely related to the problem of evil and the doctrine of participation is the problematic relationship between God's knowledge and creaturely freedom. If God knows all creatures through the knowledge of Himself as first cause, then it is easy to see how the classical model could be characterized as a form of determinism in which all human actions, including their sins, are necessary acts stemming from a divine cause, but Thomas avoids this route. For Thomas, providence includes both the means, the ends, and the proper mode of both.[61] If God wishes to decree a certain free or contingent act, then that act will be accomplished freely and contingently. To suggest anything less is to compromise God's providential freedom.[62] In short, a divine free will has freely willed that man wills contingently. A helpful Protestant explanation of this Thomistic concept is found in Stephen Charnock who wrote,

> God did not only foreknow our actions, but the manner of our actions. That is, he did not only know that we would do such actions, but that

---

61. This is another area in which, according to Muller, more historians are noticing a Thomistic influence as it pertains to Protestant thought. Muller writes: 'Looking forward to the discussion of early modern Reformed thought, on these grounds alone, the claim that the language distinguishing between impossibility and possibility, contingency and necessity found in the Reformed tradition of the seventeenth century can only have Scotist origins must be rejected. Our examination of Aristotle and Aquinas has sufficiently demonstrated that the tradition prior to Scotus contained highly a nuanced understanding of contingency – yielding the conclusion that whatever Scotus added to the discussion, he did not engineer a shift from determinism to indeterminism and, certainly, was not the first to develop a full explanation of contingency' (Richard Muller, *Divine Will and Human Choice: Freedom, Contingency, and Necessity in Early Modern Reformed Thought* (Grand Rapids: Baker Academic, 2017), 138.

62. 'St. Thomas answers the objection not by compromising the efficacy or infallibility of divine providence at all, but by deriving from it (and from the principle that grace perfects nature rather than corrupting it) the proper contingency of human events (Cf. I, 19, 8). Essentially, the objection is that because God's will is never frustrated, therefore all effects are necessary; and the answer is that precisely because God's will is never frustrated, therefore not all effects are necessary' (Kreeft, *Summa*, 173-174n167).

we would do them freely; he foresaw that *the will would freely determine itself to this or that*; the knowledge of God takes not away the nature of things; though. God knows possible things, yet they remain in the nature of possibility; and though God knows contingent things, yet they remain in the nature of contingencies; and though God knows free agents, yet they remain in the nature of liberty. God did not foreknow the actions of man as necessary, but as free; so that liberty is rather established by this foreknowledge, than removed.[63]

It should be noted, however, that Thomas's understanding of human freedom differs from more compatibilistic models such as that of Jonathan Edwards.[64] Norman Geisler refers to Thomas's model of the human will as 'self-determinism.' Geisler defines self-determinism as 'the belief that people determine their own behavior freely, and that no causal antecedents can sufficiently account for their actions.'[65] Likewise, Muller wrote, 'Aquinas stood on the assumption that human beings, as created in the image of God, have, among their likenesses to the divine, genuine freedom of choice.'[66] Still, it must be noted that this is not an absolute freedom, but as Muller explains, 'It is a "situated" freedom operating according to the capacities of an ontologically dependent nature situated in a particular context in a temporal order.'[67] *Reformed* Thomism, however, need not limit itself to Thomas's understanding of human freedom. Indeed, it is easier to explain God's knowledge of a creature's future acts in more compatibilistic or deterministic models. As such, the forthcoming argument simply demonstrates how Thomas reconciled his understanding of an *a se* divine omniscience with his understanding of self-determining human freedom.

While the topic of divine foreknowledge has taken center stage in modern conversations regarding the divine intellect, Thomas does not spend an exorbitant amount of time on this issue. Thomas has committed himself to numerous conclusions regarding the nature of God, including

---

63. See Charnock 449-50, emphasis added.

64. One may also classify Edwards's model as 'deterministic' as in Geisler, 'Freedom, Free Will, and Determinism,' 467-68.

65. ibid., 467.

66. Muller, *Divine Will and Human Choice*, 133.

67. Ibid, 137.

affirmations of divine simplicity, God's existence as pure act, divine immutability, and God's role as the universal first cause. As such, Thomas's discussion of divine foreknowledge occurs within the parameters of what has already been said of God. Some may even find Thomas's analysis of divine foreknowledge simplistic compared to modern studies. This simplicity, however, is not a weakness but a testament to how complicated certain topics become once historic beliefs about God are jettisoned.

White explains Thomas's position as follows:

> The third consequence of this identity of knowledge and being in God is that God knows all future contingent realities insofar as he is their cause. ... In other words, God knows future contingents not by any kind of foreknowledge anthropomorphically conceived (as if God were estimating future likelihoods by first observing his creatures), but through the medium of his own eternal knowledge, to which the future (which does not yet exist) is utterly transparent.[68]

Critics, however, are quick to point out the problems of necessity and contingency. Indeed, Thomas includes this critique in his objections. Thomas surmises:

> It would seem that God has no knowledge of contingent future events. For from a necessary cause there proceeds a necessary effect. But God's knowledge is the cause of things he knows. ... Since, then, his knowledge is necessary, it follows that what he knows is necessary. Therefore God does not know contingent events. (Aquinas, *ST* 1.14.13 obj. 1)[69]

To answer this critique, Thomas relies on God's use of proximate and secondary causes. Although God is the first cause of all created being, He freely works through secondary causes to accomplish His will in creation. Thomas's interlocuters mistakenly concluded that necessary causes could only have necessary effects, but Thomas explains why this conclusion should be avoided. Thomas writes:

---

68. White, *Trinity*, 331. White also writes: 'Freedom is a participative notion, in Thomistic theology, not a binary notion. Created free agents participate in the freedom of the Creator and do not exert their autonomy in opposition to him. The inverse is not the case: we do not depend for our genuine freedom on the delimitation of the Creator's causality' (White, Trinity, 332n13).

69. Kreeft is correct to point out: 'One who is seeking the strongest possible arguments against any idea of St. Thomas will rarely find any stronger ones, any more strongly argued, than those in St. Thomas himself. He is extremely fair to all his opponents' (Kreeft, *Summa*, 17).

A first cause can be necessary and yet its effects contingent because of a contingent proximate cause; thus the sprouting of a plant is contingent because of a contingent proximate cause, although the first cause, the motion of the sun, is necessary. In the same way things known by God are contingent because of their contingent causes, though the first cause, God's knowledge, is necessary. (Aquinas, *ST* 1.14.13 ad 1)

As Muller explains, 'A thing may be necessary in relation to divine knowledge but contingent in itself, inasmuch as divine knowledge, as eternal, knows all things in their actuality.'[70]

Thomas does not merely cite God's divine providence or omnipotence as the grounds of His foreknowledge but also points readers to God's eternality (Aquinas, *ST* 1.14.13). Thomas explains that what is future to mankind exists as an eternal present before God. At first glance, the reference to God's eternality may seem as if Thomas believes that God knows the future because of His observation of all time, which would necessarily require some sort of dependence within the divine intellect.[71] This apparent contradiction, however, is alleviated if one considers the two ways in which future contingent events may be known.

First, Thomas points out that future contingent events may be comprehended through a knowledge of their proximate causes. This type of knowledge, however, is conjectural, and thus uncertain, since 'a contingent event is not yet determined to one effect' (Aquinas, *ST* 1.14.13). God, of course, knows all effects present in all proximate causes, but this knowledge is not the only way by which God knows future contingent acts. Additionally, God knows contingent acts as they are actualized in time. God is eternally the first cause of a contingent act's actualization, even if this actualization is placed in the future relative to creation. Thus, God's knowledge of future contingent acts is

---

70. Muller, *Divine Will and Human Choice*, 132. Also consider Davies who writes: 'Suppose I know that you are talking to me. Aquinas does not think that my knowledge now entails that your talking to me is in any way necessitated. For him, "X knows that -p" does not mean that p is necessary in the sense that it cannot be otherwise. And, with this kind of analogy in mind, he argues that God's "all at once" knowledge of contingent events does not rob them of their contingency' (Davies, *The Thought of Thomas Aquinas*, 135).

71. Harm Gorris believes that this is a frequent interpretation of Boethius's understanding of divine eternity, which Thomas employs. See Harm Gorris, 'Divine Foreknowledge, Providence, Predestination, and Human Freedom,' in *The Theology of Thomas Aquinas*, by Rik Van Nieuwenhove and Joseph Wawrykow, eds., paperback ed. (Notre Dame, IN: University of Notre Dame Press, 2005), 110-11.

not merely conjectural but certain, and yet this certainty occurs without compromising the contingency of the act itself.

Thomas explains:

> Things which are brought to the state of actuality in the time-series are known by us in time successively, but by God in eternity, which is above time. Hence future contingents cannot be certain to us, because we know them *as* future contingents; they can be certain only to God, whose act of knowledge is in eternity, above time. (Aquinas, *ST* 1.14.13 ad 3)

This argument is significant because contingent events undergo a change in being within time. What first exists as a potential act becomes actualized by proximate causes. Knowledge of future contingents is conjectural for man, but God must eternally know these acts as they exist within their proximate causes and as they are actualized in time.[72] God's eternal knowledge, then, is certain without eliminating contingency. In Thomas's understanding, God's providence, creaturely acts, divine simplicity, transcendence, and divine omniscience are all carefully balanced without compromising God's sovereignty or the reality of contingent acts.

Middle Knowledge[73]

At this point, it is appropriate to address the concept known as 'middle knowledge.' William Lane Craig, one of the leading contemporary voices

---

72. Davies provides a helpful summary of Thomas's understanding: '1. Things or events can be necessary or contingent. God knows whether or not they are necessary or contingent. That is because his knowledge must extend to "the being" that things have in themselves (i.e., it must extend to their being necessary, if they are necessary, and contingent, if they are contingent). 2. God's knowledge would be imperfect if it did not extend to matters of contingency and necessity. But God knows all things and their causes. So God knows what is both contingent and necessary. 3. Contingent and changing effects can proceed from what is first and necessary, and contingent effects can be known to God even though he is the first and immutable cause that cannot not be. 4. Nothing is future to God since, in his eternity, God unchangeably knows all that was, is, or will be. That is so even though we, who are not eternal, speak of God as knowing what is future to us in a way that might seem to imply that God's knowledge of events precedes them in time and therefore implies that they cannot not be. 5. It is true that "God knows that such and such is the case" entails that such and such is the case. But this proposition does not entail that such and such in question is necessary in itself. So God's infallible knowledge of what was, is, and will be does not rule out the possibility that some things are but might not be, or might not be as they are' (Davies, *Summa Contra Gentiles*, 110).

73. For an overview of modal truth within a Thomistic framework, see Timothy J. Pawl Jr., 'A Thomistic Account of Truthmakers for Modal Truths' (Diss., St. Louis, MO, Saint Louis University, 2008), accessed May 24, 2022, blob:https://www.proquest.com/41ac657b-bb3a-4415-8189-c5d5994bf2b1.

promoting Molinism, a paradigm of divine sovereignty and human libertarian freedom built upon divine middle knowledge, explains his understanding of middle knowledge as such:

> The Molinists charged that the Dominicans had in effect obliterated human freedom by making counterfactual truths a consequence of God's decree, for on the Dominican account it is God who determines what each person will do in whatever circumstances he finds himself. By contrast, the Molinists, by placing God's counterfactual knowledge prior to the divine decree, made room for creaturely freedom by exempting counterfactual truths from God's decree. *In the same way that necessary truths like 2 + 2 = 4 are prior to and therefore independent of God's decree, so also counterfactual truths about how creatures would freely choose under various circumstances are prior to and independent of God's decree.* ... Since God's counterfactual knowledge lies logically in between his natural knowledge and his free knowledge, Molinists called it God's middle knowledge.[74]

This understanding of middle knowledge has been thoroughly and repeatedly rejected by Thomism and the Reformed tradition. Indeed, Muller suggests that Reformed Christians have historically rejected this idea 'with vehemence.'[75] It is, of course, uncontroversial that God knows counterfactual truth – God knows what would have happened if He had providentially willed creation to be different than it is – but the Molinistic claim of middle knowledge is a much stronger claim. In a Molinistic framework, the source of middle knowledge is placed outside of both God's essence and decree.[76] Thus, for God to grasp

---

74. William Lane Craig, 'The Middle Knowledge View,' in *Divine Foreknowledge: Four Views* (Downers Grove: IVP Academic, 2001), 122; emphasis added. For more information regarding Craig's understanding of middle knowledge, see William Lane Craig, *The Only Wise God: The Compatibility of Divine Foreknowledge and Human Freedom* (Eugene: Wipf & Stock, 2000). For more information concerning Craig's doctrine of God, see William Lane Craig, 'Anti-Platonism,' in *Beyond the Control of God: Six Views on the Problem of God and Abstract Objects* (New York: Bloomsbury, 2014), 113-26; William Lane Craig, *God over All: Divine Aseity and the Challenge of Platonism* (Oxford: Oxford University Press, 2018); William Lane Craig, 'The Tensed vs Tenseless Theory of Time: A Watershed for the Conception of Divine Eternity,' in *Questions of Time and Tense* (Oxford: Oxford University Press, 2002). See also Luis Molina, *On Divine Foreknowledge: Part IV of the Concordia* (Ithaca: Cornell University Press, 2004).

75. Muller, *Dictionary of Latin and Greek Theological Terms*, s.v. '*scientia Dei.*'

76. Muller writes: 'It is important to recognize that middle knowledge is not simply the divine foreknowledge of future possibility or contingency. If the issue were simply the divine knowledge of future possibility – even of possibilities arising out of the contingent

counterfactual knowledge of human decisions, He must look outside of Himself and receive genuine contributions from His creation. Indeed, within the Molinistic framework, this creaturely contribution would somehow occur before these creatures even existed. Therefore, these creaturely acts would occur apart from God's decree or from any existent cause.

Réginald Garrigou-Lagrange explains why the Molinistic definition of middle knowledge is incompatible with the Thomistic understanding of the divine intellect:

> One of the fundamental reasons ... why every Thomist will always reject the Molinist theory, is that this [Molinist] theory of necessity causes one to posit *a passivity in the pure Act*. If the divine causality is not *predetermining* with regard to our *choice* ..., the divine knowledge is fatally *determined* by it. To wish to limit the universal causality and absolute independence of God, necessarily brings one to place a passivity in Him, a passivity in the *self-subsisting Being*, in the *self-subsisting Intellect*. ... It becomes consequently quite clear for one who speaks seriously and does not wish to trifle with words, that *the foreknowledge is passive* when one positively asserts that this *difference* does not at all come from God; just as I am a *passive* spectator *when I see* that this man, independently of me, is seated, whereas the other is standing. ... A new passivity has entered into the pure Act, who henceforth is no more like to God than is the false diamond like the true. ... it is only *afterwards that God*, although He is Being itself, Intelligence itself, Goodness itself, saw and willed it determinately.[77]

According to Garrigou-Lagrange, a divine intellect determined by the free actions of its creatures must be marked by passivity.

---

interaction of finite creatures – it could be easily understood under the rubric of the divine *scientia necessaria* or necessary knowledge of all possibility. If the issue were simply the divine foreknowledge of contingency in the usual sense, namely, a foreknowledge of contingencies arising out of the world order willed or actualized by God, it could easily be understood under the rubric of *scientia voluntaria*, the divine knowledge of all that God has willed past, present, and future. *Scientia media*, however, is a kind of divine knowing intentionally placed *between* God's necessary and voluntary knowledge. It is a foreknowledge of future conditionals or conditional future contingencies arising from the free choice of creatures prior to the divine willing' (Richard A. Muller, *Post-Reformation Reformed Dogmatics: The Rise and Development of Reformed Orthodoxy, ca. 1520 to ca. 1725*, vol. 3, *The Divine Essence and Attributes* [Grand Rapids: Baker Academic, 2003], 418-19).

77. Réginald Garrigou-Lagrange, *God, His Existence and Nature*, 5th ed., trans. Dom Bede Rose (St. Louis: Herder, 1955), 538-39. Cited in Stump, 22-23.

An introduction of passive potency, however, not only eliminates the concept of *actus purus* but also requires a rejection of the classical doctrines built on its premise. Thomas's commitment to immutability, simplicity, and transcendence prevents the admittance of such intellectual potency. Furthermore, in addition to God's simple essence being acted upon, God's providence becomes conditioned by the will of creatures. God must work within the bounds provided to Him by independent and external actors. Without reference to the divine Ideas or transcendent omniscience, God's knowledge and will become identical to man's, as far as God must practice abstraction and data collection to build *a priori* knowledge and base His will on the conditions set before Him.

Traditionally, theologians have discussed two categories of God's simple divine knowledge: (1) natural knowledge, which is grounded in God's knowledge of His omnipotence and thus includes knowledge of all that is possible; and (2) God's free knowledge, which is grounded in God's knowledge of His will, and thus includes knowledge of all possibilities that have been actualized.[78] The Molinistic theory of middle knowledge, however, requires possibilities external to God which are thus left ungrounded by the divine essence. This untethered potentiality is virtually meaningless in a Thomistic framework. Davison explains:

> Aquinas saw all possibility, as well as actuality, as having an absolute, participatory origin in God: God is the cause of all things, including possible things, and there is no possibility independent of God. This aligns with Aquinas' insistence that actuality is prior to possibility: every possibility depends upon some actuality, and the broadest bounds of possibility *per se* are grounded in the supreme actuality of God.[79]

---

78. It should be noted that these categories are not to be understood as parts of God's knowledge, which would undermine divine simplicity. In God, knowledge, power, and will are all the same divine essence.

79. Davison, *Participation*, 167, Further Note 4. Also note Davies who writes: 'It cannot be said that what is known by God is the cause of his knowledge; for things are temporal and his knowledge is eternal, and what is temporal cannot be the cause of anything eternal. Similarly, it cannot be said that both are caused by one cause, because there can be nothing caused in God, seeing that he is whatever he has. Hence, there is left only one possibility: his knowledge is the cause of things' (Davies, *The Thought of Thomas Aquinas*, 138). Or consider Geerhardus Vos who writes: 'If in this way God must expect an increase in His knowledge of things outside Himself, if He must, as it were, wait if

Readers can note this concept in Thomas's understanding of human freedom:

> Free-will is the cause of its own movement, because by his free-will man moves himself to act. But it does not of necessity belong to liberty that what is free should be the first cause of itself, as neither for one thing to be cause of another need it be the first cause. God, therefore, is the first cause. Who moves causes both natural and voluntary. And just as by moving natural causes He does not prevent their acts being natural, so by moving voluntary causes He does not deprive their actions of being voluntary: but rather is He the cause of this very thing in them: for He operates in each thing according to its own nature. (Aquinas, *ST* 1.83.1 ad 3)

As such, Thomas believes that God could have genuine knowledge of future contingent events without compromising literal contingency and non-necessary creaturely acts while avoiding a source of divine knowledge external to the divine essence.

The Divine Intellect and the Divine Life

It is interesting to note that Thomas immediately follows his analysis of the divine intellect with an examination of the divine life. Life, Thomas argues, can be properly attributed to God because of the *opera ad intra*, the internal operations of God, namely, the divine intellect and will. Thomas writes: '… life is attributed to certain things because they act of themselves and not as moved by other things; hence the more perfectly this is verified in a thing the more perfectly does it possess life' (Aquinas, *ST* 1.18.3). This operation is found most perfectly in God because 'that Being whose own nature is its act of knowledge, *which also does not have what belongs to it by nature determined for it by another*, is the Being which has life in the highest degree. Such a Being is God' (Aquinas, *ST* 1.18.3). The divine intellect and will are the only operations in God and are thus the reason Christians may appropriately speak of a living God. Notice, furthermore, that Thomas believes that the operations, to demonstrate the type of life God possesses, cannot be moved by another.

He thus must take up within Himself the influence of the temporal, then this destroys His eternity' (Geerhardus Vos, *Reformed Dogmatics*, vol 1. *Theology Proper*, ed. and trans. Richard B. Gaffin Jr. [Bellingham, WA: Lexham Press, 2014], 19).

Indeed, Thomas differentiates man's knowledge and life from God's knowledge and life. Thomas writes:

> [A]lthough our intellect is self-actuated in certain ways, still certain things are provided for it by nature, e.g. first principles, about which it has no choice, and the ultimate end, which it is not free not to will. Hence, although the intellect moves itself to some extent, still it must in some things be moved by another. (Aquinas, *ST* 1.18.3)

This limited intellectual self-actuation is not the case, however, with divine knowledge, as has been mentioned above. It is, in fact, 'because his intellect is most perfect and always in the state of actuality' that Thomas may conclude that God 'has life most perfect and eternal' (Aquinas, *ST* 1.18.3).[80] God has life because God is His transcendent and independent act of knowing. In other words, 'God's life is his actual knowing' (Aquinas, *ST* 1.18.4).

The Relationship between Omniscience and Omnipotence

At this point, some may wonder if a totally independent and actualized divine intellect may result in divine voluntarism. Would it not be that a self-determining God could act unbounded by any moral or rational principle? In light of this popular post-Enlightenment theological presupposition, one must explain how the inner operations of the divine life in Thomistic theology differ from modern models of theism on this point. To that end, the discussion of truth we put forth will not rely on a modernistic portrayal of divine voluntarism.

Divine voluntarism is a belief grounded in the incomprehensibility of the divine essence. Since God is beyond human comprehension, creatures should not presume to understand or predict the divine will. Indeed, within this post-Enlightenment framework, the capricious, and borderline arbitrary, will of God became the focal point of divinity. God is defined as the being who can do whatever He wants, even if the divine will defies wisdom, logic, or goodness. If God were to decree

---

80. On this point, Thomas cites Aristotle, *Metaphysics*, 12.7.1072b 27-31. In this work Aristotle writes: 'Life also belongs to God; for the actuality of thought is life, and God is that actuality; and God's essential actuality is life most good and eternal. We say therefore that God is a living being, eternal, most good, so that life and duration continuous and eternal belong to God; for this *is* God.'

the antithesis of the Decalogue tomorrow, this antithesis would then become the standard of morality and ethical goodness.

Voluntarism has seeped into the modern consciousness and has become the latter's settled model of theism. An ungrounded omnipotent freedom has become the routinely accepted model of divinity. Rather than the classical definitions of divine perfections or attributes, divine freedom has become the lens through which all matters related to the doctrine of God are measured. Indeed, this idea exists even in conservative Reformed Christianity. That is, some Reformed Christians have argued that God, in His ungrounded omnipotent freedom, can even change His divine essence if He so willed. God can thus become mutable, passible, or enter into composition with His creation because His divine will is completely free from restraints or boundaries.

A classical Thomistic model of theism differs significantly from the voluntaristic model. Within Thomism, God's divine will is defined by His wisdom.[81] God has a perfect knowledge of His divine essence, which, in turn, is His goodness. Additionally, God is motivated to love that which is good. God's will, therefore, will always be framed by that which God knows to be desirable and the utmost good. God's will is not capricious, and certainly not arbitrary, but is grounded in that which is ontologically and unquestionably the highest possible good.[82] While the limiting function of goodness and wisdom upon the divine will does not mean that mankind may comprehend the divine will perfectly, it does mean that mankind may have confidence that God's will is not unstable or erratic. As Thomas states, 'Since good as perceived by intellect is the object of the will, it is impossible for God to will anything but what his wisdom approves' (Aquinas, *ST* 1.21.2 ad 2).

This distinction is especially pertinent to the discussion of truth. If God's will is indeed totally free, even to the point of contradiction,

---

81. See also Gilson's overview of Malebranche in *God and Philosophy*. Gilson writes, 'As a theologian, he would maintain that God always acts in conformity with that which He is and that the only end of God in His action is His own glory in the person of Jesus Christ' (ibid., 92).

82. Muller explains how this does not quench the divine freedom: 'Aquinas argues that the end or goal of God's willing is the divine goodness itself. And although God's goodness is manifested in the present order of things, it could just as well be manifested in different creatures in a different order. In the absolute sense, then, God could do otherwise' (Muller, *Divine Will and Human Choice*, 123). God's will, thus, is free but not capricious.

then there cannot exist an eternally guaranteed basis of truth, regardless of creaturely epistemic confidence. Even the most secure scientific, moral, or religious truth would always be tentative in light of divine freedom. At that point, truth itself verges on nonsense. Indeed, it is unsurprising that various postmodern theories of metaphysical truth followed the shift in modernity's voluntaristic model of God. Even if there were a God's eye view of truth, that truth would be erratic and would be impossible to obtain. The Thomistic model, however, serves as the grounds of epistemic confidence in an eternal metaphysical truth. God's wisdom, desiring that which is the highest good, is immutable, stable, and the theological basis of truth.

This idea of the first and most universal cause helps readers to understand the relationship between divine providence and omniscience. A perfect comprehension of the divine essence extends to a knowledge of the range of divine power. To comprehend a cause, one must know all possible effects relative to the cause. As noted, there is no potentiality in God, but there is in God the power of active potency. God does not passively receive effects, but He can cause effects without compromising His identity as *actus purus*. Therefore, a knowledge of divine omnipotence includes all possible effects, which God is free to cause.[83]

Gordon Clark and the Storehouse of All True Propositions

A popular view of divine omniscience within twentieth-century evangelicalism sees the divine intellect as a storehouse of all true propositions.[84] Gordon

---

83. 'Since there is no potentiality in God, and since God is the first cause of things being changed, his knowledge of creatures cannot be a case of them acting on him so as to bring it about that he knows them. It must rather be the case that creatures are as they are (and therefore known to God) by virtue of God' (Davies, *The Thought of Thomas Aquinas*, 138).

84. This terminology stems from Katherine Sonderegger's overview of omniscience. Sonderegger writes: 'To defend properly the doctrine of Omniscience we must be able to affirm that God is Knowledge itself, perfect Intelligibility and Insight, such that He in His very Being is not simply a storehouse of every particular and all universals, but is rather the very life, the very heart and veins, the very taste of each living thing, in its own manner and way, its own indelible mark as this very one. Anything short of this is not proper Omniscience, not the full glory of the Creator of all flesh, not the Light that illumines what is not, and brings it into being.' See Katherine Sonderegger, *Systematic Theology*, vol. 1, *The Doctrine of God* (Minneapolis: Fortress Press, 2015), 360. At times, Sonderegger comes close to supporting 'omnisubjectivity' in which God, in His divine

Clark will serve as an appropriate case study to demonstrate the distance between Thomas's model of divine propositional knowledge and the view embraced by some evangelicals. In the theology and philosophy of Clark, the commitment to a conservative bibliology led to an overemphasis on propositional truth.[85] Eventually, propositional truth, and as an extension propositional knowledge, became the only possible form of both. Indeed, Clark stated publicly: 'I would not know what the word "truth" meant unless as a quality of proposition. I cannot conceive of anything that is of truth that is not a proposition.'[86] Again, elsewhere Clark reiterates: 'Truth is a characteristic of propositions only. Nothing can be called true in the literal sense of the term except the attribution of a predicate to a subject.'[87]

This propositional nature of truth extends to and includes the knowledge of God.[88] Knowledge, according to Clark, 'means the possession of truth,' and truth is strictly propositional.[89] Therefore, God is omniscient because He knows all true propositions. The only reason that Clark can attest that omniscience is an incommunicable attribute

essence, knows human experiences because He personally experiences all events with His creation. Thomas, however, rejects omnisubjectivity while moving beyond the storehouse metaphor of omniscience.

85. The role Clark's bibliology plays in his understanding of truth is not because of any specific statement. Rather, the reason that Clark pushes propositional truth is because the Bible, which is the grounds of all truth, is written propositionally. If non-propositional truth existed, then the Bible's sufficiency as the well of all truth could be called into question. See, for instance, Gordon Haddon Clark, 'The Bible as Truth,' *Bibliotheca Sacra* 114, no. 454 (1957): 157-70. Davison would disagree with this position, as '[r]evelation participates in divine truth not simply, or mainly, as we have already noted, through propositional statements, which feature relatively rarely in the Bible, but also through such deeply human forms as narrative and poetry, through questions as well as answers, through laments, hymns, prayers, cautionary tales and so on' (Davison, *Participation*, 319).

86. Meeting of the Presbytery of the Orthodox Presbyterian Church, at 2328 Germantown Avenue, Phila. PA, 'In Regards to the Examination in Theology of Gordon H. Clark,' July 7, 1944, 1, lines 18-20.

87. Clark, 'The Bible as Truth,' 158. The word 'only' is underlined in the original manuscript to demonstrate emphasis. Elsewhere Clark writes: 'It is hard to credit the idea that truth can be non-propositional. The single word *cat* is neither true nor false' (Gordon Clark, *What Is Saving Faith?* [Jefferson, TN: The Trinity Foundation, 2004], 27).

88. 'Meeting of the Presbytery,' 1, lines 14-17.

89. Gordon Clark, *A Christian View of Man and Things* (Grand Rapids: Eerdmans, 1952), 323. Clark acknowledges that people may describe *true* scholars or *true* churches, but emphasizes that this use is derivative, and more importantly, figurative. See Clark, 'The Bible as Truth,' 159.

is that God knows an infinite number of propositions which simply requires too much time to pass on to temporal creatures.[90]

Clark's argument concerning the relationship between man's knowledge and divine knowledge was a centerpiece of controversy. Clark believes that for any given proposition to be true, it must be a shared belief by God and man. While the *mode* of the content could differ qualitatively, as God's knowledge is not discursive or acquired, the content had to be the same.[91] The *reason* that the proposition 'David was king of Israel' was true was that the content of the proposition was literally believed by both God and man. A group of leaders within the Orthodox Presbyterian Church interpreted Clark's ideas as a denial of God's incomprehensibility and called for the rejection of his ordination.

Furthermore, Clark refused to accept analogical similarities and suggested that the overlapping content in the minds of God and man were univocal. Clark explains: 'If both God and man know, there must with the difference be at least one point of similarity; for if there were no point of similarity, it would be inappropriate to use the one term *knowledge* in both cases.'[92] Thus, when Cornelius Van Til and other Orthodox Presbyterians brought objections against Clark, specifically as Clark's view relates to analogical predication, Clark responded that the concept of analogy is Neo-Scholastic skepticism in disguise.[93] Clark concludes: 'An analogical

---

90. Clark defines God's incomprehensible knowledge as 'that God knows every proposition and that those propositions are infinite in number and that we shall not exhaust them when He reveals them to us one at a time' ('Meeting of the Presbytery,' 27, lines 18-21).

91. Clark, 'The Bible as Truth,' 170.

92. Ibid., 164. Interestingly enough, Clark also dismissed the correspondence view of truth because he believed that it too closely resembled the argument for analogical thought. See ibid., 168.

93. Clark, 'The Bible as Truth,' 166. Clark specifically mentioned Thomas in ibid., 167. Clark's opponents wrote: 'Now even if it could be assumed that human knowledge has this propositional character, it would still involve a tremendous assumption to conclude that the divine knowledge must possess the same character. Since our thinking is pervasively conditioned by our creaturehood, we may not safely infer from the character of our knowledge what must be true of the knowledge of the Creator. Even if we could be sure that human knowledge might be resolved into distinct propositions, it would not necessarily follow that the knowledge of God, who penetrates into the depths of his own mind of all things at a glance, would be subject to the same qualifications. And it may not be overlooked in this connection that Dr. Clark does not claim Scriptural proof for his fundamental assumption as to the character of knowledge.' See Cornelius Van Til, 'The Text of a Complaint: Against Actions of the Presbytery of Philadelphia in the

truth, except it contain a univocal point of coincident meaning, simply is not the truth at all.'[94] Thus, for mankind to possess truth, there must be univocity of intelligible content between God and man.

There are obviously significant differences between the models of omniscience presented by Thomas and that which was presented by Clark. Both Thomas and Clark agree that God's intellect is not discursive, but Thomas's stance is much stronger. Thomas writes: 'In God's knowledge there is no discursiveness. ... God sees everything in one, that is, in himself, as we have concluded. Hence he sees everything at once and not successively' (Aquinas, *ST* 1.14.7). When Clark was asked whether or not he believed that 'God's intuitive knowledge is the same as our discursive knowledge,' he answered, 'Well, I guess not ...'[95] Clark repeatedly affirmed that God's knowledge was intuitive rather than discursive, but he could not explain how God's intuitive knowledge aligned with his understanding of propositional knowledge.

Thomas, however, presents a clear argument on how God could know all propositions:

> Since to form propositions is in the power of our intellect, and God knows whatever is in his own power or that of the creature, as we have said above, God must know all possible propositions. But, just as he knows material things immaterially, and composite things by a simple act of knowledge, so he knows propositions not in the way they are formed, i.e. not by putting

---

Matter of the Licensure and Ordination of Dr. Gordon H. Clark,' https://gordonhclark. reformed.info/the-complaint/. It should be noted that Van Til is not the sole signatory of this document, but he is the one most often associated with the complaint because Clark often attributed the document to Van Til.

94. Clark, 'The Bible as Truth,' 166. Clark continues: 'God has spoken his Word in words, and these words are adequate symbols of the conceptual content. The conceptual content is literally true, and it is the univocal, identical point of coincidence in the knowledge of God and man' (Clark, 'The Bible as Truth,' 171). Clark, an outspoken critic of Thomas and the Thomists who followed him, used the same argument as the Neo-Thomists used against the *nouvelle theologia*. Boersma explains: 'The Neo-Thomists appeared to jump from the one extreme to the other, from equivocity to univocity: they did not seem to acknowledge a differentiation between human knowledge and divine knowledge, but regarded the church's dogmatic statements as true in the same way that God's eternal truth was true. ... Once symbolism had given way to dialectic, the participatory approach to truth was lost to a univocal approach according to which truth was something to be mastered' (Hans Boersma, *Heavenly Participation: The Weaving of a Sacramental Tapestry* [Grand Rapids: William B. Eerdmans Publishing Company, 2011], 166).

95. 'Meeting of the Presbytery,' 27, lines 11-13.

together or separating their terms in his mind; he knows each thing by simple understanding, by knowing the essence of each thing. (Aquinas, *ST*, 1.14.14)[96]

The difference, however, is that Thomas recognizes that propositions are the mode of creaturely thought and need not apply to God whereas, for Clark, God knows by means of propositions, even though this knowledge is not discursive. Rather, God knows every proposition because He knows every thought that creatures have had in the past, are having currently, or will have in the future. As such, divine knowledge of propositions is an extension of God's knowledge of creatures.

The strong link between knowledge and propositions proposed by Clark overlooks the medium through which God possesses His knowledge – the divine essence.

> God does not have abstract thoughts nor does he think through the medium of concepts, propositional beliefs, syllogistic chains of reasoning, or processes of logic. … Therefore, it is problematic to apply to God any form of knowledge that implies discursive syllogisms, logical chains of reflection, propositional knowledge of facts, or developmental beliefs as contingent properties of his person.[97]

This statement is quite contrary to Clark's analysis, which concluded that 'logic is how God thinks.'[98] Muller explains: 'God is a simple being who does not know by means of propositions – particularly not

---

96. Clark and Thomas also both acknowledge God's immutable knowledge of propositions. Thomas writes: 'It must be granted, then, that "Whatever God knew, he knows" is not true if the reference is to facts as stated in propositions. But it does not follow that God's knowledge is changeable. There is no change in the divine knowledge through his knowing that one and the same thing at one time exists and at another time does not; and in the same way, there is no change in the divine knowledge through his knowing that a certain proposition is at one time true, at another time false. His knowledge would thereby be changeable if he knew propositions in the way they are formed, putting together and separating different notions, as our mind does' (Aquinas, *ST* 1.14.15 ad 3).

97. White, *Trinity*, 327. 'As intellectual creatures, human beings form propositions about the world around them, acquire beliefs, and grow in knowledge progressively, based upon an ongoing study of the structure of a reality that pre-exists their own intellectual life. … God knows directly the plenitude of his own being, and knows all other things "in himself" in a comprehensive way, not because he learns about them gradually by studying them, but insofar as he is the cause of their very existence' (White, *Trinity*, 326).

98. Gordon H. Clark, *An Introduction to Philosophy* (Unicoi, TN: Trinity Foundation, 2017), 108.

by means of an ordered series of propositions. There are, in addition, no "propositions from eternity," since propositions are, by nature, of human construction.'[99] Due to Clark's application of a creaturely mode of knowledge unto the divine intellect, and because of his rejection of analogical predication in favor of univocal thought, Clark could not replicate the Thomistic commitment to a transcendent omniscience. God's knowledge includes all propositions, but it is not limited to propositions.

The Divine Intellect in Reformed Theology

There are plenty of examples of Reformed Protestants affirming God's independent divine intellect. Consider, for instance, what Thomas Ridgely wrote about the topic:

> With respect to [God's] knowledge or wisdom, he doth not receive *Ideas* from any object out of himself, as all intelligent creatures do, and in that respect, are said to depend on the object; so that if there were no such objects, they could not have the knowledge or *Idea* of them in their minds; therefore the object known must first exist, before we can apprehend what it is. But this must not be said of God's knowledge, for that would be to suppose the things that he knows antecedent to his knowing them. *The independency of his knowledge is elegantly described in scripture; Who* hath directed the Spirit of the Lord, or, being his counsellor, has taught him? With whom took he counsel, and who instructed him, and taught him in the path of judgment, and taught him knowledge, and shewed to him the way of understanding? (Isaiah 40:13, 14).[100]

Or one may consider William Perkins's view of the divine intellect:

> The wisdom or knowledge of God, is that by which God doth, not by certain notions abstracted from the things themselves, but by his own essence: nor successively and by discourses of reason, but by one eternal and immutable act of understanding, distinctly and perfectly know himself, and all other things, though infinite, whether they have been or not.[101]

Summarizing the Reformed position, Muller writes:

---

99. Muller, *PRRD* 3:416.

100. Ridgley, *Body of Divinity*, 55, col. 2. Originally cited in Muller, *PRRD* 3:239; emphasis added. Muller adds: 'The central point, that God knows externals not on the basis of externals but in and through the divine essence, certainly derives from Aquinas' (Muller, *PRRD* 3:239).

101. Perkins, *Golden Chain*, 3 (para. 12, col. 1). Originally cited in Muller, *PRRD* 3:397.

> The divine knowledge of the created order is not, therefore, a knowing *ad extra* resting on examination of the individual existents in the finite order, that is to say, neither a contingent knowledge grounded on contingent existences nor an indefinite knowledge, but a knowledge of the possibilities and actualities known and willed by the divine essence itself.[102]

The clearest and most thorough exposition of divine knowledge in Protestant literature may have come from Stephen Charnock, and Charnock's model of the divine intellect has much in common with Thomas's understanding. In *The Existence and Attributes of God*, Charnock writes: 'God knows himself, and only knows himself. ... Herein consists the infiniteness of God's knowledge, that he knows his own essence, that he knows that which is unknowable to any else.'[103] Charnock reiterates: 'He only knows what he is, and what he knows, what he can do, and what he hath decreed to do.'[104] Charnock, like Thomas, emphasizes that the divine essence is the primary object of divine knowledge and the means through which God knows all things external to Himself. As God's knowledge pertains to creatures, Charnock writes: 'God knows himself, because his knowledge, with his will, is the cause of all other things that can fall under his cognizance: ... he is the first truth, and therefore is the first object of his own understanding.'[105]

God knows all things past, present, and future because He knows Himself as first cause of all things. More specifically, God knows all perfections that exist in creatures because they first existed in Him. Again, Charnock writes: 'He knows his own power, and therefore everything through which his omnipotence is diffused. ... He therefore knows distinctly the properties of every creature, because every property in them is a ray of his goodness.'[106]

Likewise, Charnock consistently affirmed the independence and immutability of divine knowledge. He writes: 'God knows all things

---

102. Muller, *PRRD* 3:412.

103. Charnock, 414.

104. ibid.

105. ibid., 415. Thomas also refers to God as the First Truth. See, for instance, Thomas Aquinas, *Super Boethium de Trinitate*, 1, 3 obj. 1.

106. Charnock, 421. Charnock specifically refers to God as the exemplary and efficient cause. See Charnock, 421.

independently. This is essential to an infinite understanding. He receives not his knowledge from anything without him; ... If he knows things by his essence, then, as his essence is independent from the creatures, so is his knowledge.'[107] Charnock makes his point clear:

> Again, since knowledge is a perfection, if God's knowledge of the creatures depended upon the creatures, he would derive an excellency from them, they would derive no excellency from any idea in the Divine mind; he would not be infinitely perfect in himself, but be under an indigence, which wanted a supply from the things he had made, and could not be eternally perfect till he had created and seen the effects of his own power, goodness, and wisdom, to render him more wise and knowing in time than he was from eternity.[108]

Finally, if the quotations above do not remind readers of Thomas, then Charnock's final proposition most certainly will. Charnock concludes the expositional portion of his work on the divine knowledge by writing: 'God knows all things perpetually, *i.e.* in act. Since he knows by essence, he always knows, because his essence never ceaseth, but is a pure act; so that he doth not know only in habit, but in act.'[109] An independent, *a se* omniscience runs through the entirety of Charnock's work on the divine intellect. This model is by no means peculiar to Thomas, but repeatedly has found a home within Protestant theology.

God Is Truth

After Thomas explains his views concerning the divine intellect, he moves on to the important topic of truth. Significantly, he asks whether God is truth. Thomas writes:

> You find truth in the mind when it apprehends the thing as it is, and truth in the thing when it possesses being conformable to mind. This is verified most of all in God. For his being is not only in conformity with his intellect, but is his very act of knowing; and his act of knowing is the measure and cause of all other being and all other intellect; and he

---

107. Charnock, 456. Charnock even uses the illustration of the sun that was mentioned earlier. Charnock writes: 'The earth sends not light to the sun, but the sun to the earth. Our knowledge, indeed, depends upon the object, but all created objects depend upon God's knowledge and will' (Charnock, 456).

108. Charnock, 457.

109. ibid., 461.

himself is his own being and his own act of knowing. Hence it follows not only that truth is in God but also that he is the supreme and original truth. (Aquinas, *ST* 1.16.5)

As is obvious, a correct understanding of the divine intellect provides the basis for Thomas's understanding of God's relationship to truth. God is not called the Truth simply because He knows the truth, as if truth is a standard to which God must conform. Rather, the doctrine of divine simplicity and God's *a se* independent omniscience are on full display. God is truth because He perfectly apprehends the divine essence through which He knows all things. In God, the knower, His act of knowing, and the object of knowledge are all one and the same. Indeed, God's self-comprehension is the 'measure and cause of all other being and all other intellect.' God's knowledge of Himself, which is the divine essence, is the standard of all truth.

Since God is truth, Thomas can affirm that truth is both eternal and immutable. Thomas explains: 'If no intellect were eternal, no truth would be eternal. But since the divine intellect alone is eternal, truth has eternity in it alone. Nor does it follow from this that anything other than God is eternal; because truth in the divine intellect is God himself, as we have shown' (Aquinas, *ST* 1.16.7). Notice again that Thomas does not position truth as anything external to God which He must acquire or conform. Rather, '[T]ruth in the divine intellect is God himself.' Likewise, Thomas writes:

> If there should be an intellect in which there cannot be alternation of opinions, and whose grasp no thing can escape, in such an intellect truth is unchangeable. Therefore truth in the divine intellect is unchangeable. ... The truth whereby material things are said to be true is the truth in the divine intellect; and that is altogether unchangeable. (Aquinas, *ST* 1.16.8)

It is, of course, not surprising, then, that so many thinkers have recognized divine qualities embedded in the concept of truth. How this divine truth relates to creaturely truth will be the topic of the next chapter.

Conclusion

Thomas's model of divine omniscience is dependent upon a doctrine of God that emphasizes transcendence, aseity, and independence. God knows all things through His perfect self-comprehension. Since His perfect self-comprehension includes all the effects that His power may bring about, then this knowledge includes a comprehension of all created being. This perfect knowledge is obtained without any contribution from His creatures whatsoever. To suggest otherwise would either compromise the doctrine of divine simplicity, which Thomas was unwilling to do, or suggest that God's very being is dependent upon His creatures for actualization, which would place creatures on the level of divinity.

Thomas's model of divine omniscience may seem foreign to modern thinkers. Evangelicals have grown accustomed to limiting God's knowledge to terms of propositions, much like Gordon Clark. Others may follow the theistic mutualists and suggest that God learns over time, thus punting a classical understanding of immutability. Furthermore, deviations from Thomas's model of the divine intellect may result in a misunderstanding of what it means to describe God as truth. The simple, comprehensive, self-knowledge of God provides the basis for naming God as truth and, as will be shown in the next chapter, the basis for all creaturely truth.

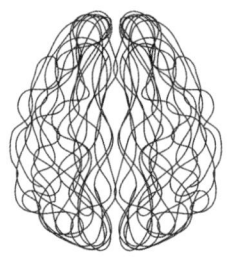

CHAPTER SEVEN

Thomistic Participation

Having discussed the relationship between truth and divinity, the legitimacy of Thomas as a source of theological retrieval for Protestants, and the Thomistic understanding of the divine intellect, readers are now equipped to examine the participatory theory of truth that has been referenced since the beginning. In order to promote this theory, the chapter will begin with an analysis of the Thomistic form of participation before considering an overview of Thomas's doctrinal understanding of the divine Ideas – the connecting point between the doctrines of creation and divine omniscience. Participation and the divine Ideas will prove to be essential in the proper understanding of truth. Much of what will be said concerning participatory truth will resemble the correspondence theory, but a few major distinctions will be highlighted. The principal difference between the participatory theory and the correspondence theory is twofold. First, the participatory theory *requires* a belief in God as the standard of all truth. Second, the participatory theory defines truth through a creature's participation in divine self-knowledge. It will be shown that truth is what God is, and all creaturely truth receives its being by participating in the likeness of the divine Ideas.

At this juncture, it is helpful to remember Thomas's primacy as a biblical exegete and theologian. In many ways, the following overview of participation and the proceeding analysis of the divine Ideas flow out of an extended application of Acts 17. Verse 28 teaches us that in God we 'live and move and exist,' which just echoes the teaching of verse 25 – 'He himself gives to all people life and breath and all things.'

The argument in Acts 17 is straightforward: human beings cannot meet any hypothetical divine needs because everything humans possess flows directly from God. As such, divine independence is contrasted with humanity's extreme dependence on the *a se* God. These verses are easy to affirm but any analysis of these concepts is going to require metaphysical consideration made clear by some translations' use of 'being' in verse 28. The doctrine of participation, then, is an attempt at explaining how divine being sustains creaturely being while avoiding the extreme ends of pantheism and deism.

Analogy and Participation

In order for readers to understand the participatory theory of truth, a working knowledge of two concepts will prove necessary – participation and analogical predication. Analogical predication is narrowly understood as an aspect of linguistic theory in the philosophy of religious language. How can finite words developed within historical contexts adequately describe an infinite God existing outside of time, space, and chronological development?[1] Thomas believes that univocal and equivocal predication both fail to represent the relationship between Creator and creature. There is an analogous similarity between God and man that makes religious language possible, but this similarity is not univocal and exists on the forefront of a greater dissimilarity.

Standing behind the concept of analogical predication, however, is a driving metaphysical commitment. Being a metaphysical realist,

---

1. Paul Tyson expresses this concern well through his analysis and summarization of Frederich Nietzsche's thought. Tyson summarizes: 'As a language specialist and a penetrating scholar of ancient culture [Nietzsche] was particularly sensitive to the fact that all thinking and all human action is only meaningful to us because of words. But words are very fragile and malleable things. Their meanings are a function of culturally situated use, and all cultural and historical situations are contingent and shifting artifacts of imagination, desire, and power, and provide us with no fixed or objectively factual grounding in truth. Any reasoned thought about "objective truth" is thus a self-deception because it must of necessity rely on words shaped and interpreted by culture and by the contingencies of one's particular community, life, and times. Contingency is the inescapable context for all human ideas, thus human ideas simply do not have the power to be universally and eternally valid (and anyone who tells you they do is selling something).' See Paul Tyson, *Returning to Reality: Christian Platonism for Our Times, Kalos* 2 (Eugene: Cascade Books, 2014), 55.

Thomas believes that human language is genuinely connected to reality.[2] Terms such as 'genus' or 'species' are not mere notional concepts without a foundation in creation but genuinely reflect something that exists outside the speaker. Andrew Davison shows how analogical predication, metaphysical realism, and the concept of participation are closely related:

> We can use our human vocabulary, learned from creaturely things, to speak about God, because God is the cause, or creator, of those creatures. Everything about them has been given to them by God. Their goodness, wisdom, strength, and so on, is given to them by God as an image or trace of God's own goodness, wisdom or strength. We call this a *participatory* account: everything the creature has comes as a participation in God. ... This trace or participation is what allows our talk about God to be more than equivocation and also what means that it is not univocation either: these names say something about God's very self, Aquinas writes, but they certainly do not capture everything about him (*ST* I, 13, 2). ... The name for a likeness to God in things is participation and the name for a likeness in language is *analogy*.[3]

Religious language may transcend equivocation because human knowledge is capable of truly reflecting the objective world order via intellectual abstraction and, furthermore, because this objective order receives its being and perfection from the Creator. The difference between the Creator and His creatures, however, prevents the mistakes of univocal language, in which perfections in God and man are spoken of in the same qualitative manner.

---

2. Jordan Cooper writes: 'It has been the assumption in the West that there is objective reason which stands behind reality, making the external world really knowable to the subject. When we use words, these are linguistic signifiers which identify something external to the self. When I say "triangle," for example, I am identifying the idea "triangle," which for Plato is the form, or for the Christian Platonist is an idea in the mind of God. ... My words are making an objective claim about the external world, and are therefore understandable to the people around me who hear the vocalization. Words have actual meaning, as they refer to real things. This is, for many postmodern philosophers, wrong' (Jordan Cooper, *In Defense of the True, the Good, and the Beautiful: On the Loss of Transcendence and the Decline of the West* [Ithaca: Just and Sinner, 2021], 61-62).

3. Andrew Davison, *The Love of Wisdom: An Introduction to Philosophy for Theologians* (London: SCM Press, 2013), 141. 'So analogy,' writes John Dunne, 'is participation's consequence in the realm of definition' (John S. Dunne, 'St. Thomas' Theology of Participation,' *Theological Studies* 18, no. 4 [December 1957]: 493).

Creatures, and all the perfections they possess, are linked to their Creator as a lesser effect is linked to a more perfect and eminent cause. 'Although creatures in their multifarious perfections *do resemble* God,' writes Thomas Joseph White, 'they nevertheless do so neither in essence and nature, nor in genus.'[4] Rather, according to Thomas Aquinas, 'Creatures are said to resemble God, not by sharing a form of the same specific or generic type, but only analogically, inasmuch as God exists by nature, and other things partake existence' (Aquinas, *ST* 1.4.3 ad 3).[5] It is because God is the ultimate origin of all creaturely 'being, good, and truth' that 'we can ascribe the perfection names (like being and goodness) to God supremely, as denoting perfections that must exist in God.'[6]

Univocity and Equivocity of Being

While Thomas promoted the doctrine of analogy, other thinkers preferred to think of being in terms of univocity, a theory of being most popularly tied to the thought of John Duns Scotus.[7] This concept has become a hallmark of modern theology, and many thinkers have suggested that the Protestant Reformers typically followed Scotus on this regard, although that claim is often debated.[8] For Scotus, 'God cannot be known naturally unless being is univocal to the created

---

4. Thomas Joseph White, *The Trinity: On the Nature and Mystery of the One God*, Thomistic Ressourcement Series 19 (Washington, DC: The Catholic University of America Press, 2022), 267.

5. Thomas also explains that this is 'the sort of analogy that holds between all things because they have existence in common ... for precisely as things possessing existence they resemble the primary and universal sources of all existence' (Aquinas, *ST* 1.4.3).

6. White, *Trinity*, 267.

7. Scotus's understanding and clear commitment to the univocity of being can be overstated. At some points in his works, Scotus holds that '"being" is an analogous notion and thereby logically equivocal,' whereas elsewhere he suggests that 'analogy and univocity may be compatible.' For more information, see Peter King, 'Scotus on Metaphysics,' in *The Cambridge Companion to Duns Scotus*, ed. Thomas Williams (Cambridge: Cambridge University Press, 2003), 58n13.

8. Richard A. Muller has repeatedly demonstrated that the Reformers' relationship with the medieval Scholastics is eclectic, and one should not overstate the influence of Scotus on Protestants. For more information, see Richard A. Muller, 'Not Scotist: understandings of being, univocity, and analogy in early-modern Reformed thought,' *Reformation and Renaissance Review* 14, no. 2 (2012): 127-50.

and uncreated.'[9] The difference between perfections in creatures and perfections in God are a matter of God's infinity. 'For in so far as [perfections] pertain to God,' argues Scotus, 'they are infinite, whereas in so far as they belong to creatures, they are finite.'[10] As such, Scotus rejected the need for analogical predication and deemed a perfection as 'univocal' if it 'has sufficient unity to serve as the middle term of a syllogism, so that wherever two extremes are united by a middle term that is one in this way, we may conclude to the union of the two extremes among themselves.'[11] 'Being,' therefore, could serve as a middle term between God and man once God's infinity was taken into account.

A contemporary advocate of Scotus's univocity of being is Thomas Ward, whose depiction of the divine Ideas will be discussed below. Ward argues:

---

9. John Duns Scotus, *Concerning Metaphysics*, in *Philosophical Writings*, trans. Allan Wolter (Indianapolis: Hackett Publishing, 1987), 5. Elsewhere Scotus clarifies: 'In the present life no concept representing reality is formed naturally in the mind except by reason of those factors which naturally motivate the intellect. Now these factors are the active intellect, and either the sense image or the object revealed in the sense image. ... Now, no concept could arise in virtue of the active intellect and the sense image that is not univocal but only analogous with, or wholly other than, what is revealed in the sense image. In the present life, since no other such analogous concept could arise in the intellect naturally, it would be simply impossible to have any natural concept of God whatsoever. But this is false' (John Duns Scotus, *Man's Natural Knowledge of God*, in *Philosophical Writings*, trans. Allan Wolter (Indianapolis: Hackett Publishing, 1987), 22.

10. Scotus, *Concerning Metaphysics*, 2. Thomists would not disagree that God's infinity played a large part in the correct understanding of being. Consider for instance the analysis of Sebastian Morello: 'Two important notions follow from the source possessing a perfection by essence, and so without composition. First, the source must be unique, for were there two sources both possessing the same perfection by essence in perfect simplicity, they could not be in any way distinguished. *Second, the perfection must be infinite in the source.* The reason for this is the same as that for its unicity: the perfection is present in perfect simplicity, therefore it forms no "mixture" with something else which could limit it. As we have said, Aquinas's entire ontology is a single participation structure, and the source on which this structure depends must be, then, perfectly simple, unique, and infinite' (Sebastian Morello, *The World as God's Icon: Creator and Creation in the Platonic Thought of Thomas Aquinas* [Brooklyn: Angelico Press, 2020], 47; emphasis added).

11. Scotus, *Man's Natural Knowledge of God*, 20. Compare Scotus's definition of univocity with William of Ockham's: '"univocal" denotes a concept common to things which are perfectly alike in all essentials without any dissimilarity' (William of Ockham, *The Possibility of a Natural Theology*, in *Philosophical Writings*, trans. Philotheus Boehner [Indianapolis: Hackett Publishing, 1990], 106). For an overview of Scotus's model of being, see Hans Boersma, *Heavenly Participation: The Weaving of a Sacramental Tapestry* (Grand Rapids: William B. Eerdmans Publishing Company, 2011), 73-76.

> [T]he being of a creature is exactly like God's being, even though his is infinite, and his the archetype. And this, by the way, is nothing more and nothing less than Scotus's doctrine of the univocity of being, the doctrine that we can correctly conceive both God and creatures under one concept, univocally. The doctrine of the univocity of being does not imply some third thing, being, which God and creatures share. Nor does it imply that the being of God is the very being which is the being of creatures, numerically identical with it. No, the doctrine of univocity simply means that a creature's being, just insofar as it is being, is exactly like God's.[12]

Ward, like Scotus, also applies this univocity to specific perfections found both in God and man. To illustrate his belief, Ward cites the property of 'lovingkindness' as it exists in his mother. 'As far as lovingkindness itself goes,' Ward writes, 'it is the same for my mom and for God – it's lovingkindness she has and lovingkindness he is – and what my mom lacks is not lovingkindness but infinite lovingkindness. But, whether finite or infinite, lovingkindness is lovingkindness.'[13] Again, readers will notice that the only difference cited between creaturely perfections and divine perfections is that perfections that exist infinitely in God are restrained by finitude in creatures.

One alternative to the univocity of being would be the equivocity of being, in which there exists no likeness between God's being and man's being. If this were the case, then 'we could say that such a view regards human knowledge of God as purely equivocal: there is no correspondence whatsoever between the language that we use about God and the reality of God himself.'[14] This view stresses the reality of divine transcendence and seeks to uphold the Creator–creature distinction, but if divine and creaturely being are equivocal, then man's goodness, wisdom, or power is in no way comparable with the divine goodness, wisdom, or power.

Analogy of Being

First, it is clear that Thomas rejects univocity between God and man. 'An effect,' Thomas writes, 'that does not receive a form specifically the same as that through which the agent acts cannot receive according

---

12. Thomas M. Ward, *Divine Ideas*, Cambridge *Elements: Religion and Monotheism* 6 (New York: Cambridge University Press, 2020), 53.

13. ibid., 51.

14. Boersma, *Heavenly Participation*, 165.

to a univocal predication the name arising from that form' (Aquinas, *SCG* 1.32.2).[15] As such, '[T]he forms of the things God has made do not measure up to a specific likeness of the divine power; for the things that God has made receive in a divided and particular way that which in Him is found in a simple and universal way' (Aquinas, *SCG* 1.32.2). Thomas goes on to claim that in order for univocal predication to be warranted, the mode of being between God and creatures would have to be identical. Everything that is in God is God according to the doctrine of divine simplicity; therefore, for man and God to share being univocally, creatures would have to be divine (Aquinas, *SCG* 1.32.3).

In concluding his argument, Thomas specifically draws from the doctrine of participation because 'nothing is said of God by participation, since whatever is participated is determined to the mode of that which is participated and is thus possessed in a partial way and not according to every mode of perfection' (Aquinas, *SCG* 1.32.6). In Thomas's estimation, if God and creatures share the same mode of being, then God would receive divine perfections via participation, which would necessarily mean possessing those perfections in a limited form. One can see, then, that the analogy of being and doctrine of participation are inseparably intertwined, and thus, to affirm univocal predication, one must reject the participatory ontology of Aquinas.

Likewise, Thomas rejects the equivocity of being. If creatures and the Creator do not possess any shared likeness, then it would be impossible to discern any truth regarding the divine as ascertained through creation (Aquinas, *SCG* 1.33.4). Humans, however, truly do possess a knowledge of the divine perfections through their understanding of creation. Thinkers first observe and experience wisdom, goodness, and love in creatures, but if God and man's being are purely equivocal, then these terms cannot be applied to God in

---

15. Davison provides a creaturely illustration to Thomas's point: 'Even to share a word between one creature and another (humans and gorillas are both "social", for instance) involves stretching a word, not using it univocally and, it goes without saying, God is more different from us that we are from gorillas. For another thing, many words apply to our fellow humans as accidents: this person, thank goodness, is wise, but he only happens to be wise. God does not just happen to be wise; God is wisdom itself. We do not understand what it means for someone to be wisdom itself, so when we call God wise we cannot be using the word in the same way as when we apply it to a creature' (Andrew Davison, *Participation in God: A Study in Christian Doctrine and Metaphysics*, paperback ed. [New York: Cambridge University Press, 2020], 140).

any appropriate manner (Aquinas, *SCG* 1.33.6). Indeed, since God has revealed Himself through words, a purely equivocal relationship between God and man would render Scripture useless. In order for man to grasp God's goodness, for example, then he must have some point of reference for what it means for God to be good. If the word good, however, is completely equivocal, then nothing in the created order provides this necessary point of reference. As such, 'goodness' loses its objective meaning and becomes a sort of wax nose. If taken thus far, the equivocity of being could lend itself to the defense of any religious claim, regardless of how inappropriate it may be, since all language would be equally ill-equipped to truly describe God's being.[16] If no religious speech accurately describes God, then all descriptions of God are equally valid.

It is important to remember that the analogy of being, and the use of analogical predication, is proposed as a legitimate third option situated between univocity and equivocity.[17] There is no hidden reliance on univocity lurking beneath the surface of analogy.[18] Wolfhart Pannenberg, for example, mistakenly believed that the

---

16. For an example of such use of religious language, see Robert B. Steward, ed., *Can Only One Religion Be True? Paul Knitter and Harold Netland in Dialogue* (Augsburg: Fortress, 2013).

17. There are those who suggest that analogy is listed as a type of equivocal predication among the Reformed, but Thomas treated analogical predication as a middle ground between univocity and equivocity. Still, even if one included analogy as a form of equivocity it would obviously be a special case in which the words were not *totally* different. Therefore, even if the classification of analogical predication changed, the concept itself would not.

18. 'It is utterly crucial to understand that there is no "common logos" of an ever so subtly hidden univocity at play in Thomas's understanding of ontological participation. For beings, by way of the measuring perfection of essence, are *intrinsically* diversified. Hence, in analogical predication of existence there is no univocity of the nature of essence whatsoever involved. Nevertheless, there still obtains an analogical unity, since all intrinsically diversified beings receive their specific limited perfection from the primary instance in which the respective perfection subsists without limitation. ... Thomas conceives transcendental analogy as a causal, as well as formal, ontological dependence of every being (*id quod est*) with respect to the *ipse esse subsistens*, God. Being (*ens*) is never univocal because it is always participated' (Reinhard Hütter, 'Attending to the Wisdom of God, from Effect to Cause, from Creation to God: A "Relecture" of the Analogy of Being According to Thomas Aquinas,' in *The Analogy of Being: Invention of the Antichrist or the Wisdom of God?*, ed. Thomas Joseph White [Grand Rapids: William B. Eerdmans Publishing Company, 2011], 233).

doctrine of analogy was simply univocal being in disguise.[19] Likewise, Gordon Clark was mistaken in conflating analogy with equivocity and Neo-Scholastic skepticism. Analogical predication, based on the understanding of the analogy of being, was presented as a legitimate option from the onset of Thomas's writing ministry.[20] Critiques against the univocity or equivocity of being cannot be properly applied to analogy as Thomas understood it.[21]

The analogy of being between God and man is experienced as a hierarchy of being in creation. Higher classes of beings participate analogously in divine being to a higher degree and thus experience creaturely being to a higher degree. As Nieuwenhove states, 'A stone has less being or actuality than a horse, and a horse has less actuality or being than a human.'[22] Reality, then, is a single participatory hierarchy in which all creatures receive being from a perfect and transcendent source in various degrees. 'Aquinas's entire ontology,' therefore, 'is a single participation structure, within which are substructures of participation accounting for the various relations with the matrix

---

19. ibid., 209-11; See also Elizabeth A. Johnson, 'The Right Way to Speak about God? Pannenberg on Analogy,' *Theological Studies* 43 (1982): 685.

20. 'Any attempt to understand the analogy of being in Aquinas has to come to terms with the simple fact that the topic of analogy is present from the very first moment of Thomas's written work. At the danger of overstating the matter, there is simply no instance in Thomas's work where analogy is not tacitly presupposed or being treated without being named or simply being silently at work in the exercise of *sacra doctrina* itself' (Hütter, 214).

21. According to W. Norris Clarke and many other existential Thomists, many critiques against analogy conflate the concept with univocity or equivocity. Clarke writes: 'Here is the central and clear-cut point of contention between Professor Nielsen and the Thomistic tradition in the very meaning of analogy itself. Thomists would admit ... that in some significant sense there must be some common core of meaning in all analogous predications of the same term, for otherwise it could not function as one term and concept. But they insist, on the other hand, that this common core of meaning is not therefore univocal, but remains analogous, similar-in-difference, or diversely similar. If it is any consolation to Professor Nielsen, his objection is exactly the same as that brought against Thomistic analogy by Duns Scotus and William of Ockham shortly after the time of Thomas himself' (W. Norris Clarke, 'Analogy and the Meaningfulness of Language about God,' in *Explorations in Metaphysics: Being, God, Person* [Notre Dame, IN: University of Notre Dame Press, 1994], 126).

22. Rik Van Nieuwenhove, *An Introduction to Medieval Theology*, 2nd ed. (Cambridge: Cambridge University Press, 2022), 278.

of contingent reality.'[23] In this structure, the transcendent, and thus independent, divine source does not receive any perfection from His creatures. Rather, as Morello explains:

> The essence of the source must be identical and convertible with [the perfection]; if it were merely to *have* the perfection as part of its essence, it too would be a participant. In turn, it cannot merely *have* the perfection, it must *be* this perfection, and *be* it in purity and simplicity.[24]

Any creaturely perfection, therefore, exists primarily in God with no mixture of potency, dependence, or shortcomings and is one and the same with the divine essence.

God's willing and generous sharing of His own being and perfections provides reality with its ontological structure. Indeed, 'The *analogia entis* is the origin, ground of truth, content and extent of our natural knowledge of God.'[25] Furthermore, Thomas believes that God's provision of creaturely being is a completely free act and is distinguished from the Platonic understanding of necessary emanation, in which God must create necessarily. What exists in God as pure actuality is given, out of pure and 'overflowing' goodness, to creatures in an analogous fashion and thus limited by the potency inherent in all composite beings. This point regarding creaturely composition brings readers to a critical Thomistic distinction.

---

23. Morello, 46. See also Tyson who writes, 'If I say that God is real *in the same way* that I say the book is real or that my friend is real, then "being" (realness if you like) is independent of or "bigger than" God, and *God becomes one being among other beings* (albeit a very different type of being from other beings). Both of these notions are radical departures from the long tradition of Christian Neoplatonist metaphysics, which envisioned reality itself as multi-layered and composed of different orders of being nested within one another, all nested within God. That old ontological outlook held sway in Western theology from Plato to Paul to Augustine and to Aquinas, but Scotus abandons it with his univocity of being idea' (Tyson, 65). Likewise, Clarke ties this concept to participation: 'The term, participation, therefore, is a condensed technical way of expressing the complexus of relations involved in any structure of dependence of a lower multiplicity on a higher source for similarity of nature' (W. Norris Clarke, 'The Meaning of Participation in St. Thomas,' in *Explorations in Metaphysics: Being, God, Person* [Notre Dame, IN: University of Notre Dame Press, 1994], 93).

24. Morello, 46.

25. Betz, 71. Betz quotes Erich Przywara, *Schriften* (Einsiedeln: Johannes Verlage, 1962), 2:10.

Esse Participating in *Ipsum Esse*

Thomas's modification and implementation of participation has recently become a center point of Thomistic studies, even inspiring a Thomistic school of thought known as Existential Thomism.[26] A hallmark of contemporary Existential Thomism is the recognition of Platonic elements within Thomas's philosophical system. It is not unusual for these thinkers to describe Thomas as a great synthesizer of Platonic and Aristotelian thought.[27] As has been mentioned, Thomas specifically modified Aristotle's understanding of act and potency by means of Plato's understanding of participation. One can understand Thomas's use of Platonic participation by reference to the relationship between an object's existence and its essence. Indeed, this distinction is often portrayed as the chief contribution of Thomas's theological system.[28]

Thinkers such as W. Norris Clarke, Cornelio Fabro, Louis Geiger, and more recently, Sebastian Morello have emphasized the synthetic nature of Thomas's philosophy rather than aligning him closely with Aristotle alone. Thomas did not strictly follow Aristotle nor did he perfectly align with Plato, but rather, Thomas accepted some classical ideas, modified others, and still rejected those classical ideas he saw as being incompatible with revealed Christian doctrine. Thomism, then, is not merely a form of Aristotelianism, as has often been presented

---

26. Morello writes: 'For those with some knowledge of the *Existential Thomist* School, it ought not to be a surprise that in the works of the scholars belonging to this movement I found support – as well as reason for ample alteration and development – for much of my general worldview. I first discovered the books of W. Norris Clarke, S.J., and subsequently became interested in Cornelio Fabro, C.P.S. and Louis-Bertrand Geiger, O.P., and later John F. Wippel and Gregory T. Doolan' (Morello, 7-8). Readers will notice that these men have been referenced frequently throughout the preceding chapters.

27. Clarke, 'The Limitation of Act by Potency in St. Thomas: Aristotelianism or Neoplatonism?,' 65–88, especially 66, 79-80; W. Norris Clarke, 'The Meaning of Participation in St. Thomas,' in *Explorations in Metaphysics: Being, God, Person* (Notre Dame, IN: University of Notre Dame Press, 1994), 89-101.

28. Thomas was not, however, the first to note the distinction between essence and existence. That honor belongs to Avicenna. '[B]ehind these arguments [the Five Ways] another argument is operative, what [Brian Davies] calls the *Existence* argument. We find in in *ST* I.65.1. Here Thomas teaches that the fact that there are actual things in the world ultimately means that something exists independently of any cause outside itself, and accounts for the existence of everything else. *The argument hinges on a key insight inspired by Avicenna: in created things, there is a distinction between essence and existence*' (Nieuwenhove, *An Introduction to Medieval Theology*, 273; emphasis added).

throughout the secondary literature, but is a genuine and original synthesis worthy of attention in its own right. To suggest otherwise would be to continue the mischaracterization of the history of ideas as if students could 'skip from Classical Antiquity to Early Modernity without missing much in-between.'[29] In addition to the synthetic nature of Thomas's system, the use of participation in particular has become a hallmark of Existential Thomism and is perceived as one of the keys to understanding Thomas's overall thought.

In Thomistic thought, only God lacks distinction between His existence and His essence. The composition of existence and essence is experienced by all creatures and is the simplest form of composition available. The fact that God does not experience composition at this foundational level necessitates that God cannot experience composition at any level. The division of existence and essence is the ground floor of creaturely composition.

Humans are capable of knowing an object's essence before they know whether or not an object exists.[30] For instance, my three-year-old son is very familiar with unicorns, horses, and zebras, and he can describe the differences between these animals in great detail. Yet, his familiarity of these animals does not mean that he is capable of identifying which of these animals could actually be found in the wild. He may find the idea of a zebra to be entirely fictional and clearly a fabrication – a mischaracterization of a horse after an encounter with black paint – or he may be disappointed to find that the local zoo lacks a unicorn exhibit and question when one will become available. The point is that he could grasp the essences of these animals without knowing which ones truly exist. Not only does this possibility suggest an epistemic priority of essence over existence, but it demonstrates how essence and existence

---

29. Ralph Stefan Weir, 'Foreword' in *The World as God's Icon: Creator and Creation in the Platonic Thought of Thomas Aquinas,* by Sebastian Morello (Brooklyn: Angelico Press, 2020), 2.

30. 'Essence' is defined as 'what a thing is; the internal principle whereby a thing is *what it is* and has its specific perfections; quiddity; internal constitutions of a thing' (Bernard Wuellner, *Dictionary of Scholastic Philosophy* [Fitzwilliam, NH: Loreto Publications, 2012], s.v. 'essence.' See also Richard A. Muller, *Dictionary of Latin and Greek Theological Terms: Drawn Principally from Protestant Scholastic Theology* [Grand Rapids: Baker Academic, 2017], s.v. *'essentia.'* Muller's definition reads, 'the whatness, or *quidditas,* of a being, which makes the being precisely what it is; e.g., the essence of Peter, Paul, and John is their humanity; the essence of God is deity or divinity.'

exist in composition. One can theoretically separate the concepts of essence and existence.

In Thomas's system, however, existence receives ontological priority and essence is identified as a negative and limiting principle. God is infinite subsistent existence. In other words, God is existence essentially – by His very nature. One cannot separate existence from essence in God.[31] He is, therefore, the ground of all being, self-subsistent being Himself, and existence is His alone to share. This divine act of sharing that which essentially belongs to divinity to creatures who imperfectly receive being from a common source is the basis for Thomas's doctrine of participation. In a participatory structure, a creature's essence is that which denotes a limited possession of that which belongs essentially to God alone.[32] If participation, however, occurs at this lowest level of creaturely composition, then all perfections that a creature possesses must be the result from its participation in its first cause. To put it in biblical terms, 'What do you have that you did not receive?' For 'in him we live and move and have our being' (1 Cor. 4:7; Acts 17:28).

Transcendental-Analogical Participation

It should be noted that Existential Thomists typically identify two types of participation within Thomas's understanding, one of which is much more pertinent to the present discussion than the other. Broadly, Thomas identifies three ways in which participation may occur, and those three ways can be separated into two categories. Thomas explains:

---

31. This is the foundation for Anselm's ontological argument. While Thomas rejects the use of this particular apologetic method due to the epistemic priority of essence in creatures as illustrated by the zoo example above, he does not reject the metaphysical principles contained within it.

32. 'Like any Thomist, Geiger holds that a contingent being is composed of two really distinct principles, essence and *esse*, with the former as the principle of limitation. However, he questions how *esse* can be limited by a purely "negative principle," that is, it seems incoherent to assign a function to a principle which does not exist. He posits that essence can be accounted for independently by reference to a kind of participation prior to that of composition, namely that of formal hierarchy "by which participants share in a greater or lesser likeness to the First Perfection." Geiger describes this in the following way: "The essence that participates *in* existence is itself a participation *of* the First Perfection, of which it conveys only a limited and fragmentary aspect." The principle of essence, then, is a created emanation of the divine essence, to which *esse* is granted, conveying a "limited and fragmentary aspect" of its source' (Morello, 57).

For 'to participate' is, as it were, 'to grasp a part.' And, therefore, when something receives in a particular way that which belongs to another in a universal way, it is said 'to participate' in that, as human being is said to participate in animal because it does not possess the intelligible structure of animal according to its total commonality; and in the same way, Socrates participates in human. And similarly, too, a subject participates in accident, and matter in form, because a substantial form, or an accidental one, which is common by virtue of its own intelligible structure, is determined to this or that subject. And similarly, too, an effect is said 'to participate' in its own cause, and especially when it is not equal to the power of its cause, as for example, if we should say that 'air participates in the light of the sun' because it does not receive that light with the brilliance it has in the sun. However, setting aside this third way of participating, it is impossible that 'to be' itself participate in anything in the first two ways.[33]

Notice, then, that the division of participation into two categories is not arbitrary but is found in Thomas's own words. Out of the three forms of participation listed below, two cannot apply to being itself. These first two types of participation are grouped together under the label of 'predicamental-univocal participation.'[34]

In predicamental-univocal participation, the 'participating object shares fully in something else,' albeit in a limited degree.[35] Thomas's first example applies to particular members of a species. What exists universally in the species is found particularly in individuals participating in that species. As Hans Boersma illustrates, 'My dog Trooper, for

---

33. Thomas Aquinas, *An Exposition of the 'On the Hebdomads' of Boethius*, trans. Janice L. Schultz and Edward A. Synan, Thomas Aquinas in Translation (Washington, DC: The Catholic University of America Press, 2001),19.

34. The terms 'predicamental-univocal participation' and 'transcendental-analogical participation' both come from the work of Cornelio Fabro. See Cornelio Fabro, *La Nozionoe Metafisica di Partecipazione*, 2nd ed. (Turin: Societa Editrice Internazioonale, 1963), 317-18; cited in Morello, 52-53. Louis Geiger also identifies two types of participation in Thomism but prefers the titles 'participation by composition' and 'participation by similitude' or 'formal hierarchy.' Fabro's and Geiger's categories are not identical, but neither are they contradictory. John Wippel has shown how Fabro's and Geiger's understanding can work together, in John F. Wippel, 'Thomas Aquinas and Participation,' in *Studies in Medieval Philosophy*, ed. John F. Wippel (Washington, DC: The Catholic University of America Press, 1987), 117-58. Since I have focused on the transcendental nature of truth along with the Thomistic understanding of analogical predication, Fabro's terminology has been retained.

35. Boersma, *Heavenly Participation*, 185.

instance, fully shares in the canine species; there is nothing in the species of "canineness" in which Trooper does not share.'[36] Yet, Trooper's participation in canineness need not suggest that he demonstrates all possible ways in which canineness may be particularized. He is truly a dog, but he is not all a dog could be. Or, in Thomas's illustration, that which applies to all humans in commonality also applies to Socrates as a particular member of humanity. Again, Socrates was not everything a human could be, but he was truly human. As such, terms describing humans may be used univocally for other humans despite accidental differences among the genus.[37]

Second, the mode of participation that will receive focus from this point forward is labeled 'transcendental-analogical participation.'[38] This mode of participation, according to Thomas, is when an effect participates in its cause, especially when the power of the effect is not equal to the power of its cause. Transcendental-analogical participation is the primary form of participation within Thomas's writings and runs through the transcendental properties of being.

According to Aristotle, there are nine categories of accidents commonly adopted by medieval theologians. 'These categories,' summarizes Davison, 'are quality, quantity, relation, place, time, position, state (or possession), action and passion (or receptivity).'[39] Commonly,

---

36. ibid.

37. Readers can see how this resembles Geiger's 'participation by similitude.' Morello explains: 'Participation by similitude, on the other hand, "expresses the diminished, particularized, and, in this sense, participated state of an essence each time it is not realized in the absolute fullness of its formal content." To return to our last example, both the greyhound and the pug (or any instance of any other breed) imitate the form "dog" for their perfection, but neither realizes the fullness of the formal content of "dog." In turn, if two or more beings both imitate the same source for their perfection, they do so to their own particular degrees' (Morello, 55).

38. 'In contrast to this first mode, transcendental participation refers specifically to the possession by finite beings of the transcendental attributes; that is, the participation of participant subjects in some perfection "according to a deficiency of likeness." The perfection in question here has an existence of its own independently of the participant, "either as a property of a higher entity or in itself as a pure and subsistent formality in its full possession, for example, as beings (entia) participate in esse." The participated perfection is shared in by participant subjects according to different degrees, and therefore cannot be predicated of them univocally. Transcendental participation is, then, an analogical mode, and Fabro considers it to be the primary meaning of the term "participation" for Aquinas' (Morello, 52-53).

39. Davison, *Love of Wisdom*, 44.

medieval Scholastics also considered 'substance' to be numbered among the categories. Reinhard Hütter describes these categories as 'the most comprehensive genera by way of which we conceptually understand all of contingent reality. Ontologically considered, the categories, or predicamentals, are the most universal modes of being, and as such, subsist independently of human conceptual formation.'[40]

Yet there are certain concepts that do not neatly fall within any of the ten categories but instead refer to a more general or universal sense of being as a whole. These terms transcend any generic (i.e., genus oriented) limitation and function as near synonyms of being. At first glance, the list of transcendentals may seem strange, or even arbitrary, to modern readers, but they would have been commonplace within Thomas's day. According to Thomas, the transcendentals are 'one,' 'good,' 'true,' and for many Thomists also 'beauty.' These terms apply to all being according to their mode of existence.

For instance, 'good' describes being insofar as the actualization and perfection of being is desirable. 'One' refers to being insofar as any existent thing avoids internal contradiction and fits into the unified whole of reality, which, in turn, leads readers to 'true' being. All being is intelligible, knowable, and therefore, true.[41] Anything with being, be it act or potentiality, can be known, and the form present in the intellect of the knower will agree with the form present in the object of knowledge. Therefore, there is no such thing as 'false being.' Anything that can be truly known, per the classical definition of 'knowledge,' must possess being, and 'falsity' refers to the mischaracterization of being rather than the non-existence of being. One can see, then, how 'true' and 'being' are virtually synonymous. Wherever being resides, truth is not far away.

---

40. Hütter, 216.

41. As previously mentioned in Chapter 3, this does not mean that all humans are capable of knowing all truth. Peter Kreeft explains: 'The intellect is by nature capable of knowing anything that is intelligible; and all being is intelligible (in itself, though not necessarily to us: not every being is intelligible at every moment to every mind). There is no curtain of darkness around *being*, only around less-than-omniscient *minds*. So to say that the intellectual soul has universal being as its object, and to say that truth, or intelligibility, is a "transcendental" or universal property of all being as such, are equivalent statements. Some Scholastic philosophers have called this "the principle of intelligibility": that mind and reality, intellect and being, are open to each other' (Peter Kreeft, ed., *Summa of the Summa: The Essential Philosophical Passages of St. Thomas Aquinas' Summa Theologica Edited and Explained for Beginners* [San Francisco: Ignatius Press, 1990], 265n26).

Since 'true' serves as a transcendental in Thomas's philosophy, then there exists a significant overlap between several important perfections. For instance, when Thomas discusses whether goodness differs from being, he writes:

> Goodness and being are really the same, and differ only in idea. ... The essence of goodness consists in this, that it is in some way desirable. ... Now it is clear that a thing is desirable only in so far as it is perfect; for all desire their own perfection. But everything is perfect so far as it is actual. ... Hence it is clear that goodness and being are the same really. But goodness presents the aspect of desirableness, which being does not present ... (Aquinas, *ST* 1.5.1).

Likewise, Thomas describes a similar relationship between truth and being:

> As good has the nature of what is desirable, so truth is related to knowledge. Now everything, *in as far as it has being, so far is it knowable*. Wherefore it is said in *De Anima* iii that *the soul is in some manner all things*, through the senses and the intellect. And therefore, as good is convertible with being, so is the true. But as good adds to being the notion of desirable, so *the true adds relation to the intellect* ... (Aquinas, *ST* 1.16.3; emphasis added).

Thomas's discussion of the transcendentals differs from his explanation of the divine attributes. Christians, utilizing the *Triplex Via*, may see diverse perfections in creation and attribute this variety of perfections to the divine essence. Grounding this process, however, is the belief that God is entirely simple and, thus, what exists as a diversity in creation exists simply as the divine essence *ad intra*. The transcendentals function differently. While truth and goodness are identical in God due to divine simplicity, truth and goodness are also unified in creation as transcendentals. The transcendentals are inherent in created being and not something exclusive to the Creator's being. In theological terms, the transcendentals fall under the category of creation rather than the doctrine of God. As such, the relationship between the 'true' and 'being' pertains to creaturely truth and creaturely being.

As a part of Thomas's discussion regarding whether it is necessary that every being be created by God, Thomas writes,

> It must be said that every being in any way existing is from God. *For whatever is found in anything by participation, must be caused in it by that to which it belongs essentially*, as iron becomes ignited by fire. Now it has

been shown above (*ST* I, 3, 4) when treating of the divine simplicity that God is the essentially self-subsisting Being; and also it was shown (*ST* I, 11, 3-4) that subsisting being must be one. ... *Therefore all beings apart from God are not their own being, but are beings by participation.* Therefore it must be that ... things which are diversified by the diverse participation of being, ... are caused by one First Being ... (Aquinas, *ST* 1.44.1)

So, in Thomas's understanding, that which does not pertain to an object essentially must pertain to that object via participation. Furthermore, that participation is grounded in a cause that does possess that perfection essentially. As an example, a stack of papers dropped in a puddle may be said to participate in 'wetness' because they have shared in an essential property of water. Likewise, creatures participate in being because they receive their being from God who is subsistent being Himself.

Thomas reaches a similar conclusion concerning the ontological and participatory nature of goodness when he discusses the final end of all creatures. In his response to one objection, Thomas writes, 'All things desire God as their end, when they desire some good thing, whether this desire be intellectual or sensible, or natural, *i.e.*, without knowledge, because *nothing is good and desirable except forasmuch as it participates in the likeness of God ...*' (Aquinas, *ST* 1.44.4 ad 3). Following the structure of Thomas's previous arguments, it can be concluded that Thomas's use of participatory language suggests that creatures do not possess goodness essentially, even though they are most certainly good. That is, they are not good in the same way that God is good. Rather, they receive their goodness from God who is subsistent goodness Himself. Elsewhere,

For it is clear that good has the nature of an end; wherefore, a particular end of anything consists in some particular good; while the universal end of all things is the Universal Good; Which is good of Itself by virtue of Its Essence, Which is the very essence of goodness; whereas a particular good is good by participation. Now it is manifest that in the whole created universe there is not a good which is not such by participation. Wherefore that good which is the end of the whole universe must be a good outside the universe ...' (Aquinas, *ST* 1.103.2).

Likewise, Thomas uses this participatory language to discuss the source of creaturely beauty.

The beautiful and beauty are distinguished with respect to participation and participants. Thus, we call something 'beautiful' because it participates in some way in beauty. Beauty, however, is a participation in the first cause, which makes all things beautiful. So that the beauty of creatures is simply a likeness of the divine beauty in which things participate.[42]

If creatures have their being, goodness, and beauty through participation, and if 'true' is a transcendental alongside good, being, and beauty, then it stands to reason that creatures will possess their truth through participation as well, where 'truth' refers to the intelligibility of being itself. As has already been discussed, Thomas is clear in his understanding of the divinity–truth connection. When answering whether God is Truth, Thomas writes, 'He Himself is His own ... act of understanding. Whence it follows not only that truth is in Him, but that He is truth itself' (Aquinas, *ST* 1.16.5). If truth is related to being as that which is capable of intellectual comprehension, then there is no higher form of truth than God who *is* His own act of intellectual self-comprehension. One may then speak of God, then, as subsistent Truth – a personal, living, and operative Truth who freely shares His being in an analogous way with His creatures. As such, a person possesses truth participatorily, even though he is not truth essentially.

Indeed, it is unsurprising that Thomas is willing to apply divine terms to truth. For instance, Thomas affirms the eternality of truth: '*I answer that*, ... it has been already said that things are called true from the truth of the intellect. Hence, if no intellect were eternal, no truth would be eternal. Now because only the divine intellect is eternal, in it alone truth has eternity' (Aquinas, *ST* 1.16.7). Likewise, Thomas affirms the immutability of truth, which

> properly speaking, resides only in the intellect, as said before; but things are called true in virtue of the truth residing in an intellect. ... If, then, there is an intellect wherein there can be no alternation of opinions, and the knowledge of which nothing can escape, in this is immutable truth. (Aquinas, *ST* 1.16.8)

There is an inseparable connection between the divine intellect and the perfection of truth.

---

42. Aquinas, *Commentary on the Sentences*, 1252, quoted in Umberto Eco, *The Aesthetics of Thomas Aquinas*, trans. Hugh Bredin (Cambridge, MA: Harvard University Press, 1988), 27. Thanks to Samuel G. Parkison for pointing this out.

Still, it is clear that humanity does not possess truth in this way. While a simple God may be the perfect coherence of intellect, act of understanding, and object of knowledge, composite humanity falls short of this unity. Furthermore, man's judgment, unlike God's, is fallible and can fall short even when perfect conditions are met. With such a great divide between the creature and Creator, how can truth apply to both God and man? In the same way Thomas can speak of a hierarchy of being, he can discuss a hierarchy of truth.

Thomas's Fourth Way

One of Thomas's most famous contributions to theology is one that has been left unaddressed up to this point – the five proofs of God's existence. These proofs (or ways, if one were to limit examination to the *Summa Theologiæ*), are not original to Thomas, but his name is now most closely associated with them.[43] Each argument consists of three basic principles: a logical presupposition, one datum drawn from ordinary experience, and one metaphysical conclusion.[44] The five points of experiential data associated with each proof are motion, efficient causality, necessity and contingency, gradation, and the order of creation. Thomas's fourth way, that of gradation, is of significant pertinence to the analysis of participatory truth.

According to Thomas, God's existence can be demonstrated through the observation of gradated perfections in creation. In short, since good things exist and people acknowledge that some things are truly 'more good' than others, then readers are left to believe that some being would then be the best of all beings (Aquinas, *ST* 1.2.3). This metaphysical apex is what people typically call 'God,' and God would necessarily be the 'most fully in being' (Aquinas, *ST* 1.2.3). Note, however, that Thomas does not apply this argument to all properties, as if God must be the 'tallest' or 'shiniest' of all beings, but limits his argument to the transcendental properties, most notably goodness,

---

43. On the distinction between 'proofs' and 'ways,' Kreeft writes: 'These five are not the *proofs* themselves but *ways*, i.e., indications or summaries of proofs. The proofs themselves are elsewhere worked out in much greater detail; e.g., in the *Summa Contra Gentiles* the first way takes thirty-one paragraphs (Bk I, chap. 13); here [in the *Summa Theologiæ*], it takes only one' (Kreeft, *Summa*, 61n19).

44. Kreeft, *Summa*, 61-62n19.

beauty, and truth.[45] Timothy McDermott clarifies: 'If, however, the perfection is not such as to be definable specifically by genus and difference it can be shared in or "participated" with a constancy of meaning that admits differences of degree. Thus the transcendental attributes of being – truth, unity, goodness, and perhaps beauty.'[46] Again, McDermott draws attention to the close relationship between participation and analogical language: 'These perfections are called analogical,' writes McDermott, 'that is they can be predicated variously of diverse subjects, and it with these ... that the argument is concerned.'[47]

The application to truth is easy to track. If there exists any truth, then there must be a being which is 'most true' in the ontological sense of the word. Matthew Levering explains it thus:

> The predication of 'more' or 'less' good or true requires that there be a measure of the degree to which something 'resembles' goodness or truth. This measure must be maximal goodness or truth, for otherwise it would itself be measured rather than being the measure. For a maximum in perfection to exist, it must be maximal actuality, 'for those things that are greatest in truth are greatest in being.'[48]

45. 'One objection to this Way is that if God were the most good, true, and noble being, he would also be the "perfect maximum of conceivable smelliness," or indeed the maximum of any attribute. This in fact would not be the case as it is not the *accidental predicates*, only attributed to *particular* beings, which need explaining by reference to what is understood by Aquinas to be God. He is instead concerned with the attributes of being *in general*, those "transcendental attributes" which are called such because they are above every genus and common to every being, "unrestricted to any particular category or individual." In turn, to the extent that these attributes of *being* come in degrees, they must be traceable to a maximum. The transcendental attributes are the attributes of substance *per se*, not accidents of particular beings. Furthermore, as we have said, these attributes are held by Aquinas to be convertible with one another, i.e., they are all one but differing in aspect' (Morello, 88-89). Additionally, the fact that the transcendentals are convertible explains why they can all be traced back to one source, rather than positing an independent first cause for each transcendental perfection.

46. Timothy McDermott, 'Appendix 9: The Fourth Way,' in *Summa Theologiæ*, vol. 2, *Existence and Nature of God* (1a. 2-11), by Thomas Aquinas, trans. Timothy McDermott, 62 vols. (Cambridge: Cambridge University Press, 2006), 204.

47. McDermott, 'Appendix 9: The Fourth Way,' 204.

48. Matthew Levering, *Proofs of God: Classical Arguments from Tertullian to Barth* (Grand Rapids: Baker Academic, 2016), 67.

With this statement, the analogy of being, the division of being into act and potency, and God's identity as *actus purus* all intersect with metaphysical truth.

Kreeft includes a helpful note on this matter:

> The fourth way presupposes something which everyone except a few Sophists in ancient Greece and Skeptics in ancient Rome accepted until modern times, but which the modern mind tends to find incomprehensible: viz., that 'values' are objective, that value judgments are judgments of fact – e.g., that a man *really* has more value than an ape.[49]

As opposed to postmodern assumptions, the gradation of perfections present in creation are not based on subjective estimation but genuinely reflect an objective, ontological reality.[50] These gradated ontological perfections are 'something we *discover* rather than invent.'[51] Some aspects of creation truly do reflect a greater degree of God's goodness than other things; humanity truly does image God in higher ways than non-rational animals; and some creatures possess a higher correspondence to the divine essence than lesser creatures. Beauty is indeed not in the eye of the beholder but is grounded in an object's reflection of divinity. While it may be difficult to gauge such gradations, this epistemic shortcoming does not eliminate the chain of being that truly exists.

This clarification is important because modern minds are conditioned to distinguish only truth from falsehood, rather than permitting degrees of ontological truth. If Thomas's ontology is correct, however, there exists in creation a hierarchy of truth, properly understood. This hierarchy is not limited to epistemic evaluation but is closely related with an object's being. Since God is infinite, perfect being, then it makes

---

49. Kreeft, *Summa*, 68.

50. Edward Feser calls the Fourth Way 'the most difficult for modern readers to accept, or even to understand' (Edward Feser, *Aquinas: A Beginner's Guide*, Oneworld Beginner's Guides [2009; repr. London: Oneworld Publications, 2020], 100). Also, for an overview of the proofs of God, Thomistic or otherwise, see Edward Feser, *Five Proofs of the Existence of God* (San Francisco: Ignatius Press, 2017).

51. Feser, *Aquinas*, 101. Feser specifically rejects a purely Platonic interpretation of the Fourth Way, as if a non-material realm of forms was necessary for Thomas's argument to be cogent. However, Feser's interpretation, based on Aristotelian hylomorphism, is virtually identical to the Existential Thomistic interpretation. As long as the divine Ideas are found within the divine intellect, Feser's objections against a Platonic interpretation of the Fourth Way are not a problem.

sense that He would be the measurement of all truth. The hierarchy of truth among creatures, then, reflects how much a class of creatures imitates and reflects God's being. The higher the correspondence, the greater the truth. Again, this argument is similar to what has been previously stated regarding the doctrine of participation and the divine Ideas as exemplary causes. At this point, our next chapter may focus its attention on these divine Ideas.

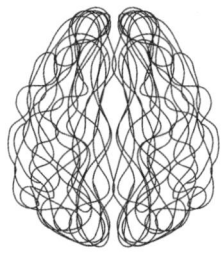

CHAPTER EIGHT

Truth Ad Extra: A Participatory Model of Truth

God's independent omniscience stands at the center of all creaturely truth, but Thomas and the tradition that he received were more specific than a broad reference to God's knowledge. Specifically, Thomas, and authors like him, navigated God's knowledge of creatures through the means of the divine Ideas. The formal blueprints of each creature pre-exists within the mind of God. Through an understanding of how His essence may be finitely imitated in creation, God has intimate knowledge of creatures without depending on them for this knowledge. God knew creaturely truth long before we did because He knew how a likeness of divine truth would be manifested in time.

The Divine Ideas

Thus far, we have argued that a proper understanding of divine omniscience is intimately tied with a proper understanding of divine transcendence and independence. God knows Himself perfectly, and this divine self-knowledge includes a perfect knowledge of creation. Specifically, the divine intellect is linked to the doctrine of creation via the concept of the divine Ideas.[1] It will be shown that this doctrine allows Thomas to avoid the charge of pantheism (or panentheism), despite the existence

---

1. Gregory Doolan writes, 'Without a doctrine of exemplarism, Thomas's metaphysics would reduce God to an Aristotelian "thought thinking itself" that thinks only itself: a first principle that is blissfully unaware of the world that it moves' (Doolan, 250-51).

of a strong participatory link between God and man. The forthcoming examination of divine Ideas will lead to a defense of divine exemplarism, which will, in turn, lead to a participatory theory of metaphysical truth. In short, it will be shown that a Thomistic model of the divine intellect necessitates that divine Truth be independent of creation but knowable by creatures through their grasp of the divine Ideas. The divine Ideas, then, link divine metaphysics with creaturely epistemology.

A Thomistic Definition of the Divine Ideas

Thomas's understanding of divine omniscience differs from the alternative models previously discussed, specifically where that understanding interacts with the doctrine of creation. Theistic mutualism argues that God's knowledge must depend on creation in some fashion if a real and loving relationship is to exist between the Creator and His creatures. Hans Urs von Balthasar, for example, claims that nothing short of divine 'receptivity' is fitting for a divine being. Von Balthasar writes:

> This capacity to *receive truth* is among the supreme values of existence. ... Accordingly, it would not be a sign of perfection if a subject were already so well-equipped, so stuffed with truths, that it no longer needed another to share anything with it and would not know what to do with such a communication anyway. ... An all-knowingness that precluded any communication or sharing would be the height of boredom, and the idea of having to deal with someone or thing that displayed this kind of knowing would be the least attractive prospect imaginable.[2]

Von Balthasar's argument is incompatible with Thomas's doctrine of God due both to Thomas's theological commitments, such as immutability, and philosophical commitments, namely, the division of all being into act and potency and the confession of God as *actus purus*. It has already been said that God knows all creatures through the means of His perfectly comprehensive self-knowledge. Thomas, however, offers further explanation. God not only perfectly comprehends His omnipotence, which is referred to as His *natural knowledge*, and perfectly comprehends His will and decree, which is called His *free knowledge*, but also knows exactly how His divine essence may be imitated by His creatures – the

---

2. Hans Urs von Balthasar, *Theo-Logic: Theological Logical Theory*, vol. 1, *Truth of the World*, trans. Adrian J. Walker (San Francisco: Ignatius Press, 2000), 46.

divine Ideas. To be clear, this description is not a map of the divine mind *per se*, which knows all things through one simple act of knowledge, but is rather a map of how contingent and composite creatures may understand the divine intellect.

As previously stated, the primary object of God's knowledge is the divine essence. A divine Idea, according to Gregory Doolan, is 'God's knowledge of the particular relationship that a particular creature bears (or can bear, as regards possible creatures) to His essence. Hence, it is His knowledge of the divine essence *as imitable* that is the central characteristic of a divine Idea.'[3] Notice that priority in this definition is given to the divine essence as the means by which God knows His creatures. God knows everything there is to know about His essence and this knowledge necessarily includes an understanding of how His essence could be imitated by creatures external to Himself. God's grasp of the divine Ideas, however, can be logically distinguished from His knowledge of the divine essence. While the divine essence refers to all that God is, the divine Ideas specifically pertain to the forms of participatory creatures.

Thomas describes the divine Ideas as such: 'By "Ideas" we understand forms of other things, existing apart from the things themselves' (Aquinas, *ST* 1.15.1). These Ideas have two possible functions: (1) as the 'exemplar or pattern of the thing whose form it is said to be' or (2) as the 'principle of knowing that thing in the sense in which the forms of the knowable things are said to be in the knower' (Aquinas, *ST* 1.15.1). Thomas claims that it is necessary to posit divine Ideas for both of these reasons.

Thomas connects the divine Ideas to efficient causation. He writes: '[T]he form must be the end in view in every kind of generation. Moreover for the agent to act for the sake of the form, the likeness of the form must be in the agent' (Aquinas, *ST* 1.15.1). Some creatures may only generate by passing on their generic or species-specific likeness to others, such as when fire produces fire or cats produce more cats.[4]

---

3. Gregory T. Doolan, *Aquinas on the Divine Ideas as Exemplar Causes* (Washington, DC: The Catholic University of America Press, 2014), 92. Doolan's work is the authoritative work on the doctrine of the divine Ideas in Thomas's works and, as such, will provide critical assistance throughout this chapter.

4. Doolan explains: 'An individual man cannot be the cause of human nature absolutely, for he would then be the cause of himself. Rather, a univocal cause can only cause the form of another individual in the same species inasmuch as that form exists in matter. In short, it causes *this* matter to acquire *this* form. Thus, even though one man

Intellectual beings, however, may move beyond this form of generating by accessing the forms in their intellect. This claim will lead readers to Thomas's favorite illustration of the divine Ideas – God as the divine artist and architect.

On that subject Thomas writes: '[T]he form of the house already exists in the mind of the architect. This can be called the idea of the house; because the architect intends to make the house to the pattern of the form which he has conceived in his mind' (Aquinas, *ST* 1.15.1). Thus, the divine Ideas serve primarily as the exemplars, or blueprints, of creatures in the divine mind. In this way, the divine Ideas reverse the intellectual abstraction mentioned in Chapter 4. Rather than God receiving forms from creatures by the means or abstraction, the forms of creatures first exist within the divine mind and are then given to creatures.

Divine Simplicity and a Plurality of Divine Ideas

On one hand, many different creatures exist, which would suggest a plurality of divine Ideas within God's mind. On the other hand, God knows all creatures through His simple divine essence, which would suggest that the divine essence serves as the only genuine divine Idea. As one would expect, Thomas distinguishes between these two true statements. First, Thomas makes clear, 'God in his essence is the likeness of all things. Hence an Idea in God is simply the divine essence' (Aquinas, *ST* 1.15.1 ad 3). Second, Thomas clarifies: 'Idea is not the name for the divine essence as such, but in so far as it is the likeness or intelligible nature of this or that thing' (Aquinas, *ST* 1.1.15.2 ad 1). Therefore, there is one divine essence, through which God knows all things, but that divine essence is imitable in various ways, and God knows every which way His essence may be imitated by possible creatures. God thus knows many divine Ideas through His simple divine essence.

It must not be missed that Thomas uses participatory language to describe this imitative relationship.[5] Thomas writes:

---

cannot be the cause of human nature absolutely, he can be the cause of human nature as it exists in *this* man. It is this mode of causality that Thomas terms "generation," according to which an agent's action presupposes determinate matter' (Doolan, 172).

5. To be clear, Thomas clarifies this use of 'relationship.' Thomas writes: 'The relations which multiply Ideas are not in created things but in God. Yet they are not real relations, like those which distinguish the divine Persons, but relations understood by God' (Aquinas, *ST* 1.15.2 ad 4). See Doolan, 102-06.

Now the divine essence can be known not only as it is in itself, but as it can be *participated* in some degree of likeness by creatures. On the other hand every creature has its own nature in so far as it *participates* in some way the likeness of the divine essence. In this way then God, in knowing his essence as imitable in this particular way by this particular creature, knows his essence as the nature and Idea proper to that creature ... (Aquinas, *ST* 1.15.2)

Embedded in this explanation is a crucial claim – a creature cannot have a nature without participating in the likeness of the divine essence. Every created thing that exists does so via participation, and God knows exactly how each particular being participates in a likeness of the divine essence.[6] At this point in the *Summa Theologiæ*, Thomas transitions to a discussion regarding divine exemplarism, but before following Thomas's thought, a few clarifying notes should be offered.

The Divine Ideas as Opposed to the Platonic Forms

As has been shown, Thomas believes that the opening lines of John's Gospel implicitly reject the Platonic Forms. Thomas writes:

Plato, however, thought that the Ideas of all the things that were made were subsistent, i.e., existing separately in their own natures; and material things exist by participating in these. ... So lest you supposed, as did Plato, that this Idea through which all things were made be Ideas separated from God, the Evangelist adds, *and the Word was with God*.[7]

---

6. The doctrine of participation is thus the metaphysical basis for analogical predication: 'Since every agent reproduces itself so far as it is an agent, and everything acts according to the manner of its form, the effect must in some way resemble the form of the agent. If therefore the agent is contained in the same species as its effect, there will be a likeness in form between that which makes and that which is made, according to the same formality of the species; as man reproduces man. If, however, the agent and its effect are not contained in the same species, there will be a likeness, but not according to the formality of the same species; as things generated by the sun's heat may be in some sort spoken of as like the sun, not as though they received the form of the sun in its specific likeness, but in its generic likeness. Therefore if there is an agent not contained in any *genus*, its effects will still more distantly reproduce the form of the agent, not, that is, so as to participate in the likeness of the agent's form according to the same specific or generic formality, but only according to some sort of analogy; as existence is common to all. In this way all created things, so far as they are beings, are like God as the first and universal principle of all being ... (Aquinas, *ST* 1.4.3).

7. Aquinas, *Commentary on the Gospel of John, 1-5*, 29. Notice, also, the Christological emphasis embedded in Thomas's understanding of the Ideas.

This statement, however, does not dismiss the Platonic *influence* on Christian thought.[8] As Frederick Christian Bauerschmidt explained, 'Christianity had long before made a kind of peace with Platonic thought. ... For example, Christians had long before appropriated Plato's notion of a realm of "forms" as a way of speaking of the Christian notion of divine ideas in the mind of God.'[9]

The significant difference between the Platonic Ideas and Thomas's divine Ideas is, once again, connected to divine transcendence, independence, and aseity. The blueprints for creation are not external to God, as if God found Himself limited to creating beings with corresponding plans from some sort of metaphysical or cosmic database, as Molinism implies. Without God, there would be no divine Ideas, no exemplars, and no forms. As Davies writes: 'Aquinas is not here saying that there are many subsistent forms in which things in the world "participate" in some way. He does not believe that there are, and he rejects Plato's theory of forms as it is commonly construed, as holding that forms exist as objects in a nonmaterial realm.'[10] There are no subsistent Platonic

---

8. Indeed, the proceeding argument for participatory thought will sound reminiscent of Plato. Davison demonstrates: 'Christians might take it for granted that something (or Someone) lies beyond this world, not least as its origin. This chimes with Plato, although that role was taken not by God but by these "Forms". They stand behind created things, in all their fragility and mutability, as the source of their existence and order. The Forms are also the ultimate standard of truth and the proper objects of human desire. Underlying all goodness in the world, Plato would say, is the *Good*; animating all beautiful things is the true and eternal *Beauty*; every example of justice is an expression of *Justice*; when a carpenter makes a bed he consults the perfect plan of the true *Bed*' (Davison, *The Love of Wisdom*, 17).

9. Frederick Christian Bauerschmidt, *The Essential Summa Theologiae: A Reader and Commentary*, 2nd ed. (Grand Rapids: Baker Academic, 2021), xvi-xvii. See also, Michael Bergmann and Jeffrey Brower, 'A Theistic Argument against Platonism (and in Support of Truthmakers and Divine Simplicity),' in *Oxford Studies in Metaphysics* (Oxford: Oxford University Press, 2006), 2:358. As an editorial note, there does not seem to exist any formal agreement on how to capitalize 'divine Ideas.' As such, readers will find several different styles in the pertinent literature.

10. Brian Davies, *Thomas Aquinas's Summa Contra Gentiles: A Guide and Commentary* (Oxford: Oxford University Press, 2016), 104. Compare this quote with White's analysis: 'Some critics of Aquinas's theology claim that he has a concept of God as a set of abstract properties, in which terms like perfection or goodness are attributed to God as pre-existent abstract objects. The arguments of this chapter suggest, however, that Aquinas rejects the notion that we can attribute properties to God as abstract entities. His criticism of the Platonic notion of the good is telling in just this respect. Goodness, for Aquinas, is not a "form," that is, a universal property found in all things that can be apprehended in a generic way, which would indicate a pre-existing abstract object in which all things are said to participate. There are no such separated properties or abstract forms for Aquinas' (White, *Trinity*, 277).

Forms that God consults in order to create. Rather, the forms are redefined as divine Ideas within the divine intellect and are concretized within individuals, as Aristotle believed.

Still, one of the most significant developments in Christian thought was Augustine's adaptation of the Platonic forms. As Davison states:

> Augustine of Hippo deserves particular credit for finding a way to relate the Forms to God in such a way that they are not external to God. His formulation is brilliant: what Plato called the eternal Forms are in fact *ideas in the mind of God*. With this simple move, Augustine secured a place within Christian thought for all he had found wise and perceptive in the Platonic tradition: a tradition he had studied in great detail, and which was instrumental in leading him towards Christianity.[11]

Indeed, some Thomistic scholars, especially those thinkers who believe divine Ideas endanger Thomas's previous commitment to divine simplicity, have wondered if Thomas included his thoughts on the Ideas only out of respect to Augustine.[12] This connection between Augustine and Thomas is unsurprising considering that Thomas frequently cited Augustine when discussing the divine Ideas.[13] However, Thomas's understanding of the divine Ideas differs further still from a Platonic or even Augustinian formulation.[14]

Thomas's formulation of the divine Ideas stood as a midpoint between Platonic and Aristotelian models. The key difference separating

---

11. Davison, *Love of Wisdom*, 25.

12. See, for instance, Etienne Gilson, *Introduction à la Philosophie Chrétienne* [Paris: N.p., 1960], 170-83, esp. 174-75; Etienne Gilson, *Le Thomisme* [Paris: N.p., 1965], 146-48. Originally cited in Vivian Boland, *Ideas in God According to Saint Thomas Aquinas: Sources and Synthesis,* Studies in the History of Christian Thought 69 (New York: E. J. Brill, 1996), 7. Doolan also draws attention to Gilson's thought. Doolan writes: 'Why then, we might ask, do the divine ideas reappear in the *Summa theologiæ*. According to Gilson, it is not because Thomas is "adding one more piece to a sort of philosophical mosaic." Indeed, Gilson does not even consider Thomas's doctrine of divine ideas to be philosophical at all; rather, he concludes, it represents a theological effort to reconcile an otherwise Augustinian doctrine with "the strictest philosophical truth." To speak of a multiplicity of ideas, he insists, is to employ a Platonic language foreign to the Aristotelianism of Thomas's theology' (Doolan, 112).

13. See, for instance, Aquinas, *ST* 1.15.2; Aquinas, *SCG* 1.53; and *n Hebr.* 11.2.

14. Indeed, Boland writes: 'Saint Thomas frequently shows himself to be quite independent of Augustine and his contemporaries ... he is by no means an uncritical student of Augustine and ... was engaged in radically revising the philosophical resources deemed suitable for use in Christian theology' (Boland, 7).

Thomas from Plato was Thomas's understanding of intrinsic forms. The Platonic Forms were theorized as subsistent entities transcendent of creation, whereas Thomas believed forms to exist within individual beings. 'Plato,' White explains, 'seems to have considered these ideas to be the truest expression of singular realities, such that what Socrates and Alexander are in essence is the idea of man, a separate or distinct form in which each participates.'[15] Thomas, however, following the thought of Aristotle, rejected Plato's idea and held that Socrates was 'formally a man in virtue of the intrinsic form, his individualized nature, which is that of a human being.'[16]

This concept not only makes forms immanent but also supplies each creature with a certain ontological dignity. White continues: 'In the same way, [a man] also has an intrinsic goodness. His individual human nature is good. There are no separate, subsisting forms.'[17] At the same time, Thomas differed from Aristotle, having agreed with Plato that a transcendent source of all forms is necessary. In Thomas's system, unlike Aristotle's, there was a self-subsisting exemplar of all creaturely forms and perfections. White concludes: 'God is himself essential existence and goodness, and all secondary, created beings participate in the existence and goodness of God. God, who is himself essentially good, is the transcendent cause and exemplar of all created goodness.'[18]

The forms of creatures indwell each and every individual, and yet the forms have prior existence within the mind of God. In this way, a creature's form will always cohere with its corresponding divine Idea. There is no gradation of resemblance between the divine Ideas and creatures, and this correspondence means that knowledge of a creature's form is knowledge of its corresponding idea. Creatures made to resemble the divine Ideas cannot fail to participate in the likeness of the divine essence. The limiting aspects of participation, then, are already embedded within the divine Ideas before the forms exist within a creature. A creature's essence is the limiting principle of existence, because the divine Idea is a *likeness* of the divine essence and not the

---

15. White, *Trinity*, 276.
16. ibid.
17. White, *Trinity*, 277.
18. ibid.

divine essence itself. This limitation does not mean that divine Ideas somehow possess some negative principle that God lacks but rather means that each divine Idea lacks something that God is.

Pantheism, the Divine Ideas, and Aristotelian Causation

At times, the Thomistic description of divine omniscience and the divine Ideas has invited the charge of pantheism or panentheism, based on certain Thomistic claims. They are: (1) God knows the forms of all creatures through the knowledge of His own essence; (2) since God is an entirely simple being, all that is in God is God; and (3) the forms do not only exist in the mind of God but are also a part of a creature's essence. At first glance, therefore, it seems that the charge of pantheism might be warranted. Thomas, however, addressed this problem by means of Aristotelian causation. Whereas God is the efficient and final cause of all created being, He is not the material cause. In other words, the created order is not made up of pieces of divinity.

Gilles Emery offers a helpful explanation:

> The *order* [of creation] consists in the relation of a thing with its principle. It is comprised of three elements, which, in the case of creation, are as follows: (1) the fundamental distinction of God and of the world (the exclusion of pantheism); (2) the fact that God is absolutely first (*primum, prius*), while the created world is second, existing through participation in the divine perfection (participation through creation, analogy); (3) the threefold causality – efficient, exemplar, and final – that characterizes God as *principle* with regard to the world.[19]

---

19. Gilles Emery, 'Trinity and Creation,' in *The Theology of Thomas Aquinas*, by Rik Van Nieuwenhove and Joseph Wawrykow, eds., paperback ed. (Notre Dame, IN: University of Notre Dame Press, 2005), 60. See also the words of Francis O'Rourke: 'The divinity who is cause of all … neither has contact nor mingles with its participants in its communion with them. He is participated wholly by all participants but in such a manner that none has any part of him. All that they are, is a share in his infinite richness, but he is in no manner received within creatures. Beings are fully participations in God but do not participate in his fullness. The being and essence of the creature is to be a participation in God; without this sharing they would cease to be. They share the perfection created by him in a manner which in no way diminishes his transcendence or enters as a real relation into his nature. God's essence and Being are not participated. This is the mystery of creation: creatures participate exclusively and exhaustively in the infinite causal perfection of God who is in no wise participated according to his essence.

215

There are several ideas worth noticing in Emery's analysis. First, the transcendent independence of God is upheld. The identity between divinity and creatures as that which occurs in pantheism would conflict entirely with all that Thomas has written regarding the transcendent nature of God. Second, creatures exist through qualified participation, as Emery specifically cites participation through creation and analogy. As such, creatures do not have to share in the fullness of divinity to exist via participation as would be the case if predicamental-univocal participation was the only type of participation present in Thomas's works. Finally, Emery highlights a threefold causality of God's relation to the world and intentionally neglects to include material causation. This threefold model of causation is completely in line with Thomistic thought.

Readers should also note the distinction that Thomas makes throughout his account of the divine Ideas. Creatures do not participate in the divine essence directly but rather participate in a *likeness* of the divine essence. Sebastian Morello writes:

> Generally Aquinas adds that such participation is by some 'likeness,' or imitation. By such a qualification Aquinas is being clear that he ought not to be read as a pantheist; he is not positing that created beings possess some small part of God's *esse*. Rather, each finite being has a particular likeness to the divine *esse*, for each possesses its own *actus essendi*, which has God as its efficient cause. The divine nature itself remains uncommunicated and unparticipated; nevertheless its *likeness* is communicated to all created beings. Both the *actus essendi* of each finite being, and the *esse commune* of all finite being, depend upon *esse subsistens* – the First *Esse* – for their explanation, which is the exemplar, efficient, and final cause of every created substance.[20]

This participation in the *likeness* of divinity means that perfections do not exist in creatures and God in the same manner. Man's goodness is *like* God's goodness; man's intelligence is *like* God's intelligence; man's life is *like* God's life; and man's being is *like* God's being, but behind

---

We have thus, in summary, the following triadic structure: 1, God as he is in himself, in whom nothing participates and who participates in nothing (*améthektos*); 2, God as efficient cause who is participated by the effects into which he proceeds (*méthektos*); 3, Creatures which through participation proceed from God, abide within themselves, and return to God as final cause (*metéchōn*)' (Francis O'Rourke, *Pseudo-Dionysius and the Metaphysics of Aquinas* [Notre Dame, IN: University of Notre Dame Press, 2005], 224).

20. Morello, 59-60.

this concept of 'likeness' lies a great dissimilarity between divine and human perfections.[21] If two separate entities are similar to one another, then they are not identical with one another.[22] In the same way that a drawing fails to encapsulate all that is present in a human being, the human being fails to encapsulate the fullness of being present in divinity.[23] Thomas, however, goes further still to guard the transcendent nature of God. Not only does he clearly reject God as the material cause and provide careful distinction between the divine essence and the likeness of the essence in which creatures participate, but Thomas also sets careful parameters around divine formal causation.

The Relationship between Formal and Exemplar Causation

One will note that Thomas typically avoids the term 'formal cause' to describe God's relation to creation. In general, he refers to God as the exemplar cause of created being. Therefore, some scholars have suggested that Thomas is positing a fifth type of causation while rejecting both material and formal causation as applied to God. Others believe that there exists in Thomas's thought a certain level of continuity between

---

21. 'There is only one perfect uncreated image. The first exemplar, the divine essence, cannot be represented perfectly by a single creature but must be represented by many created things' (Aquinas, *ST* 1.47.1 ad 2). As quoted in Josef Pieper, *The Human Wisdom of St. Thomas: A Breviary of Philosophy from the Works of St. Thomas Aquinas.*, trans. Drostan Maclaren, repr. ed. (San Francisco: Ignatius Press, 2002), 442.

22. John Wippel writes: 'After criticizing Averroes' account of divine knowledge, Thomas explains how it is possible for God to have a proper and certain knowledge of individuals through his single essence (ad 3, 1 Sent). This is so because no created thing perfectly imitates the divine goodness, even though all things participate in it. Hence one thing is likened to it in a way in which others are not. Therefore the divine essence is a proper likeness for each individual. Here, then, differing degrees of imitating and participating in the divine essence account for the fact that one principle – the divine essence – can be a proper likeness for individual creatures' (John F. Wippel, 'Thomas Aquinas on Divine Ideas,' in *Gilson Lectures on Thomas Aquinas*, ed. James P. Reilly [Toronto: Pontifical Institute of Mediaeval Studies, 2008], 127).

23. See C. S. Lewis, 'Transposition,' in *The Weight of Glory* (San Francisco: HarperOne, 2015), 102. Lewis wrote: 'Pictures are part of the visible world themselves and represent it only by being part of it. Their visibility has the same source as its. The suns and lamps in pictures seem to shine only because real suns or lamps shine on them; that is, they seem to shine a great deal because they really shine a little in reflecting their archetypes.' Indeed, the entirety of Lewis's essay is exceptionally helpful in explaining the participatory outlook.

exemplar and formal causation. Ultimately, Thomas presents the divine Ideas as exemplar causes due to his commitment to God's transcendence.

In *The Same God Who Works All Things*, Adonis Vidu argues that formal causality cannot be applied to God as it is traditionally understood. Vidu writes: 'If one were to choose Aristotle's four causes, only the two extrinsic causes may represent this causal relation [between Creator and creature]: the efficient and the final. Conversely, *God may never be the formal cause of a thing*, or its material cause.'[24] Vidu's argument is grounded in an Aristotelian and Thomistic understanding of form and matter:

> A formal cause is that which makes a particular thing to be the thing that it is. For example, the formal cause of a statue is the substantial form of a statue. Since a formal cause enters into composition with the matter that it informs, the formal cause itself is defined and limited in its being by the potentiality of matter. As such, a formal cause always depends on the passive potency of the matter it informs. As Aquinas explains in *Summa Contra Gentiles* 1.27.4, 'the union of form and matter results in a composite, which is a whole with respect to the matter and the form. But the parts are in potency in relation to the whole.' For this reason, God cannot be understood to become the formal cause of any created thing. *No created thing can be made to be in act by God as formal cause.* Were that the case, created things would have the form of God; they would be God. Absurdly, God would be limited by that which he informs.[25]

Readers will notice how Thomas's affirmation of intrinsic forms prevents God from being the formal cause of His creatures. The impetus behind Vidu's argument, namely, the emphasis of divine transcendence and the rejection of pantheism, is a correct and noble goal. According to Vidu: 'In restricting divine causality to the efficient/final causation, Aquinas plays a familiar tune on the instrument of Aristotelian philosophy. The familiar tune extols the supremacy and aseity of the Creator in relation to his creature.'[26] Yet, in order to safeguard divine aseity, Vidu virtually suggests that Thomas believed in a fifth type of causation.

---

24. Adonis Vidu, *The Same God Who Works All Things: Inseparable Operations in Trinitarian Theology* (Grand Rapids: William B. Eerdmans Publishing Company, 2021), 131; emphasis added.

25. ibid., 131; emphasis added. The explanation of causation through the illustration of a statue is very much in line with the history of thought. See Davison, *Love of Wisdom*, 35.

26. Vidu, 132.

Instead of assigning formal causality to God, Vidu points to the concept of exemplar causation. He defines exemplar causation, specifically as it pertains to the divine Ideas, as such:

> The divine ideas are the *ratio* of the creatures. That is to say, the divine ideas are the exemplar causes of the creatures. The idea of exemplar causes lies somewhere in between the formal and final causes. An exemplar cause is similar to a formal cause in the sense that it sketches the idea of what a thing will become. But it is never quite the formal cause, since what makes the thing to be itself must be intrinsic to the thing itself.[27]

It is difficult, however, for Vidu to maintain such a fine distinction between exemplary and formal causation. At times, Vidu seems to overstate the difference between exemplary and formal causation since even Thomas occasionally uses both phrases to describe God's relation to creatures.[28] In practice, Vidu sometimes conflates or relates the two causes, even after clearly denying formal divine causation. In a passage summarizing Thomas's position, Vidu writes: 'In this commentary [on the Gospel of John], [Thomas] further explains that the world has been created through the Son as through a *formal cause*.'[29] It is obvious, however, that Vidu is neither suggesting that the second person of the Trinity enters into composition with His creatures nor denying the divinity of the Son. Again, Vidu sometimes places exemplar causation under the banner of formal causation, as he does when he writes:

> While they all share efficient causality, the persons act as distinct exemplar causes, insofar as the effects of their inseparable actions come to resemble

---

27. ibid. Compare this line of reasoning with Thomas who writes: 'God is the efficient and final cause of things. Hence, He is also their formal cause – but as an exemplary cause, since He cannot be a form that is part of a creature.' See Thomas Aquinas, *Disputed Questions on Truth*, trans. Robert W. Mulligan, James V. McGlynn, and Robert Schmidt, 3 vols. (Chicago: Henry Regnery Company, 1952), 3.1 ad 3.

28. For instance, Thomas writes: 'And so when it says that *All things were made through him*, if the "through" denotes the efficient or movent cause, causing the Father to act, then in this sense the Father does nothing through the Son, but he does all things through himself, as has been said. But if the "through" denotes a formal cause, as when the Father operates through his wisdom, which is his essence, he operates through his wisdom as he operates through his essence' (Thomas Aquinas, *Commentary on the Gospel of John*, vol. 1, *Chapters 1–5*, trans. Fabian Larcher and James A. Weisheipl, 3 vols., Thomas Aquinas in Translation [Washington, DC: The Catholic University of America Press, 2010], 33).

29. Vidu, 146.

them distinctly. ... Such relations, however, are not in the order of efficient causality, but in the order of formal, or more exactly exemplar, causality.[30]

It would seem, then, that Vidu recognizes exemplar causes as a type of formal cause, although one that does not enter into any sort of composition with matter. The difficulty of maintaining this distinction makes sense when considering the identity of the divine Ideas as the exemplar cause. As Thomas Joseph White writes: 'Since the exemplary cause in itself implies only a mentally immanent standard of measure and not a direct extrinsic cause, appeal to it will need to somehow be related to one of the other causes.'[31]

Doolan helps to explain this distinction between formal and exemplary causation. In Doolan's estimation, exemplary causation includes aspects of multiple causes without serving as a distinct fifth cause in its own right.[32] Doolan explains: 'What we find, then, is that an exemplar idea exercises two types of causality: as a final cause, it arouses the artisan's will to produce an effect, and as a formal cause, it measures the effect that he produces. Only in the latter sense, however, can an exemplar be said to act *as* an exemplar.'[33] Furthermore, efficient causality can be seen in exemplary causation. Elsewhere Doolan explains the Thomistic definition of an exemplar:

> For Thomas, the term [exemplar] is properly defined as 'a form that something imitates because of the intention of an agent who predetermines the end for himself.' ... Following Thomas's mature use of the term 'exemplar,' we saw that only actually practical ideas should be called 'exemplars.' Inasmuch as an exemplar is properly a productive idea, then, its causality necessarily entails efficient and final causality: it entails efficient causality because the exemplar's causality is caused by the efficient cause; it entails final causality because the exemplar must first motivate the intention of the agent for him to produce his work. Nevertheless, we found that an exemplar idea, in its capacity *as* an exemplar, *is reduced to the order of formal causality since the characteristic that is proper to it as an exemplar is its imitability.*[34]

---

30. ibid., 148. Elsewhere he writes, 'So there is a causality that is proper to each of the persons, yet it is in the order of exemplary, not efficient, causality' (ibid., 151).

31. Thomas Joseph White, *Wisdom in the Face of Modernity: A Study in Thomistic Natural Theology*, second edition (Ave Marie, FL; Sapientia Press, 2016), 168.

32. Doolan, 34.

33. Doolan., 41.

34. ibid., 43; emphasis added.

The divine Ideas do not technically cause anything to come about on their own. Rather, without the movement of the divine will, the divine Ideas would only exist in God's speculative knowledge. Apart from the divine will, God would know the divine Ideas as imitative forms of creatures that He could create, if He so chose.[35] Once combined with the divine will, however, the divine Ideas are intricately tied to efficient causation. Therefore, when divine Ideas serve as exemplars, efficient causation has taken place. Hence there is no exemplary cause without an efficient cause, namely, the divine will.

Exemplary causation's relationship to final causation is similar to its relationship to efficient causation. When exemplar causation occurs, final causation has also taken place. The production of the exemplary form in creation serves as the goal of the acting agent. In other words, God wants certain divine Ideas to serve as actual exemplars and others to remain as potential exemplars. God's desire for His goodness to be imitated in certain ways by particular creatures motivates God's choice in assigning certain divine Ideas as exemplars. Hence, exemplar causation will never be separated from final causation.

Still, in the quotation above, Doolan specifies that exemplar causation 'is reduced to the order of formal causality.' This reduction is due to the content of the divine Ideas, namely, the pre-existent forms of creatures within the mind of God. These divine Ideas serve as the defining parameters for each and every creature. When a building is analogously referred to as an extension of its architect, this is not to suggest that the building is erected with pieces of its designer. Rather, the expression is meant to communicate that the building's defining form, by which it should be measured, exists within the mind of its creator. Likewise, the form of each particular creature is ultimately measured by correspondence to its proper divine idea. When properly understood, then, it is not inappropriate to refer to God as the formal cause of creatures, even though there is a technical distinction that needs to be made.

---

35. 'The knowledge of God is the cause of things. For the knowledge of God is to all creatures what the knowledge of the artificer is to things made by his art. Now the knowledge of the artificer is the cause of the things made by his art, ... [but] the intelligible form does not denote a principle of action in so far as it resides in the one who understands unless there is added to it the inclination to an effect, which inclination is through the will ...' (Aquinas, *ST* 1.14.8).

Morello is another author who helps readers to understand the tight relation between exemplars and formal causation. 'God, then,' writes Morello, 'knows the *being* of a thing as its efficient cause, and the *essence* of a thing as its exemplar cause. In this way the two modes of God's knowledge address both efficient and formal causality.'[36] Morello agrees with Vidu, and Thomas, that the divine Ideas do not enter into composition with creation. Morello writes:

> There is a *real* (ontological) distinction between the divine idea and the creature of which it is the exemplar; there is no composition between the former and the latter. If there were such a composition, 'God's essence would enter into the composition of a creature since the divine ideas are ontologically the same as the divine essence.' If the divine ideas were not identical to the divine essence, God would Himself be a composition of parts, and therefore would need an explanation beyond Himself, and so would not be God.[37]

Therefore, exemplar causation is not simply a type of formal cause, even though these two categories are intimately related. Rather, it is a full-fledged explanation of how God serves as the first cause of creation without sacrificing divine transcendence. When Thomas speaks of exemplar causes, there is an understanding embedded within the concept of God as efficient, final, and, when properly qualified, formal cause. Thus, exemplar causation is not less than formal causation but more. Davison summarizes the previous material well:

> Theologians have made a great deal of God-as-first-efficient cause, particularly as part of arguments for the existence of God: that there could be no motion without an unmoved mover or causation without an uncaused cause. The idea of God as final cause, or goal of all longing, is just as promising, although this aspect has often been passed over. It is a good example of the way in which Aristotle is not always quite as far from the religious mysticism of Plato as is sometimes assumed. ... Aristotle provided resources to be deployed but Christians knew that they would have to go far beyond him in talking about God and creation. To God as efficient and final cause, found in Aristotle, they added God as the formal cause of all things, since the essence of everything stands as a participation in God.

---

36. Morello, 69. Morello cites Doolan, 213.

37. Morello, 65.

Although God is not the material cause of creation, the idea of *creation out of nothing* makes the revolutionary claim that God is the cause of matter.[38]

All examples of causation listed by Davison above are embedded within the concept of exemplar causation. Everything that possesses created existence will trace its causal origins back to divinity.

The Mode of Existence of the Divine Ideas

As is the case of numerous doctrines, the divine Ideas are understood and expressed in a variety of ways. As such, there does not exist a uniform, universally agreed upon conception of the divine Ideas as they exist in the divine intellect. Two theologians may affirm the existence of divine Ideas and disagree significantly on classical theism, the doctrine of creation, and metaphysics. As such, the promotion of a Thomistic version of the divine Ideas will admittedly differ from alternative models. The best way to highlight the key differences between two major models is to share a tale of two Thomases – Aquinas and Ward.[39]

Thomas Ward, professor of philosophy at Baylor University, suggests there exists two main camps concerning the ontology of divine Ideas – the imitative theory and the containment theory.[40] In imitative theories, the divine Ideas are defined by God's knowledge of how His nature may be *imitated* in various finite modes, whereas containment theories suggest that various archetypal forms (ideas) of creatures are somehow contained *within* the divine nature itself.[41] Now, various versions of these two main theories exist, and Ward acknowledges that his binary categorization is intentionally broad. For instance, Anselm's and

---

38. Davison, *Love of Wisdom*, 46-47.

39. For the sake of clarity, the typical nomenclature will be altered, and Thomas Aquinas will be referred to as 'Aquinas,' while Thomas Ward will simply be called 'Ward' throughout the following discussion.

40. Ward, 23.

41. In Ward's own words: 'An imitative theory holds that God gets his ideas of creatures by understanding his own infinite essence as able to be imitated in various, finite ways …' (Ward, 23). This seems to be a fair assessment of the Thomistic view (other than the vague implications of God 'getting' Ideas), and this language of imitation is often repeated by Thomists. See, for instance, Davies who writes: 'There always remains a new way in which some copy is able to imitate the divine essence, and nothing prevents God from knowing infinite things through his essence' (Brian Davies, *Thomas Aquinas's Summa Contra Gentiles: A Guide and Commentary* [Oxford: Oxford University Press, 2016], 111).

Aquinas's theories of divine Ideas are both considered to be examples of the imitative theory in Ward's estimation, yet they need not be identical for Ward's formulation to be accurate. The imitative and containment theories agree on several pertinent claims, the most significant of which is that God knows the divine Ideas through His self-knowledge rather than gleaning any information from external sources.[42] The two camps, however, disagree on how divine self-knowledge logically leads to the proper ectypal formulation of the divine Ideas.

Ward considers Aquinas to be among those who support the imitative theory of divine Ideas. As a reminder, Aquinas explains the divine Ideas as such:

> God knows his essence perfectly; he knows it therefore in all the ways in which it is knowable. Now the divine essence can be known not only as it is in itself, but as it can be participated in some degree of likeness by creatures. On the other hand every creature has its own nature in so far as it participates in some way the likeness of the divine essence. In this way then God, in knowing his essence as *imitable* in this particular way by this particular creature, knows his essence as the nature and Idea proper to that creature; and similarly in other cases. (Aquinas, *ST* 1.15.3)

After defining the imitative theory and listing Aquinas as the main example of such an understanding, Ward moves on to dismiss imitative models of divine Ideas as untenable. Rather, Ward believes that Christians should affirm a containment theory, but, if readers follow Ward's preferred model, this necessitates rejecting a strict definition of divine simplicity. The version of the containment theory that Ward

---

42. There are, indeed, several excellent points scattered throughout Ward's book. His analysis concerning abstract objects and the Platonic forms is specifically worth noting: 'The theory of divine ideas I defend eliminates abstract objects and holds that God supplies all the ontology needed to explain anything abstract objects explain, and the spirit of the elimination is the spirit of Gideon tearing down the altar of Baal. The fact is that Goodness, Truth, and Beauty, considered as forms or properties which exist in logical space for all eternity, which are the objects of God's knowledge insofar as he has knowledge of Goodness, Truth, and Beauty, and which are the properties God exemplifies insofar as God is Good, True, and Beautiful – these abstract objects, along with the whole pantheon of which they are members, are rivals to God and have no place in a monotheistic system in which the one God is worthy to be loved with all our heart, soul, and might. Tear them down, and say instead that God is the Good, God is the True, God is the Beautiful' (Ward, 13). He specifically cites Alvin Plantinga's metaphysics as one that makes God a derivative being and thus one to be avoided (Ward, 33).

promotes claims that the divine Ideas are truly a part of the divine essence while remaining indivisible from the divine essence. Some may then ask, 'Why do certain forms exist in God in this way?' To which Ward responds:

> Here is where explanation comes to an end. I think that God contains these many ways of being, just because. Being divides up the way it does, just because. All the categories, genera, differences, right down to ultimate differences, there is no explanation of why there are just these.[43]

Hence, the divine Ideas are simply brute facts.[44]

To understand the major difference between two views, Ward's understanding of divine simplicity should be examined. Ward's chief objections to divine simplicity focus on the existence of multiple divine attributes or perfections. Power, love, mercy, and wisdom are distinct perfections and, even though they are very much interrelated, cannot be reduced to one concept.[45] Love certainly entails mercy and power certainly entails knowledge, but a proper definition of each attribute goes beyond the others. Any interpretation of simplicity that fails to recognize the multiplicity of divine attributes, such as Ward's understanding of Aquinas, is to be rejected.

There is no possibility of dismissing divine simplicity within the Thomistic framework, but it is unclear why Ward's proposal necessitates the imitative theory to be pitted against the containment theory. It is true, as Ward concludes, that Aquinas defines the divine Ideas by their imitation of and participation in the divine essence,

---

43. Ward, 38.

44. There are several components of my overarching arguments that Thomas Ward would question or reject. It's difficult to answer any of Ward's objections, however, because he does not provide any. Rather, when discussing concepts such as 'the great chain of being,' the transcendentals, the analogy of being, and analogous participation, Ward simply writes, '[S]uch a proposal is too wonderful for me' (ibid., 29).

45. Ward writes: 'The denial of composition or complexity in God stands in tension with all the traditional attributes which theologians ascribe to God – for example that God is wise, good, merciful, just, powerful, loving, and so on – to say nothing of the earthier things said of God in the Bible. The tension arises because these various attributes are clearly different from each other. Being powerful is compatible with, but not exactly the same thing as, being wise. ... So it seems that, if God really is wise, good, merciful, etc., then he has *more than one feature*: his being wise is not altogether the same as his being good, and these are not altogether the same as his being merciful, etc. But having more than one feature is in tension with not having any parts' (Ward, 27).

and indeed this definition explains *how* the divine Ideas are contained in the divine essence. As has been said numerous times above, the content of divine knowledge, the act of the divine intellect, and the divine knower are all one due to Aquinas's understanding of divine simplicity. Yet, Aquinas must place the divine Ideas somewhere if he wishes to avoid the same mistakes embodied by the Platonic Forms. Following Augustine, Aquinas places these divine Ideas in the divine mind, making them the same as the divine essence. An imitative theory is a version of the containment theory without the unsatisfying metaphysical explanation of the source of Ideas. The divine Ideas are the divine essence, and the divine Ideas exist because God knows how His essence, pure and unrestricted act, can be limited by a creature's potency.

For instance, Aquinas states: 'All creatures are nothing other than an objective expression and representation of what is *contained* in the concept of the divine Word' (Aquinas, *SCG* 3.42). Elsewhere, 'Knowledge and will means that the thing known is in the knower and the thing willed is in the willer. Thus, according to knowledge and will, *things are more in God* than God is in things' (Aquinas, *ST* 1.8.3 ad 3). In this sense, the Thomistic version of divine simplicity is the very reason why divine Ideas are 'contained' in God, and theologians need not cite brute facts to explain the existence of the Ideas. Indeed, the divine Ideas have true existence as, 'We know that everything done by God dwells in him as known, so it follows that all created things are in him as in the divine life. ... Also the natures of inanimate things are alive in God's mind, in which they have divine existence' (Aquinas, *ST* 1.18.4; 1.18.4 ad 2). This analysis of Thomas's understanding of the mode of ideas is affirmed by John Wippel who writes:

> With the analogy of the artisan in mind Aquinas describes ideas as the forms of things *as they exist in God*, and notes that they are like operative forms. He then quotes from Dionysius' *De divinis nominibus* 5, where he refers to ideas: 'We describe as exemplars the substantial reasons of existing things which *preexist* in God in uniform fashion and which theology refers to as predefinitions and as divine and good wills (*voluntates*) which are predeterminative and productive of existing things.'[46]

---

46. Wippel, *Thomas Aquinas and the Divine Ideas*, 129; emphasis added.

While Ward is not a theistic mutualist, it does seem that his system is an example of a doctrine becoming more complicated once certain load-bearing theological commitments have been weakened or lost. More can be said concerning how these Ideas are present within God, specifically by an examination of the divine Logos, to which we turn next.

The Divine Ideas and the Divine Logos

The divine Ideas have sometimes led to discussions concerning Thomas Aquinas's understanding of the triune persons. Specifically, scholars debate how Thomas understood the relationship between the divine Ideas and the second person of the Trinity. At times, Thomas draws special attention to the identity of the Word, or the divine Wisdom, and how He relates to the divine exemplars. This connection, however, may be missed if readers skip over Thomas's commentaries. For instance, in his commentary on the Gospel of John, Thomas describes the Son as 'the Word, who is the art of the Father, full of living archetypes.'[47]

Commenting on John 1:3, Thomas writes:

> If we carefully consider the words, *All things were made through him*, we can clearly see that the Evangelist spoke with the utmost exactitude. For whoever makes something must preconceive it in his wisdom, *which is the form and pattern of the thing made: as the form preconceived in the mind of an artisan is the pattern of the cabinet to be made.*[48]

This analysis means that everything that God makes is created through the divine Wisdom. 'Accordingly,' Thomas continues, 'it is impossible that he should make anything except through the Son. And so Augustine says, in *the Trinity*, that the Word is the art full of the living patterns of all things. Thus it is clear that all things which the Father makes, he makes through him.'[49]

Thomas continues to address this topic in his commentary on Galatians. According to Thomas, the author of the epistle 'says that the Son is the first-born of every creature because he is generated or begotten as the principle of every creature. And so he says, for in him

---

47. Aquinas, *Commentary on the Gospel of John*, 1:37.

48. ibid., 34; emphasis added.

49. Aquinas, *Commentary on the Gospel of John*, 1:34.

all things were created.'[50] Thomas then goes on to differentiate this idea from the Platonic understanding of the Forms. Rather than the Platonic proposal of a series of Forms in which all creation participates, *we have one, that is, the Son, the Word of God. For an artisan makes an artefact by making it participate in the form he has conceived within himself, enveloping it, so to say, with external matter; for we say that the artisan makes a house through the form of all the thing which he has conceived within himself.*[51] Specifically, this form and wisdom is the Word that Thomas refers to as an 'exemplar.'

Similarly, Thomas draws a strong connection between the Son and the divine Ideas in the first volume of his *Summa Contra Gentiles*. Analyzing this data is complicated, however, because of the scant attention the divine Ideas received from Thomas in the *SCG*. Indeed, some Thomistic scholars would suggest that, according to the *SCG*, the divine Ideas play such a small role in Thomas's theology that readers should be wary of overstating the importance of the doctrine. This position is that of Etienne Gilson, but his view has decreased in popularity over time. More scholars are beginning to recognize the presence of divine Ideas in the *SCG* under different terminology. Rather than discussing the Ideas, as Thomas does in the *Summa Theologiæ* (*Summa*; *ST*), Thomas discusses 'notions' or 'ratios' in the *SCG* and firmly connects these concepts to the Word.

Thomas suggests that the intellect, 'having been informed by the species of the thing, by an act of understanding forms within itself a certain intention of the thing understood, that is to say, its notion, which the definition signifies' (Aquinas, *SCG* 1.53.3). This passage and the concept of notion seems strikingly similar to the concept of intellectual abstraction that was discussed in Chapter 4. The rest

---

50. Thomas Aquinas, *Commentary on Colossians*, ed. Daniel Keating, trans. Fabian Larcher (Naples, FL: Sapientia Press, 2006), ch. 1, lec. 4, n37. Davison comments on this passage: 'The Son, as the divine Logos, Reason, or Word, and as the seat of the divine "ideas" concerning creation, is the exemplar for all the forms and perfections of creation, embodying already the principle of likeness as the Image of the Father' (Davison, *Participation*, 202).

51. Aquinas, *Commentary on Colossians*, 1.4.37; emphasis added. It should be noted that Thomas's use of the term 'form' to describe the Word does not suggest any sort of imperfection, finitude, or lack of identity to the divine essence, as the term suggests elsewhere. Rather, Thomas is describing the Son as the Wisdom of God through which the Father creates all things.

of the passage draws an even greater comparison: 'The intellect has this characteristic in addition, namely, that it understands a thing as separated from material conditions, without which a thing does not exist in reality. But this could not take place unless the intellect formed the abovementioned intention for itself' (Aquinas, *SCG* 1.53.3).[52] Thomas then places this notion firmly in the Word:

> Now, the divine intellect understands by no species other than the divine essence, as was shown above. Nevertheless, the divine essence is the likeness of all things. Thereby it follows that the conception of the divine intellect as understanding itself, which is its Word, *is the likeness not only of God Himself understood, but also of all those things of which the divine essence is the likeness.* In this way, therefore, through one intelligible species, which is the divine essence, and through one understood intention, which is the divine Word, God can understand many things. (Aquinas, *SCG* 1.53.5)[53]

As such, Thomas occasionally uses very similar language to describe the divine Ideas and the divine Wisdom. The correlation between these two entities can be further explained through a brief overview of Thomas's Trinitarianism, specifically an examination of the imminent acts of procession and the psychology analogy.

The Psychology Analogy

A key difference between medieval and modern Trinitarian discussions is the function of the psychology analogy. Even the medieval thinker most linked to the univocity of being, Scotus, had a place for the psychology analogy within his Trinitarian theology. Indeed, his well-known doctrine of 'formal distinctions' in the Godhead, whereby the attributes of God were ontologically distinct from one another while remaining inseparable from one another, was utilized at length

---

52. To continue the similarities, Thomas calls this intention or notion as a 'likeness of the thing understood' (Aquinas, *SCG* 1.53.2).

53. Wippel reiterates the straight-forward interpretation of this passage. Wippel writes: 'God's intellect needs no species by which it understands other than the divine essence. But the divine essence is a likeness for all things, as Thomas has established at chapter 29 [of *SCG*]. Therefore the conception of the divine intellect by which God knows himself, which is his Word, is not only a likeness of God as understood, it is also a likeness of all things of which the divine essence itself is a likeness. Therefore, by one intelligible species – the divine essence, – and on understood divine intention – the divine Word, – God understands many things' (Wippel, 'Thomas Aquinas on Divine Ideas,' 145).

to explain the psychology analogy.[54] Likewise, Thomas's Trinitarian system, as well as his explanations of the *opera ad extra*, are dependent upon the psychology analogy. Modern Trinitarian models, however, often overlook this medieval constant.

The psychology analogy posits that the immanent acts of a human mind and will offer an analogy to understand the immanent acts of procession within the Godhead. White explains the psychology analogy as that 'which inevitably considers relations in the Trinity in a qualifiedly unipersonal way, so as to depict the immaterial processions of the Word and Spirit by analogy to processions of intellectual and voluntary life in one human person.'[55] The theory is analogous to how a man must obtain an object of knowledge before addressing that object in love. The Father, speaking analogically, knows Himself perfectly and loves what He knows perfectly. God's perfect knowledge of Himself serves as the principle of the Son's eternal generation, and the love between the Father and the Son serves as the principle of the Spirit.

In creatures, mankind learns via the material world. Analyzing individual objects allows the human mind to abstract the form from an object's matter. In return, the mind can then use, or 'send forth,' that abstracted form to analyze other individual objects. This 'procession' is completely imminent within the human mind, meaning that it does not produce anything external to the person. Additionally, the human will, or rational appetite, inclines the person to pursue what is good. In this way, the will can be seen as 'going forth' from the person, driving him to that which is good. Again, this procession of will is completely imminent within the human person and does not produce anything external. These

---

54. White writes: 'Scotus distinguishes between formal distinctions and real distinctions. Things that are really distinct can be separated from one another, while things that are formally distinct cannot. Scotus claims that the divine attributes proper to God's nature (such as goodness, eternity, infinity and so on) are formally distinct in God, and thus inseparable. They are not accidents or properties of the divine nature but are identical with the divine nature due to God's simplicity. Nevertheless, they are not identical with one another ontologically. ... Scotus's thinking on this point is integrally connected with his theory of predication of divine attributes, since each attribute we ascribe to God must pertain to something truly in God, something quasi-generically or essentially distinct from all other such attributes, and must be attributed to God in such a way as to preserve some content that pertains to both God and creatures univocally' (White, *Trinity*, 376n6).

55. White, *Trinity*, 439.

psychological acts, then, can be used by means of analogy to explain how the Word and Spirit may process from the Father without producing anything external to the Father. While the psychology analogy is not sufficient to fully explain the acts of immanent procession (the Word is also called the Son for a reason), it does provide a helpful starting point for Thomas's explanation.

Modern models, however, typically deem the psychology analogy (also known as the analogy of acts of the mind) as unwarranted or a mark of the type of epistemological hubris associated with natural theology. The rejection of the psychology analogy means that modern thinkers are left to explain the distinctions of personhood within the Godhead by other means. In order to accomplish this, modern theologians turn to the opera ad extra, the economic Trinity. In this mindset, the Son is not best distinguished from the Father by the act of eternal generation grounded in the divine intellect but should be distinguished by His acts of obedience or suffering as displayed through the divine economy. Likewise, the Spirit is not the Trinitarian person marked by spiration or procession but as the revealing person who illuminates the minds of mankind. White calls this maneuver 'inverted monophysitism,' which he defines as the belief that '[t]he human nature of Jesus, in its action and suffering, is depicted as if it provided a quasi-univocal portrait of the inner life of God and the eternal communion of the persons.'[56]

It should be noted, however, that the analogy of psychology, grounded in a broader method of analogical predication, has not been overcome in modern Trinitarian discourse. Rather, the model is simply overlooked. If analogical predication is accepted as a legitimate option in understanding the divine names, then the analogy of psychology is a legitimate option in understanding the divine processions.

The Word – Proceeding from the Intellect

Thomas's frequently cited illustration of the divine architect or artist is an apt way to describe the immanent acts of procession. Emery explains:

---

56. White, *Trinity*, 17. Specifically White points to thinkers such as Wolfhart Pannenberg and Hans Urs von Balthasar to illustrate this concept, but many contemporary models of the Trinity, such as those that promote the eternal functional subordination of the Son, would fall under White's inverted monophysitism. Once the missions of the triune persons are seen as their defining characteristics, then the eternal processions are either ignored as unnecessary speculation or punted as dangerously philosophical.

> The immanent action takes place when the architect mentally conceives the plan of the building which he is going to construct, and he wills its construction; then, in the transitive action, the architect concretely realizes his plan by getting the building constructed.[57]

Immanent acts, then, are actions which terminate in the agent, such as conceiving a plan or willing a goal, whereas transitive acts are those actions that terminate outside of the agent, such as the construction of a building. The importance of the immanent acts of procession cannot be overstated in Thomistic Trinitarianism. The principal of procession is an eternal act of the Father, the fruit of which is internal to the divine essence. Without an understanding of immanent acts, the divine persons, as the fruit of an act of the Father, would be seen as external to the divine nature and thus would be creatures. This distinction between immanent and transitive acts is also important because Thomas uses the term 'procession' to describe the act of creation. In the case of creaturely being, however, the act of procession would be a transitive act.

Thomas believes that the 'Word' is the most appropriate and proper name for the second person of the Trinity because of the intellectual nature of the Word's immanent act of procession. Whereas 'Son' properly suggests generation, it must be explained that this generation does not terminate outside of God. The title 'Word' also suggests generation with the added benefit of its link to the immanent procession of a word within a mind.[58]

Emery explains, 'The word is the *expression* of the thing known in the mind of the knower; *formed* by the intellect, its existence is intrinsically relative.'[59] The Word, then, is the ultimate internal expression of God's comprehensive self-knowledge in which is contained all that God knows.[60] As such, there is perfect correspondence between the Word and the Father. The Son is the 'begotten wisdom flowing from the Father.'[61]

---

57. Emery, *Trinity*, 56.

58. See Emery, *Trinity*, 176-80.

59. ibid., 182.

60. Emery writes: 'The eternal begetting of the Word does not issue from a knowledge derived from creatures; rather, it is by knowing *himself* that God engenders his Word ...' (Emery, *Trinity*, 400). Elsewhere Emery explains: 'The word is not that *through which* the mind knows (which is the *species*) but is, rather, the *fruit* of an internal making or conceiving, the expression of the reality known within a mind' (ibid., 184).

61. Gilles Emery, *The Trinitarian Theology of Saint Thomas Aquinas*, trans. Francesca Aran Murphy (New York: Oxford University Press, 2007), 350.

If one considers Thomas's Trinitarian understanding, then the connection between the divine Ideas and the Word is unsurprising. Doolan summarizes:

> Given knowledge of the essential attributes, however, we can make use of them to 'manifest' the divine Persons, for there is some similitude or dissimiltude between a Person and an attribute. This approach to manifesting the divine Persons is termed by Thomas 'appropriation' (*appropriatio*). For example, the Son of God proceeds by way of intellect as the Word; thus those things that pertain to intellect can be appropriated to him by similitude. Now, since ideas pertain to intellect, they can be appropriated to the Son. Hence, Thomas explains, the Word can be identified as the locus of the divine ideas.[62]

The Word is appropriately referred to as God's wisdom and truth. He is the perfect image of the Father with whom He shares complete consubstantiality.

Christ as Epistemic Mediator[63]

In addition to the Son's role as the wellspring of all truth, Thomas also depicts the Son as the mediator of all truth. One can once again turn to Thomas's commentary on the Gospel of John to see the connection between the Word as the 'home' of the divine Ideas and the Son as epistemic mediator. The Son communicates what He is by essence, Truth, to men through a creaturely knowledge of participatory truth. Thomas addresses this epistemic mediation as he exegetes John 1:3.

First, the divine Ideas seated in the Son play a major role in this epistemic mediation. Thomas writes:

> For as light is not only visible in itself and of itself, but through it all else can be seen, so the Word of God is not only light in himself, but he makes known all things that are known. For since a thing is made known and understood through its form, and all forms exist through the Word who

---

62. Doolan, 119.

63. It may be surprising for some to find that Thomas Aquinas and Carl F. H. Henry addressed the epistemic illumination of the Son very similarly. For more information, see Timothy Gatewood, '"Lighted by the Logos": Carl Henry's Christological Anthropology as the Crux of His Theological Method,' Evangelical Theological Society Midwest Regional Conference, 2020, https://www.academia.edu/43389168/_Lighted_by_the_Logos_Carl_Henrys_Christological_Anthropology_as_the_Crux_of_His_Theological_Method.

is the art full of living forms, the Word is light not only in himself, but as making known all things; 'all that appears is light' (Eph. 5:13).[64]

It is because the Son is the seat of the divine Ideas, the forms of all creatures, that He may illuminate man's knowledge of all things. This illumination from the Son is not limited to religious truth, as if the Son can only reveal knowledge concerning the Father alone. Obviously, the Son reveals the Father, but Thomas goes beyond that claim to suggest that the Word, as the 'art full of living forms,' may reveal all forms that exist through Him, i.e., all things.

Thomas provides greater clarity in what it meant for Christ to be the 'art full of living forms' earlier in his commentary on John. Thomas writes:

> The archetypes which exist spiritually in the wisdom of God, and through which things were made by the Word, are life, just as a chest made by an artisan is in itself neither alive nor life, yet the exemplar of the chest in the artisan's mind prior to the existence of the chest is in some sense living, insofar as it has an intellectual existence in the mind of the artisan. Nevertheless it is not life, because it is neither in his essence nor is it his existence through the act of understanding of the artisan. But in God, his act of understanding is his life and his essence. And so whatever is in God is not only living, but is life itself, because whatever is in God is his essence. Hence the creature in God is the creating essence. Thus, if things are considered as they are in the Word, they are life.[65]

Here are several concepts which have been previously discussed. First, Thomas uses the same illustration to convey the forms seated in Christ as he does in the *Summa Theologiæ* and elsewhere to convey the concept of the divine Ideas in the mind of God. Second, Thomas explains that the 'archetypes' or forms exist 'spiritually in the wisdom of God.' These forms have an 'intellectual existence' and are yet 'divine' Ideas due to the doctrine of divine simplicity. Third, notice that Thomas here seems to support the containment theory of divine Ideas in addition to the imitative theory which he supports elsewhere.

---

64. Aquinas, *Commentary on the Gospel of John*, 1:49.

65. ibid., 1:39. It should be noted that this quote appears in a section summarizing the ideas of Augustine, but it is summarized positively and as the preferred option of interpretation.

Ultimately, all truths are granted their truthfulness due to their participation in the First Truth. First, this claim could be demonstrated as a correlation of a creature's existence, as everything that does not exist by their essence must receive their being through participating in Him whom existence and essence are identical. Thomas summarizes the Platonists when he writes:

> They noted that everything which is something by participation is reduced to what is the same thing by essence, as to the first and highest. ... And so since all things which exist participate in existence (*esse*) by its essence, i.e., whose essence is its existence. And this is God, who is the most sufficient, the most eminent, and the most perfect cause of the whole of existence, from whom all things that are participate existence (*esse*).[66]

This participated being is connected to an object's participated truth, but Thomas continues to make his thoughts explicit. Thomas writes: 'I answer that although there are many participated truths, there is just one absolute Truth, which is Truth by its very essence, that is, the divine act of being (*esse*); and by this Truth all words are words.'[67] Indeed, 'The Son of God is light by his very essence; but John and all the saints are light by participation. So, because John participated in the true light, it was fitting that he bear witness to the light; for fire is better exhibited by something afire than by anything else, and color by something colored.'[68] This is consistent with the way Scripture sometimes uses the word 'truth,' as '[s]ometimes it is contrasted with what is something by participation, as in "that we may be in his true Son" (1 John 5:20), who is not his Son by participation.'[69] As Emery writes:

> [T]he Son is the model and source of this communication in which God confers a participation in the goods of nature upon creatures. Because he proceeds by a mode of intellect as the Word of the Father, the Word is the Art by which the Father achieves his works of wisdom in the world: the Father creates through his Word.[70]

---

66. Aquinas, *Commentary on the Gospel of John*, 1:2.

67. ibid., 1:17.

68. ibid., 1:52.

69. ibid., 1:53.

70. Emery, *Trinity*, 358.

The Divine Ideas, Participation, and Creaturely Truth

Contemporary Thomistic scholarship has increasingly emphasized the role of participation within Thomas's theological framework. Additionally, the doctrine of participation is currently experiencing an intellectual revival as the concept has been the focus of several popular works dedicated to theological retrieval. This doctrine is especially pertinent when discussing divine omniscience and the doctrine of truth. Boersma suggests multiple phrases that all describe aspects of a participatory outlook of reality including participation, analogy, and sacramentality or a 'sacramental ontology.' Boersma uses all of these phrases to highlight the biblical reality that creatures have nothing that is not received. This application sees a universal perspective in Paul's words to the apostles in 1 Corinthians 4:7: 'For who considers you as superior? What do you have that you did not receive. And if you did receive it, why do you boast as if you had not received it?'

Within a participatory outlook, God shares His infinite being with finite creatures. As Gilson writes: 'The only possible explanation for the presence of such finite and contingent beings is that they have been freely given existence by "Him who is," and not as parcels of his own existence … but as finite and partial imitations of what He himself eternally is in his own right.'[71] Infinite being is limited within each creature due to the creature's unique potentiality as determined by the creature's individual essence. If a creature has life, for instance, it is because God has shared pure, unlimited life with the creature as fitting to its finite mode of existence. This rule, known as the modus principle, applies to all creaturely perfections – wisdom, truth, beauty, being, etc. Any derivative good that may be found in a creature can be found perfectly and eminently in the Creator. Renard may be helpful here as he writes: 'It is clear that the word "participated" indicates that such a perfection, limited as it is by being received in a potency, implies an unparticipated, unreceived, and, consequently, infinite perfection which is both the exemplary idea and the supreme efficient cause of the participated perfection.'[72] Creatures receive in a particular form

---

71. Gilson, *God and Philosophy*, 53.
72. Renard, 39.

appropriate to their mode of being those perfections that exist in God in a universal mode appropriate to the divine essence.

Furthermore, this participation must continue throughout the creature's existence. If a creature were to ever stop participating in God, then that creature would cease to exist. Indeed, the doctrine of participation is closely linked to the creature's dependence on a divinely independent Creator. Therefore, if a creature reflects any of the divine perfections in a derivative fashion, it is only because that creature is participating in God *in that very moment*.[73]

The Thomistic synthesis of Platonism and Aristotelianism has been repeatedly referenced above, and the synthesis is no less present in the discussion of truth. Thomas describes truth in two ways: ontological truth and logical truth.[74] Ontological truth pertains to truth as it exists in a specific being's essence and, as a transcendental, is nearly synonymous with being. Logical truth pertains to the adequation of the intellect to a specific being's essence. Even though logical truth receives priority, the two modes of truth are inseparable. Without either the transcendental or epistemological aspect of truth the participatory theory of truth will not function properly.

Ontological truth, as an extension of a creature's essence, has been addressed through the lens of participation. However, truth, properly speaking, exists as a component of an intellect. Truth requires the existence of a rational mind. If ontological truth is measured by the knowability of an object's being, then there must be an accompanying

---

73. 'God alone is a being (*ens*) through his essence because his essence is his act of being (*esse*), whereas every creature is a being by participation, and so its essence is not its act of being. Hence, Thomas concludes (following Augustine) that if God were to cease his action in governing created things, all species would cease to be and every nature would perish (*concideret*)' (Doolan, 176).

74. 'Thomas Aquinas is well-known for having defended the view that truth consists of an adequation between the intellect and a thing.... Even so, in addition to describing truth as an adequation of the intellect and a thing, he there considers a number of other definitions. Most importantly, he develops a notion of truth of being (what might be called "ontological truth") along with truth of the intellect (what might be called "logical truth"). As various scholars have pointed out, prior to Thomas's time two general traditions regarding the nature of truth had already appeared. One is heavily neoplatonic and emphasizes truth of being. It was known to Aquinas especially through the writings of Augustine, Anselm, and Avicenna. The other, more Aristotelian, stresses truth as an adequation of mind and reality, or truth of the intellect' (John F. Wippel, 'Truth in Thomas Aquinas,' *The Review of Metaphysics* 43, no. 2 [December 1989]: 295).

mind to receive or measure the truth of the object's being. An object's truth may be connected to a mind by one of two types of relationships. If an object's existence is dependent upon a mind, then Thomas refers to this type of relationship as an essential relation. If the object does not depend on a mind for its existence, then Thomas refers to this type of relationship as an incidental relation (Aquinas, *ST* 1.16.1).

For Thomas, it is the essential relation that defines the essence of an object, which leads him to suggest that 'every thing is said to be true in the absolute sense because of its relation to a mind on which it depends' (Aquinas, *ST* 1.16.1). This mind need not be the divine mind, as Thomas acknowledges that human creations, such as architecture or speech, are measured by the plans within the minds of human beings. Natural objects, however, are defined by their relation to the divine mind. 'True stone,' writes Thomas, 'is stone that has the nature proper to stone as it is conceived first in the divine mind' (Aquinas, *ST* 1.16.1).

A mind of some sort provides the exemplar form of all objects, and this exemplary cause is the source of an object's existence. Thomas is thus able to define truth as 'conformity between intellect and thing' (Aquinas, *ST* 1.16.2). All truth, then, is primarily in and dependent upon the existence of an intellect, but the order of events should be noticed. The adequation of intellect and an object of knowledge begins in the intellect that holds the exemplar form of that object. Truth does not primarily reside in an object, even though it does in a secondary sense in light of Thomas's understanding of ontological participation. In actuality, however, the origin, source, or cause of truth is not created reality but the divine mind in which the exemplars of creation are found.

Even though truth begins in an intellect, human minds are incapable of creating their own truth. Incidental relations between objects of knowledge and human intellect truly do exist. While all truth is dependent upon an intellect, this does not mean that all truth is dependent upon a human intellect. Creaturely intellect, and thus creaturely truth, is measured by its conformity to a specific object of knowledge. There are, therefore, three 'levels of truth' – (1) God, as the perfect conformity between the intellect and an object of knowledge, (2) ontological truth as present within a creature's essence, and (3) the conformity of a creature's intellect and the essence of an object.[75]

A Creature's Correspondence to the Divine Ideas

Even after acknowledging that a creature receives its identity from the divine Ideas, there is still the issue of correspondence. It would seem that a creature never truly corresponds with its unique divine Idea because the creature is in a constant state of flux. Creatures, of course, grow over time and experience significant physical changes, and even if one were to correctly attribute such changes to matter rather than form, there still exists deeper and seemingly more intrinsic progressions. Plato as a baby is significantly different than Plato as a mature philosopher, even though he remains Plato throughout. Which version of a creature, then, best corresponds to the Idea?

Remember that the divine Ideas are closely related to both formal and final causation. In terms of final causation, the exemplar provides an end for each creature as the individual's 'nature is always tending toward a more complete manifestation of the exemplar, the idea in the mind of God.'[76] In this sense, the Idea is the fullness of a creature's being – an Idea in which all potential creaturely perfections have been actualized. A creature's divine Idea, then, serves as a measuring stick of true being. The actualization of creaturely perfections moves an individual closer to that which they were always designed to be. As the exemplar cause relates to final causation, then, the divine Ideas serve as a creature's end or goal.

The divine Ideas, however, are not limited to final causation, and there is a sense in which Thomas believed the exemplar to be a type of intrinsic formal cause.[77] The Ideas, then, would function in the same

---

75. 'In sum, Thomas has singled out three levels of truth in this discussion. Truth in the full and complete sense is assigned to the intellect insofar as the intellect's grasp of a thing corresponds to that thing as it is in itself. Truth is then assigned to things themselves, but only analogically, because of their capacity to produce truth in the intellect. Finally, truth in the fullest and most perfect sense is assigned to God because he causes both the being of all other things and the acts of knowing of all other intellects. At the same time, it is clear from this discussion that Thomas reserves truth in the full and primary sense for it insofar as it is present in the intellect' (Wippel, 'Truth in Thomas Aquinas,' 299).

76. Henri Renard, *The Philosophy of Being* (Milwaukee, WI: The Bruce Publishing Company, 1947), 167.

77. Renard, 163.

way that the idea of a house in the mind of an architect can provide the form of the house-in-progress. As the house falls under construction, it increasingly becomes more aligned with the architect's plans, but these same plans dictate the house's form along the way. The house's future can therefore provide its present form. We can further explain how a seemingly future act provides a creature's internal form by remembering that act actually precedes potentiality.

Everything that comes to be is dependent on 'previously existent realities in act.'[78] The divine Ideas exist before any creatures exist (and, indeed, even 'before' time existed). Furthermore, the source of all creaturely goodness is the God described as *actus purus*. In this sense, the form of man exists in act before an individual man exists as a composite of act and potency. As such, the Idea serves both as a man's final goal and original formal source when the God of pure act chooses to create. The only reason that a man may pursue his fitting final cause is because he is given a form capable of moving toward its natural end.

Still, one must address the relationship between man's sinful tendencies and the divine Ideas. Surely it is inappropriate to say that man's sinful acts perfectly align with God's creation or intent. Even mankind's sinful operations, however, give us a glimpse of God's preceding goodness. A creature's operations flow out of its soul, but these operations are secondary acts 'because they are not necessary for the fundamental subsistence of the reality.'[79] A man is a genuine man regardless of these secondary acts. These operations, then, are accidental operations and are therefore capable of contrary states. In this case, operations intended for good may result in evil when used defectively. Man's rational operations are a good thing capable of moving a man to his final end, but this same good power may be abused and result in moral failures. The capability for evil is thus dependent upon a form's capability for good, and these operations that can produce either good or evil are dependent upon a creature's formal and final cause. As Thomas Joseph White explains:

> The next stage in this argument derives from the realization that this tendency-toward-actuation is not something that any of the aforementioned

---

78. Thomas Joseph White, *Wisdom in the Face of Modernity*, 56.
79. ibid., 57.

beings (human, sensate, or inanimate) can of themselves choose or determine. Such inscribed purposes or teleological determinations are characteristic of *what* they are *essentially*. That is to say, these essential patterns of behavior are not decided upon – or realized by one's own operational determination – but are ontologically inherited, or given in being.[80]

Mankind's capability of sin reflects mankind's capability of goodness resulting from humanity's higher and more significant participation in divine reality compared to that of other creatures.

Man's sinful acts, then, move us away from the final end of true humanity without abandoning man's human nature. When an individual abuses human operations intended for good, then he moves further away from the exemplar cause. These sinful actions are unfitting for one gifted with a human nature, which is one reason that mankind's idol worship produces animalistic or mechanistic results without the sinner losing his humanness. Furthermore, sin moves human beings away from pure act and rushes them along to non-being, the privation of good, and the lack of metaphysical truth. On the contrary, as a human aligns with its exemplar cause then he can reflect true humanity – the kind demonstrated by Christ, who existed in perfect correspondence to what a man was always intended to be.

In this relationship between humanity and the divine Ideas, Christ is emphasized as the alpha and the omega, the formal cause through which all is created and the final cause to which we all strive. One can then explain, in part, how 'this world is essentially an analogy ... not just of some general Logos, a vague principle of cosmic reason or order, but of *this* Logos, the incarnate Logos, the very one "which we have heard, which we have seen with our eyes, which we have looked upon and touched with our hands."'[81] Christ is mankind's principle and end; He is the one preceding us as Creator and the one fulfilling the goal of humanity on our behalf. Jesus is the same essence as the Father according to His divinity, and He is the same essence as us according

---

80. ibid., 242.

81. John R. Betz, *Christ the Logos of Creation: An Essay in Analogical Metaphysics* (Steubenville, OH; Emmaus Academic, 2023), 3. Betz continues elsewhere, 'Accordingly, we will need to keep in mind that the Logos is not just the "Word" of creation but also its "Reason," "Ground," and "Principle," which is also to say, in keeping with ancient usage, its "Purpose" and "End"' (Betz, 18). See also Betz, 7.

to His humanity, but He is the perfect representation of that which a human essence can be – the image of the invisible God and the goal of image bearers. As such, being made in the 'image of Christ' is to become more human, developing in genuine being, goodness, and truth.

The Analogy of Truth

If there exists a transcendental-analogical participation, and the 'true' is treated as a transcendental property of being, then a participatory theory of truth must be predicated in terms of analogy. This connection between transcendental participation and analogical predications means that human discourse is, in the thought of Boersma, similar to a sacrament. 'Human discourse,' writes Boersma, 'participates in divine truth, so that God's truth is really present in the dogmatic statements of the church; on the other hand … the mystery of divine truth infinitely transcends the human words themselves.'[82] Analogical truth, then, 'implies real heavenly participation, while at the same time it retains infinite divine transcendence.'[83]

Furthermore, if human language must be analogical as it pertains to the divine, and truth and divinity are inseparable as proposed in Chapter 1, then analogical predication should play a role in an accurate theory of truth. Human knowledge and propositional truth, then, are inescapably 'both-and.' It simultaneously fulfills its intent and is capable of grasping truth, but the truth available to humanity will always fall short of the transcendent ground of truth. This finitude does not mean, however, that human knowledge is a façade, as if creaturely truth was equivocal with the First Truth. Rather, it simply means that creaturely truth is a limited and analogical reflection of truth as it exists in God. Boersma continues:

> The 'analogy of truth' notion maintains that one can speak not only of an analogous or sacramental relationship between the *being* of God and that of the creature, but also of an analogous or sacramental relationship between the *truth* of God and of the creature. Indeed one could say of each of the three eternal transcendentals – truth, goodness, and beauty – that they are

---

82. Boersma, *Heavenly Participation*, 164. Boersma believes that the analogy of truth follows both the *nouvelle théologie* as well as the work of the Cappadocian Fathers (Boersma, *Heavenly Participation*, 164).

83. ibid., 164.

reflected in earthly truth, goodness, and beauty. Put differently, human truth, goodness, and beauty participate sacramentally in heavenly truth, goodness, and beauty.[84]

Transcendental-analogical participation is on full display in Boersma's analysis. If there exists an analogy of being, then an analogy of truth will closely follow, as 'truth, goodness, and unity ... were "basically being itself in its relationship to intelligence, appetite, and self-possession."'[85] As such, propositional truth statements should not be understood as univocal concepts capable of serving as the middle term between God and man. Truth exists in God simply and without any mixture of error, whereas creaturely truth statements are always dependent, complex, and deficient 'just as all human beings [are] complex and deficient.'[86]

Again, this analysis does not render creaturely truth obsolete or false but rather just means that human truth is not divine. Creatures possess genuine being, even if this being is analogical when compared to the transcendental being of God. Likewise, analogical truth is genuine truth, but it is a creaturely mode of truth, and human beings simply cannot rise above their mode of being. The idea of human beings inventing or creating truth, then, would require the crossing of the Creator-creature divide. Rather, readers should acknowledge with John Calvin

> that not a particle of light, or wisdom, or justice, or power, or rectitude, or *genuine truth*, will anywhere be found, which does not flow from him, and of which he is not the cause; in this way we must learn to expect and ask all things from him, and thankfully ascribe to him whatever we receive.[87]

The divine essence, as the first cause and the ground of all being, must be that in which all creaturely truth participates. To further this concept, readers may refer to the intermediary between God and man

---

84. ibid., 164.

85. Hans Boersma, 'Analogy of Truth: The Sacramental Epistemology of Nouvelle Théologie,' in *Ressourcement: A Movement for Renewal in Twentieth-Century Catholic Theology*, ed. Gabriel Flynn and Paul D. Murray (Oxford: Oxford University Press, 2011), 168. Boersma quotes Jean Marie Le Blond, 'L'Analogie de la Vérité: Réflexion d'un Philosophe sur une Controverse Théologique,' *Recherches de Science Religieuse* 34 (1947): 130.

86. Boersma, 'Analogy of Truth,' 168.

87. John Calvin, *Institutes of the Christian Religion*, trans. Henry Beveridge (Peabody, MA: Hendrickson Publishing, 2008), 2.1, 7.

already discussed – the divine Ideas. Thomas states that '[n]atural things mediate between God's knowledge and ours; for we get our knowledge from natural things, of which God is the cause through his knowledge' (Aquinas, *ST* 1.14.8 ad 3). If God's knowledge of natural things is the cause of those things, this means that God's knowledge is also the measure of those things, 'in the same way a house mediates between the knowledge of the architect who made it and that of one who gets his knowledge of the house from the house itself once it is made' (Aquinas, *ST* 1.14.8 ad 3). Knowledge of natural objects existing in creation allows humans to receive an analogical insight into the mind of God.

As such, participatory truth and analogical predication are closely aligned with divine exemplarism. 'In the production of any thing,' writes Thomas, 'an exemplar is necessary so that an effect may receive a determinate form; for an artisan produces a determinate form in matter according to the exemplar to which he looks ...' (Aquinas, *ST* 1.44.3). These determinate forms, however, must be traced back to the first cause, namely, divine Wisdom.[88] Thomas continues: 'We must say that in the divine wisdom there are notions of all things, which we have previously called "ideas" – that is, exemplar forms existing in the divine mind' (Aquinas, *ST* 1.44.3). Exemplarism, then, provides creation with all of its forms and, as such, 'provides a necessary epistemological and ontological account of the order of reality.'[89]

Doolan explains: 'As regards their ontological role, the divine ideas account for the determination of form and the directedness of nature.'[90] Without divine exemplarism, then, it would seem that creation would either be the result of random chance or the fruit of necessary emanation, both of which Thomas rejects. As regards the epistemological role,

---

88. 'Both kinds of truth – truth of the intellect and truth of a thing – are reduced or traced back to God as to their first principle. This is because God's being is the cause of all other being (*esse*) and his understanding is the cause of all other knowing. Therefore he is the first truth just as he is the first being, for each and every thing stands in relation to truth just as it does to being (*esse*). It is for this reason, Thomas continues, that Aristotle shows in *Metaphysics*, volume 2, that the first cause of being is identical with the first cause of truth and true to the maximum degree. (This passage is interesting, for in it Thomas can see some justification for finding a theory of truth of being in Aristotle as well as a theory of truth of intellect.)' (Wippel, 'Truth in Thomas Aquinas,' 298).

89. Doolan, 250.

90. ibid., 251.

divine exemplarism grounds the forms in the divine essence, allowing an eternal confidence in the availability of truth. Thomas explains:

> The second argument, concerning the eternity of the truth which the soul understands, calls for a distinction. In one way, this eternity can be taken to refer to the thing understood; in another, to that by which it is understood. In the first case, the thing understood would be eternal, but not the one who understands; in the second, eternity would be on the side of the soul which understands. Now, the understood truth is eternal, not in the latter but in the former reference; since as we have already clearly shown, the intelligible species, whereby our soul understands truth, come to us repeatedly from the phantasms through the operation of the agent intellect. It cannot, then, be inferred that the soul is eternal, but *that the truths understood are based upon something eternal; for, indeed, their foundation is in the first truth, as in the universal cause embracing all truth.* But the soul stands in relation to this eternal entity, not as subject to form, but as thing to proper end, since the true is the good of the intellect, and its end. (Aquinas, *SCG* 2.84.4)[91]

Participation in a likeness of the divine essence through a creature's correspondence to the respective divine Idea not only makes truth knowable, but it makes truth possible. In thinking of truth in this way, truth's availability to all rational souls is defended, God's transcendent, *a se*, independence is protected, and Protestants reclaim their own participation in a long-held tradition.

Conclusion

There are certain positions a Christian must take concerning the doctrine of God if he wishes to make use of Thomas's theological system. First, it has been repeatedly demonstrated that Thomas was especially convinced of an absolute divine independence. God is a transcendent being completely unformed, or un-in-formed, by His creation. To suggest otherwise does not only compromise God's

---

91. For Aristotle, see *Metaphysics* 2.1.993b23-31: 'Now we do not know a truth without its cause; and a thing has a quality in a higher degree than other things if in virtue of it the similar quality belongs to the other things (e.g. fire is the hottest. Of things; for it is the cause of the heat of all other things); so that which causes derivative truths to be true is most true. Therefore the principles of eternal things must be always most true; for they are not merely sometimes true, nor is there any cause of their being, but they themselves are the cause of the being of other things, so that as each thing is in respect of being, so is it in respect of truth' (Barnes, 2:1570).

transcendence but also jeopardizes divine simplicity, immutability, and God's pure actuality.

Second, the divine Ideas serve a mediatorial position between God's knowledge, God's essence, and God's creation. All creaturely essences have their corresponding blueprint within the mind of God through which He works to bring about the essences of creatures. He is truly the exemplar cause, which also means He is the efficient, final, and when properly understood, formal cause of all creaturely being. The divine Ideas help explain how God can serve as a type of formal cause without entering into composition with His creatures.

Third, a strong doctrine of divine simplicity positions God as the absolute Truth. Since the object of divine knowledge, the divine knower, and the act of divine knowledge are all the same in God, then God serves as the perfect correspondence between intellect and reality. God is the primary truth that Thomas's Fourth Way inclines readers to affirm. 'God's act of knowing,' writes Thomas Joseph White, 'is subsistent and is pure actuality. Furthermore, God is not qualified intellectually by the relation to another reality, by which he might become a more adequate kind of knower, and upon which he depends.'[92]

The theory of truth, which stands most in line with these previous commitments, is the participatory theory outlined above. Human truth statements truly do correspond with objects in reality, but this only matters because objects in reality correspond with a likeness of the divine essence. Likewise, truth statements are truly unified, as the coherentist view of truth proclaims, because being is truly unified in God and shared with creation. One may even say that truth statements are those that lead to a proper end, similar to the pragmatic view, because God serves not only as the efficient exemplary cause but is the final cause of all being. Thus, one can see the emphasis of the transcendentals in the various theories of truth. However, these transcendentals should not be emphasized individually but corporately, which is the ultimate advantage of the participatory theory. Human truth is analogical, but this analogical existence is ultimately a good thing because it means that truth is grounded in a participation in the likeness of divine essence. Indeed, as White concludes, 'Precisely

---

92. Thomas Joseph White, *Wisdom in the Face of Modernity*, 278.

because God alone knows the perfect plenitude of being that is his divine essence (his subsistent wisdom), he in turn knows all that derives from himself. As contemplative wisdom, God knows the created order through the medium of his divine essence without having to "exit" from himself, learn from another, or undergo any progressive noetic melioration through dependence upon another.'[93]

Indeed, this participatory theory can help readers understand how God is Truth and why Jesus proclaimed Himself to be the Truth. God is the perfect coherent and good correspondence between the act of knowledge, the object of knowledge, and the knower. Furthermore, the Son perfectly corresponds to the Father and holds within Himself the forms of all creaturely being. As such, the Son, as Truth, serves as a bridge between God and man and can fix the modern divide between metaphysics and epistemology. Truth is an entirely theocentric enterprise, in which creatures are blessed to participate.

---

93. ibid., 279.

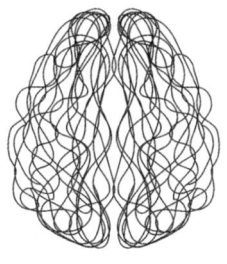

CHAPTER NINE

Concluding Remarks

The Thomistic model of the divine intellect provides an eternal, immutable, and genuinely good foundation for the existence and intelligibility of metaphysical truth. The God of pure act *is* being itself and is thus more real than even the most accurate interpretation of reality. The simple and omniscient God is simultaneously the knower, His act of knowing, and His own knowledge, which has led generations of Christians to confess Him as the Truth. The truth of creaturely beings, then, stems from their participation in the divine perfections through the divine Ideas. After summarizing the main claims put forth in the preceding chapters, we will conclude with a few practical and pastoral implications.

Summary of Argument

First, Chapter 1 highlighted the divinity–truth connection. The divinity–truth connection is an innate, frequently unexpressed but understood relationship between the concept of metaphysical truth and the nature of God. Scripture repeatedly emphasizes this connection either through associating the divine persons with the concept of truth or inserting truth as a divine name (Spirit of Truth, Jesus's identification as the Truth). Likewise, even secular and atheistic voices can recognize, and do at times articulate, the rational relationship between God and truth. A theologian's or philosopher's understanding of divinity will necessarily and ubiquitously affect his stance on the existence and nature of truth. It is unsurprising, then, that Christians have argued for the existence of God based on the universal acceptance of truth and have, at other times, argued for the existence of Truth based on the affirmation of God's existence.

The need for theological retrieval was also addressed in Chapter 1. Modern and postmodern philosophical presuppositions have separated metaphysics from epistemology. A return to premodern sources is helpful in alleviating one's personal, often unaddressed, philosophical assumptions and draws attention to theological shortcomings inherent in modernity and postmodernity. Since the rise of modernity is often linked to events occurring toward the end of the medieval period, Thomas was suggested as a prime candidate for retrieval who could help move contemporary discussion forward.

Second, as discussed in Chapter 2, the twentieth century witnessed an increase of relational models of theism which emphasize the mutual dependence between God and creation. These models, which have been classified as instances of theistic mutualism, all identify the object of divine knowledge as content external to the divine essence. Consequently, these models greatly depart from the classical Thomistic model of theism, which emphasizes divine transcendence, aseity, and independence. In the Thomistic model, the true object of divine knowledge is the divine essence itself. Indeed, in light of divine simplicity, Thomas argues that there is no distinction between the object of God's knowledge, the operation of the divine intellect, and the divine knower Himself. As belief in an externalized model of divine knowledge became the common belief, various concepts of metaphysical truth arose, including coherentism and pragmatism. If the object of divine knowledge is external to God, then one can see why the alternative models of truth are attractive. Indeed, even a traditional correspondence theory of truth, frequently associated with Christianity, stands at risk of becoming creaturely focused as God is increasingly understood as the perfect interpreter of external facts. Instead of defending a theory of truth grounded in creation, we have focused upon the participational metaphysics of truth stemming from God's independent, transcendent, and *a se* self-knowledge.

Chapter 3 then turned to demonstrate the legitimacy of the task at hand, namely a Protestant theological retrieval of Thomas's doctrine of God. The influence of Thomas on the early Reformers, Protestant

Scholastics, and the Puritans was demonstrated, and the contemporary literature was shown to note a shift regarding the development of Protestant thought. Specifically, the 'Calvin against the Calvinists' model, which had been on the forefront of this discussion, has been overtaken by an appreciation of Protestant retrieval and critique of Thomas. As such, earlier depictions of Thomas as the enemy of Protestantism do not do justice to the skilled balance of acceptance and denial of Thomistic conclusions present in Protestant works. A critical retrieval of classical and catholic works is at the very heart of Protestantism.

Chapter 3 also identified the core beliefs of Thomism that are pertinent to the current discussion. Philosophical principles such as the division of being into act and potency, analogical predication, and Aristotelian causation were discussed. Theological principles such as Nicene Trinitarianism and a classical understanding of the divine attributes were also affirmed. Additionally, in order to separate Reformed Thomism from Catholic Thomism, two other categories were examined – the function of Scripture in theological method and the affirmation of Reformed confessionalism. In order for Protestants to retrieve Thomas, it will, at times, need to be a critical retrieval based on the ultimate authority of Scripture. This affirmation of Scripture's primacy in theology, of course, would be affirmed and expected by Thomas and does not represent a major departure from Thomas's theological method.

Chapter 4 set out the specific theological aspects of the doctrine of God that are to be retrieved from Thomas, namely, his understanding of the divine intellect. Thomas's exposition of the divine intellect as presented in the *Summa Theologiæ* was explained with an eye toward the proper object of divine knowledge, the divine essence. Truth was shown to exist primarily in God as the perfect conformity between agent, operation, and intellectual content. It was shown that God's transcendent knowledge was in no way dependent upon external factors for its intellectual content.

In Chapter 5, the doctrines of the divine Ideas, participation, and the analogy of being were examined. Since creatures must possess perfections either via their own essence or through participation, it was concluded that creaturely truth is participated truth. There necessarily exists a correspondence between a creature and its respective divine idea. This relationship produces an analogical understanding of truth that can be trusted and approved by creatures. While one cannot know truth as God knows it, this does not mean that creatures cannot know truth at all. Humans instead can know creaturely analogical truth, which is entirely appropriate for a creaturely mode of existence and operation. In the end, it has been shown that a participatory model of truth should accompany a correct belief in an *a se*, transcendent divine omniscience.

Acts 17 teaches its readers that all creatures live, move, and have their being in the transcendent God who has bridged the metaphysical–epistemological divide. If creaturely being comes from God, as Paul has taught, then creaturely goodness and truth must come from God as well. Indeed, all creaturely being, goodness, truth, and beauty owe their existence to an exemplar cause within the mind of God. As God has granted humanity the ability to abstract these forms, our knowledge of truth and our knowledge of the God of Truth becomes possible. Truth, then, is grounded in a most secure foundation – the God not served by human hands.

Pastoral Application

Aligning one's soul with Truth results in right practice, so it is fitting to end on a note of practical application. First, because of God's good omniscience genuine, objective, transcendental truth exists. We are not left to our own devices in a world of intellectual chaos but can pursue the chief end of our minds with hope of actually accomplishing the task. The truth *is* out there. Perspectives, of course, vary among people groups, faith traditions, and even individuals, but this variety of interpretation does not negate the universality and objectivity of truth. The knower is capable of transcending the boundaries of their intellectual upbringing as creaturely truth guides these sojourners further up and further in the Truth.

Second, truth is knowable. As image bearers gifted with rational souls, we may tap into the creaturely being of others in a unique way. We are not limited to a conceptual world of our own making but can actually interact with the world as it is. Furthermore, the knowledge obtained through our intellectual friendship with the world is not a cold or sterile knowledge but one brimming with dynamic goodness and beauty.

The being, life, breath, and existence of all creaturely reality is a gift that flows from the goodness of our Creator, and human beings can celebrate and participate in this goodness by the right use of our minds. A popular caricature depicts the knowledgeable man as aloof, discontent, and frustrated with the state of the world, but this picture of a 'scholar' stands in stark contrast with the joyful God-ordained structure of reality. The more you know, the more goodness you come to recognize, and the more beauty you begin to appreciate, even in a world distorted by sin. Rather than secularism's grumpy genius, the wise man need not be marked by a state of constant resentfulness but a deep and sometimes confusing cheerfulness.

Third, by recognizing the forms and secondary causes of the world around us, our recognition of the First Cause can grow as well. The intimate link between the divine Ideas and creaturely natures can prevent us from elevating the gift over the giver. The goodness, beauty, and yes, even truth of the world around us is a limited reflection of the fountain of all being. The created world encourages mankind to 'seek God, if perhaps they might grope for Him and find Him, though He is not far from each one of us; for in Him we live and move and exist …' (Acts 17:27-28). The transcendent Creator is exceptionally close to all creatures and our very souls, forms, and natures testify to our divine exemplar cause. The link between creation and the divine Ideas does not necessitate a salvific form of rationalism, as if mankind could reason our way to the Trinity and the incarnation, but does render man without excuse as divinity is actively involved with and reflected by all creaturely being.

Finally, readers should apply the weight of these claims to their own being. God's perfect knowledge of our being – your nature and mine – existed before we did. His perfect will worked through the divine Ideas to produce individual creatures, and each individual exists as a manifestation of God's goodness. Even though none of us have attained perfect likeness of our exemplar cause, we currently reflect a genuine likeness of our Creator, and the God who creates out of pure freedom is pleased by this truth. The goodness, truth, and beauty that fills the whole world did not skip over you!

This reality, however, must not produce sloth or necessitate affirmation of our sins, as if these acts of rebellion were simply the by-product of how God made us. Indeed, as God calls us to Himself He is also calling us to a higher and truer form of ourselves. As we grow in the image of Christ, we grow in likeness to that which we were always intended to be. So, while we currently participate in goodness, truth, and beauty, we can expect greater participation in these realities as the Spirit leads and moves us through sanctification.

These two truths help us mediate between two possible conclusions: (1) While we are sinful and in need of redemption, the goodness of our being is not totally eradicated. This goodness is not the product of our white-knuckle efforts or merit but the result of our First Cause. It is good to be a person, and sin will never completely overtake that goodness. God's creation through the divine Ideas ensures that mankind reflects our divine benefactor, even after the Fall. (2) Affirmation of our individual goodness does not eliminate an external standard by which we are measured. Christ is both true God, in that He is the image of the invisible God, and true man, in that He took on a real human nature and demonstrated what humanity was always designed to be. His life testifies to our failings and prevents us from believing that we set the bar for humanity's divine reflection. In this way, we acknowledge that we possess and reflect real goodness, but it is a little 'g' goodness. Likewise, the truth that surrounds us is as genuine as any creaturely reality, but the standard of little 't' truth is the Truth standing behind it, granting it life.

The existence of a Truth not served by human hands, then, is very good news for humanity. Knowability and even relational knowledge is embedded into every aspect of the cosmos. Human beings are not left to manufacture truth, as if its existence was dependent upon our innovations, but can happily receive that which God is pleased to share. Creaturely truth reflects divine Truth by the means of God's creation through His perfect will and intellect. A retrieval of doctrines such as God's independent omniscience and the divine Ideas can lead us to a rediscovery of truth's objective existence and knowability. In light of this reality, we can echo Thomas's words that opened this project: '*The ultimate end of the universe must, therefore, be the good of an intellect. This good is truth.*'

Bibliography

Adler, Mortimer J. *Aristotle for Everybody: Difficult Thought Made Easy.* Touchstone ed. New York: Simon & Schuster Inc., 1997.

Allen, Michael and Scott R. Swain, eds. *Christian Dogmatics: Reformed Theology for the Church Catholic.* Grand Rapids: Baker Academic, 2016.

———. *Reformed Catholicity: The Promise of Retrieval for Theology and Biblical Interpretation.* Grand Rapids: Baker Academic, 2015.

Anselm. *On Truth. Anselm of Canterbury: The Major Works.* Edited by Brian Davies and G. R. Evans. Oxford World's Classics. Oxford: Oxford University Press, 2008.

Aquinas, Thomas. *An Exposition of the 'On the Hebdomads' of Boethius.* Translated by Janice L. Schultz and Edward A. Synan. Thomas Aquinas in Translation. Washington, DC: The Catholic University of America Press, 2001.

———. *Aquinas: Selected Philosophical Writings.* Translated by Timothy McDermott. Oxford World's Classics. 2008 Oxford World's Classics paperback ed. Oxford: Oxford University Press, 1993.

———. *Commentary on Colossians.* Edited by Daniel Keating. Translated by Fabian Larcher. Naples, FL: Sapientia Press, 2006.

———. *Commentary on Isaiah.* Translated by Louis St. Hilaire. Steubenville, OH: Emmaus Academic, 2021.

———. *Commentary on the Gospel of John.* Translated by Fabian Larcher and James A. Weisheipl. 3 vols. Thomas Aquinas in Translation. Washington, DC: The Catholic University of America Press, 2010.

————. *Compendium of Theology*. Translated by Richard J. Regan. Oxford: Oxford University Press, 2009.

————. *Disputed Questions on Truth*. Translated by Robert W. Mulligan, James V. McGlynn, and Robert Schmidt. 3 vols. Chicago: Henry Regnery Company, 1952.

————. *On Being and Essence*. Translated by Armand Maurer. Toronto: Pontifical Institute of Mediaeval Studies, 1968.

————. *Summa Theologiæ*. Vol. 1 (1a.1), *Christian Theology*. Translated by Thomas Gilby. 62 vols. Cambridge: Cambridge University Press, 2006.

————. *Summa Theologiæ*. Vol. 2 (1a2–11), *Existence and Nature of God*. Translated by Timothy McDermott. 62 vols. Cambridge: Cambridge University Press, 2006.

————. *Summa Theologiæ*. Vol. 3 (1a12–13), *Knowing and Naming God*. Translated by Herbert McCabe. 62 vols. Cambridge: Cambridge University Press, 2006.

————. *Summa Theologiæ*. Vol. 4 (1a14–18), *Knowledge in God*. Translated by Thomas Gornall. Cambridge paperback. 62 vols. Cambridge: Cambridge University Press, 2006.

————. *Summa Theologiæ*. Vol. 8 (1a44–49), *Creation, Variety and Evil*. Translated by Thomas Gilby. 62 vols. Cambridge: Cambridge University Press, 2006.

————. *Summa Theologiæ*. Vol. 12 (1a84–89), *Human Intelligence*. Translated by Paul T. Durbin. 62 vols. Cambridge: Cambridge University Press, 2006.

————. *Summa Theologiæ*. Vol. 13 (1a90–102), *Man Made to God's Image*. Translated by Edmund Hill. 62 vols. Cambridge: Cambridge University Press, 2006.

Aristotle. *Metaphysics*. Vol. 2, *The Complete Works of Aristotle*. Edited by Jonathan Barnes. Princeton, NJ: Princeton University Press, 1984.

Armstrong, Chris R. *Medieval Wisdom for Modern Christians: Finding Authentic Faith in a Forgotten Age with C. S. Lewis*. Grand Rapids: Brazos Press, 2016.

Augustine. *Against the Academicians and the Teacher*. Translated by Peter King. Indianapolis: Hackett Publishing Company, Inc, 1995.

———. *Eighty-Three Different Questions*. Translated by David L. Mosher. The Fathers of the Church. Washington, DC: The Catholic University of America Press, Burleigh. The Library of Christian Classics. Louisville: Westminster John Knox Press, 2006.

———. *On Christian Doctrine*. Translated by J. F. Shaw. Mineola, NY: Dover Publications, 2009.

———. *On Order*. Translated by Silvano Borruso. South Bend, IN: St. Augustine's Press, 2007.

———. *On the Free Choice of the Will, On Grace and Free Choice, and Other Writings*. Edited and translated by Peter King. Cambridge Texts in the History of Philosophy. Cambridge: Cambridge University Press, 2010.

———. *The City of God against the Pagans*. Edited and translated by R. W. Dyson. 3rd printing. Cambridge Texts in the History of Political Thought. Cambridge: Cambridge University Press, 2018.

———. *The Soliloquies. Earlier Writings*. Edited and translated by J. H. S. Burleigh. The Library of Christian Classics. Louisville: Westminster John Knox Press, 2006.

———. *The Trinity*. The Works of Saint Augustine. 2nd ed. Edited by John E. Rotelle. Translated by Edmund Hill. Hyde Park: New City Press, 2015.

———. *The Usefulness of Belief. Earlier Writings*. Edited and translated by J. H. S. Burleigh. The Library of Christian Classics. Louisville: Westminster John Knox Press, 2006.

———. *Tractates on the Gospel of John 1-10*. Vol. 1. Translated by John W. Rettig. 2 vols. The Fathers of the Church: A New Translation, vol. 78. Washington, DC: The Catholic University of America Press, 1988.

Ball, James. *Post-Truth: How Bull**** Conquered the World*. London: Biteback, 2018.

Barr, James. *Fundamentalism*. Philadelphia: Westminster, 1978.

Barrett, C. K. *The Gospel According to St. John*. Louisville: Westminster John Knox Press, 1958.

Barrett, Matthew. *Simply Trinity: The Unmanipulated Father, Son, and Spirit*. Grand Rapids: Baker Books, 2021.

Basinger, David and Randall Basinger, eds. *Predestination and Free Will: Four Views*. Spectrum Multiview Books. Downers Grove: IVP Academic, 1986.

Bauerschmidt, Frederick Christian. *The Essential Summa Theologiae: A Reader and Commentary*. 2nd ed. Grand Rapids: Baker Academic, 2021.

Bavinck, Herman. *Reformed Dogmatics*. Vol. 2, *God and Creation*. Edited by John Bolt. Translated by John Vriend. Grand Rapids: Baker Academic, 2004.

Beeke, Joel and Paul M. Smalley. *Reformed Systematic Theology*. Vol. 1, *Revelation and God*. Wheaton: Crossway, 2019.

Beilby, James K. and Paul R. Eddy, eds. *Divine Foreknowledge: Four Views*. Spectrum Multiview Books. Downers Grove: IVP Academic, 2001.

Bell, Bernard Iddings. *Postmodernism and Other Essays*. Harrisburg: Morehouse Publishing Co., 1926.

Bergmann, Michael and Jeffrey Brower. 'A Theistic Argument against Platonism (and in Support of Truthmakers and Divine Simplicity).' In *Oxford Studies in Metaphysics*, 2:357-85. Oxford: Oxford University Press, 2006.

Berkhof, Louis. *Systematic Theology*. New combined ed. Grand Rapids: William B. Eerdmans Publishing Company, 1996.

Betz, John R. *Christ, the Logos of Creation: An Essay in Analogical Metaphysics*. Steubenville: Emmaus Academic, 2023.

Blackburn, Simon. *On Truth*. Oxford: Oxford University Press, 2018.

Boersma, Hans. 'Analogy of Truth: The Sacramental Epistemology of Nouvelle Théologie.' In *Ressourcement: A Movement for Renewal in Twentieth-Century Catholic Theology*, edited by Gabriel Flynn and Paul D. Murray, 157-71. Oxford: Oxford University Press, 2011.

―――. *Five Things Theologians Wish Biblical Scholars Knew*. Downers Grove: IVP Academic, 2021.

―――. *Heavenly Participation: The Weaving of a Sacramental Tapestry*. Grand Rapids: William B. Eerdmans Publishing Company, 2011.

―――. 'The Sacramental Reading of Nicene Theology: Athanasius and Gregory of Nyssa on Proverbs 8.' *Journal of Theological Interpretation* 10, no. 1 (2016): 1-30.

Boland, Vivian. *Studies in the History of Christian Thought*. Vol. 69, *Ideas in God According to Saint Thomas Aquinas: Sources and Synthesis*. New York: E. J. Brill, 1996.

Bordeianu, Radu. 'Maximus and Ecology: The Relevance of Maximus the Confessor's Theology of Creation for the Present Ecological Crisis.' *Downside Review* 127, no. 447 (April 2009): 103-26.

Boyd, Gregory A. *God of the Possible: A Biblical Introduction to the Open View of God*. Grand Rapids: Baker Books, 2000.

Buschart, W. David and Kent D. Eilers. *Theology as Retrieval: Receiving the Past, Renewing the Church*. Downers Grove: IVP Academic, 2015.

Carson, D. A. *The Gospel According to John*. Pillar New Testament Commentary. Grand Rapids: William B. Eerdmans Publishing Company, 1991.

Carter, Craig A. *Contemplating God with the Great Tradition: Recovering Trinitarian Classical Theism*. Grand Rapids: Baker Academic, 2021.

―――. *Interpreting Scripture with the Great Tradition: Recovering the Genius of Premodern Exegesis*. Grand Rapids: Baker Academic, 2018.

Cessario, Romanus. *A Short History of Thomism*. English ed. Washington, DC: The Catholic University of America Press, 2005.

Chesterton, G. K. *St. Thomas Aquinas*. Mansfield Center, CT: Martino Publishing, 2011.

Clark, D. K. 'Truth.' *Evangelical Dictionary of Theology*. 2nd edition. Edited by Walter A. Elwell. Grand Rapids: Baker Academic, 2001. 1219-20.

Clarke, W. Norris. 'Analogy and the Meaningfulness of Language about God.' In *Explorations in Metaphysics: Being, God, Person*, 123-49. Notre Dame, IN: University of Notre Dame Press, 1994.

―――. 'The Limitation of Act by Potency in St. Thomas: Aristotelianism or Neoplatonism?' In *Explorations in Metaphysics: Being, God, Person*, 65-88. Notre Dame, IN: University of Notre Dame Press, 1994.

―――. 'The Meaning of Participation in St. Thomas.' In *Explorations in Metaphysics: Being, God, Person*, 89-101. Notre Dame, IN: University of Notre Dame Press, 1994.

―――. 'The Problem of the Reality and Multiplicity of Divine Ideas in Christian Neoplatonism.' In *The Creative Retrieval of Saint Thomas Aquinas: Essays in Thomistic Philosophy, New and Old*, 66-88. New York: Fordham University Press, 2009.

Cleveland, Christopher. *Thomism in John Owen*. New York: Routledge, 2013.

Cobb, John B., Jr. *A Christian Natural Theology: Based on the Thought of Alfred North Whitehead*. 2nd ed. Louisville: Westminster John Knox Press, 2007.

―――. and Clark H. Pinnock, eds. *Searching for an Adequate God: A Dialogue between Process and Free Will Theists*. Grand Rapids: William B. Eerdmans, 2000.

Cooper, Jordan. *In Defense of the True, the Good, and the Beautiful: On the Loss of Transcendence and the Decline of the West*. Ithaca: Just and Sinner, 2021.

Coppins, McKay. 'A Carnival of Disinformation: Republicans Warmly Welcomed Voters into Their Post-Truth Convention.' *The Atlantic*, August 28, 2020, https://www.theatlantic.com/politics/archive/2020/08/trumps-rnc-was-loaded-disinformation/615838/.

Craig, William Lane. *God over All: Divine Aseity and the Challenge of Platonism*. Oxford: Oxford University Press, 2016.

―――. 'Propositional Truth—Who Needs It?' *Philosophia Christa* 15, no. 2 (2013): 355-65.

————. *The Only Wise God: The Compatibility of Divine Foreknowledge and Human Freedom*. Eugene: Wipf & Stock, 2000.

Davies, Brian. *Post-Truth: Why We Have Reached Peak Bull**** and What We Can Do About It*. Boston: Little, Brown, & Company, 2017.

————. *The Thought of Thomas Aquinas*. Oxford: Clarendon Press, 1993.

————. *Thomas Aquinas's Summa Contra Gentiles: A Guide and Commentary*. Oxford: Oxford University Press, 2016.

Davison, Andrew. *Participation in God: A Study in Christian Doctrine and Metaphysics*. Paperback ed. New York: Cambridge University Press, 2020.

————. *The Love of Wisdom: An Introduction to Philosophy for Theologians*. London: SCM Press, 2013.

DeSpain, Benjamin R. *Thinking Theologically about the Divine Ideas: Reexamining the Summa of Thomas Aquinas*. Brill's Series in Catholic Theology 11. Leiden: Brill, 2021.

Dew, James K. and Mark W. Foreman. *How Do We Know? An Introduction to Epistemology*. Downers Grove: IVP, 2014.

Dewan, Lawrence. 'St. Thomas and Analogy: The Logician and the Metaphysician.' In *Form and Being: Studies in Thomistic Metaphysics*, 81-95. Washington, DC: The Catholic University of America Press, 2006.

Dodds, Michael J. *The One Creator God in Thomas Aquinas and Contemporary Theology*. Washington, DC: The Catholic University of America Press, 2020.

Dolezal, James E. *All That Is in God: Evangelical Theology and the Challenge of Classical Christian Theism*. Grand Rapids: Reformation Heritage Books, 2017.

————. *God without Parts: Divine Simplicity and the Metaphysics of God's Absoluteness*. Eugene: Pickwick, 2011.

Donnelly, John Patrick. *Calvinism and Scholasticism in Vermigli's Doctrine of Man and Grace*. Leiden: E. J. Brill, 1976.

————. 'Calvinist Thomism,' in *Viator* 7 (1976): 441-55.

Doolan, Gregory T. *Aquinas on the Divine Ideas as Exemplar Causes.* Reprint ed. Washington, DC: The Catholic University of America Press, 2014.

Duby, Steven J. *Divine Simplicity: A Dogmatic Account.* Paperback ed. Edited by John Webster, Ian A. McFarland, and Ivor Davidson. T & T Clark Studies in Systematic Theology 30 New York: T&T Clark, 2018.

———. "'For I am God, Not a Man'": Divine Repentance and the Creator-Creature Distinction.' *Journal of Theological Interpretation* 12, no. 2 (2018): 149-169.

———. *God in Himself: Scripture, Metaphysics, and the Task of Christian Theology.* Studies in Christian Doctrine and Scripture. Downers Grove: IVP Academic, 2019.

Dunne, John S. 'St. Thomas' Theology of Participation.' *Theological Studies* 18, no. 4 (December 1957): 487-512.

Emery, Gilles. *The Trinitarian Theology of Saint Thomas Aquinas.* Translated by Francesca Aran Murphy. New York: Oxford University Press, 2007.

———. *The Trinity: An Introduction to Catholic Doctrine on the Triune God.* Translated by Matthew Levering. Thomistic Ressourcement Series 1. Washington, DC: The Catholic University of America Press, 2011.

Erickson, Millard J., Paul Kjoss Helseth, and Justin Taylor, eds. *Reclaiming the Center: Confronting Evangelical Accommodation in Postmodern Times.* Wheaton: Crossway, 2004.

Evans, C. Stephen. 'Wisdom as Conceptual Understanding: A Christian Platonist Perspective.' *Faith and Philosophy* 27, no. 4 (October 2010): 369-81.

Fabro, Cornelio. 'The Intensive Hermeneutics of Thomistic Philosophy: The Notion of Participation.' Translated by B. M. Bonansea. *The Review of Metaphysics* 27, no. 3 (March 1974): 449-91.

Feinberg, John S. *No One Like Him: The Doctrine of God.* Foundations of Evangelical Theology. Wheaton: Crossway, 2001.

Feser, Edward. *Aquinas: A Beginner's Guide.* Oneworld Beginner's Guides. 2009. Reprint. London: Oneworld Publications, 2020.

————. *Editiones Scholasticae*. Vol. 39, *Scholastic Metaphysics: A Contemporary Introduction*. Postfach, Heusenstamm: Editiones Scholasticae, 2014.

————. *Five Proofs of the Existence of God*. San Francisco: Ignatius Press, 2017.

————. *The Last Superstition: A Refutation of the New Atheism*. South Bend, IN: St. Augustine's Press, 2008.

Fesko, J. V. *Reforming Apologetics: Retrieving the Classic Reformed Approach to Defending the Faith*. Grand Rapids: Baker Academic, 2019.

Frankfurt, Harry G. *On Bull*****. Princeton: Princeton University Press, 2005.

Geisler, Norman. 'The Concept of Truth in the Inerrancy Debate,' *Bibliotheca Sacra* (1980): 327-39.

————. *Thomas Aquinas: An Evangelical Appraisal*. Eugene: Wipf and Stock Publishers, 2003.

Gerson, Lloyd P. *Aristotle and Other Platonists*. Cornell Paperback Edition. Ithaca, NY: Cornell University Press, 2006.

Gettier, Edmund. 'Is Justified True Belief Knowledge?' *Analysis* 23, no. 6 (1963): 121-23.

Gillespie, Michael Allen. *The Theological Origins of Modernity*. Chicago: The University of Chicago Press, 2008.

Gilson, Etienne. *God and Philosophy*. New Haven, CT: Yale University Press, 2002.

————. *The Christian Philosophy of St. Thomas Aquinas*. New York, NY: Random House, 1956.

————. *Thomist Realism and The Critique of Knowledge*. San Francisco, CA: Ignatius Press, 1983.

Grenz, Stanley J. and John R. Franke. *Beyond Foundationalism: Shaping Theology in a Postmodern Context*. Louisville: Westminster John Knox Press, 2001.

————. and Roger E. Olson. *20th Century Theology: God and the World in a Transitional Age*. Downers Grove: InterVarsity Press, 1992.

————. *A Primer on Postmodernism*. Grand Rapids: William B. Eerdmans, 2006.

————. 'Beyond Foundationalism: Is a Nonfoundationalist Evangelical Theology Possible?' *Christian Scholar's Review* 30, no. 1 (Fall 2000): 57-82.

————. *Reason for Hope: The Systematic Theology of Wolfhart Pannenberg*. 2nd ed. Grand Rapids: William B. Eerdmans, 2005.

————. *Theology for the Community of God*. Grand Rapids: William B. Eerdmans, 2000.

Groothius, Douglas. 'Truth Defined and Defended.' In *Reclaiming the Center: Evangelical Accommodation in Postmodern Times*, edited by Millard J. Erickson, Paul Kjoss Helseth, and Justin Taylor, 59-79. Wheaton: Crossway, 2004.

Gruenler, Royce Gordon. *The Inexhaustible God: Biblical Faith and the Challenge of Process Theism*. Eugene: Wipf & Stock, 1983.

Hankey, W. J. *God in Himself: Aquinas' Doctrine of God as Expounded in the Summa Theologiae*. Oxford Theological Monographs. Oxford: Oxford University Press, 1987.

Hartshorne, Charles. *Omnipotence and Other Theological Mistakes*. Albany: State University of New York Press, 1984.

Hodge, Charles. *Systematic Theology*. Vol. 1, *Theology*. Peabody, MA: Hendrickson Publishing, 2016.

Hoenen, M. J. F. M. *Marsilius of Inghen: Divine Knowledge in Late Medieval Thought*. Studies in the History of Christian Thought 50. Leiden: Brill, 1993.

Hollingsworth, Andrew and Jordan L. Steffaniak. 'Craig Carter on Creatio Ex Nihilo and Classical Theism: Some Objections.' *Philosophia Christi* 23, no. 2 (2021): 249-69.

Holmes, Christopher R. J. *A Theology of the Christian Life: Imitating and Participating in God*. Grand Rapids: Baker Academic, 2021.

Hughes, John. 'Creatio Ex Nihilo and the Divine Ideas in Aquinas: How Fair Is Bulgakov's Critique?' *Modern Theology* 29, no. 2 (April 2013): 124-37.

Hütter, Reinhard. 'Attending to the Wisdom of God, from Effect to Cause, from Creation to God: A "Relecture" of the Analogy of Being According to Thomas Aquinas.' In *The Analogy of Being: Invention of the Antichrist or the Wisdom of God?*, edited by Thomas Joseph White, 209-45. Grand Rapids: William B. Eerdmans Publishing Company, 2011.

Hyman, Arthur, James J. Walsh, and Thomas Williams, eds. *Philosophy in the Middle Ages: The Christian, Islamic, and Jewish Traditions.* 3rd ed. Indianapolis: Hackett Publishing Company, Inc., 2010.

'Is God Dead?' *Time Magazine* 87, no. 14 (1966).

'Is Truth Dead?' *Time Magazine* 189, no. 12 (2017).

James, William *Pragmatism: A New Name for Some Old Ways of Thinking.* Reprint ed. New York: Longmans, Green and Col., 1928.

Johnson, Jeffrey D. *The Failure of Natural Theology: A Critical Appraisal of the Philosophical Theology of Thomas Aquinas.* New Studies in Theology. Conway, AR: Free Grace Press Academic, 2021.

Jordan, Mark D. 'The Intelligibility of the World and the Divine Ideas.' *Review of Metaphysics* 38, no. 1 (September 1984): 17-32.

Junius, Franciscus. *A Treatise on True Theology: With the Life of Franciscus Junius.* Translated by David C. Noe. Grand Rapids: Reformation Heritage Books, 2014.

Kakutani, Michiko. *The Death of Truth: Notes on Falsehood in the Age of Trump.* New York: Tim Duggan Books, 2018.

Kempis, Thomas à. *The Imitation of Christ.* Wheaton: Christian Classics Ethereal Library, 1998.

Kerr, Fergus. *Very Short Introductions.* Vol. 214, *Thomas Aquinas: A Very Short Introduction.* Oxford: Oxford University Press, 2009.

Koterski, Joseph. 'The Doctrine of Participation in Thomistic Metaphysics.' In *The Future of Thomism*, edited by Deal W. Hudson and Dennis W. Moran, 185-96. Notre Dame, IN: University of Notre Dame Press, 1992.

Kreeft, Peter, ed. *Summa of the Summa: The Essential Philosophical Passages of St. Thomas Aquinas' Summa Theologica Edited and Explained for Beginners.* San Francisco: Ignatius Press, 1990.

Levering, Matthew. *Proofs of God: Classical Arguments from Tertullian to Barth.* Grand Rapids: Baker Academic, 2016.

Lewis, C. S. *The Screwtape Letters with Screwtape Proposes a Toast.* HarperCollins Edition. San Francisco: HarperCollins, 2001.

———. 'Transposition.' In *The Weight of Glory*, 208. San Francisco: HarperOne, 2015.

Lyotard, Jean-François. *The Postmodern Condition: A Report on Knowledge.* Minneapolis: University of Minnesota Press, 1984.

Macgregor, Kirk R. *Contemporary Theology: An Introduction.* Grand Rapids: Zondervan, 2019.

Marsh, Harry Clarke, Jr. 'Cosmic Structure and the Knowledge of God: Thomas Aquinas's "In Librum Beati Dionysii de Divinis Nominibus Expositio."' Dissertation, Vanderbilt University, 1994.

Marshall, Bruce D. *Trinity and Truth.* Cambridge *Studies in Christian Doctrine* 3. Cambridge: Cambridge University Press, 2000.

McDuffie, Adam. 'Searching for Truth in a Post-Truth World: The Southern Baptist Schism as Case Study in the Power of Narrative for the Construction of Truth.' *Baptist History and Heritage* 52, no. 2 (2017): 75-90.

McGraw, Ryan M. *Reformed Scholasticism: Recovering the Tools of Reformed Theology.* Paperback edition. New York, NY: T&T Clark, 2020.

McIntosh, Mark A. *The Divine Ideas Tradition in Christian Mystical Theology.* Oxford: Oxford University Press, 2021.

———. 'The Maker's Meaning: Divine Ideas and Salvation.' *Modern Theology* 28, no. 3 (July 2012): 365-84.

McIntyre, Lee. *Post-Truth.* MIT Press Essential Knowledge Series. Cambridge: MIT Press, 2018.

Milbank, John, Catherine Pickstock, and Graham Ward, eds. *Radical Orthodoxy: A New Theology.* New York: Routledge, 1999.

Molina, Luis. *On Divine Foreknowledge: Part IV of the Concordia.* Ithaca: Cornell University Press, 2004.

Moltmann, Jürgen. *God in Creation.* Minneapolis: Fortress Press, 1993.

———. *The Trinity and the Kingdom.* Minneapolis: Fortress Press, 1993.

———. *Theology of Hope.* Minneapolis: Fortress Press, 1993.

Morello, Sebastian. *The World as God's Icon: Creator and Creation in the Platonic Thought of Thomas Aquinas.* Brooklyn: Angelico Press, 2020.

Muller, Richard A. *Post-Reformation Reformed Dogmatics: The Rise and Development of Reformed Orthodoxy, ca. 1520 to ca. 1725.* Second Edition. 4 vols. Grand Rapids, MI: Baker Academic, 2006.

———. 'Reading Aquinas from a Reformed Perspective: A Review Essay.' *Calvin Theological Journal* 53, no. 2 (January 1, 2018): 255-88.

Nash, Ronald H. *Faith and Reason: Searching for a Rational Faith.* Grand Rapids: Zondervan, 1988.

———. *The Concept of God: An Exploration of Contemporary Difficulties with the Attributes of God.* Grand Rapids: Zondervan, 1983.

Nichols, Tom. *The Death of Expertise: The Campaign against Established Knowledge and Why It Matters.* Oxford: Oxford University Press, 2017.

Nieuwenhove, Rik Van. *An Introduction to Medieval Theology.* 2nd ed. Cambridge: Cambridge University Press, 2022.

——— and Joseph Wawrykow, eds. *The Theology of Thomas Aquinas.* Paperback ed. Notre Dame, IN: University of Notre Dame Press, 2005.

Origen. *On First Principles.* Translated by John Behr. Reader's ed. Oxford: Oxford University Press, 2019.

Ortlund, Gavin. *Theological Retrieval for Evangelicals: Why We Need Our Past to Have a Future.* Wheaton: Crossway, 2019.

Oxford Languages. 'Word of the Year 2016.' Accessed February 6, 2020, https://languages.oup.com/word-of-the-year/2016/.

Pannenberg, Wolfhart. *Basic Questions in Theology*. Vol 2. Translated by George H. Kehm. Philadelphia: Fortress Press, 1972.

———. *Systematic Theology*. Vol 1. Paperback edition. Translated by Geoffrey W. Bromiley. Grand Rapids: William B. Eerdmans, 2009.

———. *The Idea of God and Human Freedom*. Philadelphia: Westminster Press, 1973.

Pawl, Timothy J., Jr. 'A Thomistic Account of Truthmakers for Modal Truths.' Dissertation, Saint Louis University, 2008.

Peckham, John C. *Divine Attributes: Knowing the Covenantal God of Scripture*. Grand Rapids: Baker Academic, 2021.

Peirce, Charles Sanders. 'How to Make Our Ideas Clear.' In *Selected Writings (Values in a Universe of Chance)*. Edited by Philip P. Wiener. New York: Dover, 1958.

Pieper, Josef. *The Human Wisdom of St. Thomas: A Breviary of Philosophy from the Works of St. Thomas Aquinas*. Translated by Drostan Maclaren. Reprint ed. San Francisco: Ignatius Press, 2002.

Pine, D. W. 'Is Truth Dead? Behind the Time Cover.' *Time*, March 23, 2017, accessed August 27, 2020, https://time.com/4709920/donald-trump-truth-time-cover/.

Pinnock, Clark H. *Most Moved Mover: A Theology of God's Openness*. Grand Rapids: Baker Academic, 2001.

———. *Reason Enough: A Case for the Christian Faith*. Downers Grove: InterVarsity Press, 1980.

———. *The Openness of God: A Biblical Challenge to the Traditional Understanding of God*. Downers Grove: InterVarsity Press, 1994.

———. *Tracking the Maze: Finding Our Way through Modern Theology from an Evangelical Perspective*. San Francisco: Harper & Row, 1990.

——— and Barry L. Callen. *The Scripture Principle: Reclaiming the Full Authority of the Bible*. 2nd ed. Grand Rapids: Baker Academic, 2006.

Piper, John, Justin Taylor, and Paul Kjoss Helseth, eds. *Beyond the Bounds: Open Theism and the Undermining of Biblical Christianity*. Wheaton: Crossway, 2003.

Plantinga, Alvin. *Does God Have a Nature?* Milwaukee: Marquette University Press, 1980.

———. 'How to Be an Anti-Realist.' *Proceedings and Addresses of the American Philosophical Association* 56, no. 1 (1982): 47-70.

Poythress, Vern S. *Redeeming Mathematics: A God-Centered Approach.* Wheaton: Crossway, 2015.

Pseudo-Dionysius. *Pseudo-Dionysius: The Complete Works.* Translated by Colm Luibheid. The Classics of Western Spirituality. Mahwah, NJ: Paulist Press, 1987.

Quinn, Benjamin T. *Studies in Historical and Systematic Theology.* Vol. 24, *Christ, the Way: Augustine's Theology of Wisdom.* Bellingham, WA: Lexham Academic, 2022.

Renard, Henri. *The Philosophy of Being.* Second edition. Milwaukee: The Bruce Publishing Company, 1947.

Rogers, Katherin A. *Perfect Being Theology.* Reason and Religion Series. Edinburgh: Edinburgh University Press, 2000.

Sanders, John. *The God Who Risks: A Theology of Divine Providence.* Revised ed. Downers Grove: IVP Academic, 2007.

Schnackenburg, R. *The Gospel According to St. John.* Vol. 1. New York: Herder and Herder, 1968.

Schreiner, Thomas. *Commentary on Hebrews.* Edited by T. Desmond Alexander, Andreas J. Köstenberger, and Thomas R. Schreiner. Biblical Theology for Christian Proclamation. Nashville: B&H Publishing, 2015.

Soll, Jacob. 'The Long and Brutal History of Fake News.' *Politico Magazine*, December 18, 2016, https://www.politico.com/magazine/story/2016/12/fake-news-history-long-violent-214535.

Sonderegger, Katherine. *Systematic Theology.* Vol 1: *The Doctrine of God.* Minneapolis: Fortress Press, 2015.

Stump, Eleonore. *The Aquinas Lectures.* Vol. 80, *The God of the Bible and the God of the Philosophers.* Milwaukee: Marquette University Press, 2016.

Svensson, Manfred and David VanDrunen. 'Introduction: The Reception, Critique, and Use of Aquinas in Protestant Thought.' In *Aquinas among the Protestants*. Edited by Manfred Svenson and David VanDrunen. Oxford: Wiley Blackwell, 2018.

Swinburne, Richard. *The Coherence of Theism*. 2nd ed. Oxford: Oxford University Press, 2016.

Tanner, Kathryn. 'Creation Ex Nihilo as Mixed Metaphor.' *Modern Theology* 29, no. 2 (2013): 138-55.

———. *Current Issues in Theology*. Vol. 7, *Christ the Key*. 1st ed. Cambridge: Cambridge University Press, 2010.

te Velde, Rudi. *Ashgate Studies in the History of Philosophical Theology*. Vol. 4, *Aquinas on God: The 'Divine Science' of the Summa Theologiae*. New York: Routledge, 2016.

———. *Participation and Substantiality in Thomas Aquinas*. Leiden: Brill, 1995.

The Baptist Confession of Faith 1689. Carlisle, PA: Banner of Truth Trust, 2012.

The Belgic Confession. Faith Alive Christian Resources, 2011.

Thiel, John E. 'Sonderegger's Systematics: The Divine Attributes as the Divine Being,' in *International Journal of Systematic Theology* 19.2 (2017): 187-99.

Thiselton, A. C. 'Truth.' *New International Dictionary of New Testament Theology*. Edited by Colin Brown. Grand Rapids: Zondervan, 1978. 3:874-902.

Tomarchio, John. 'Aquinas's Division of Being According to Modes of Existing.' *The Review of Metaphysics* 54, no. 3 (March 2001): 585-613.

———. 'Thomistic Axiomatics in an Age of Computers.' *History of Philosophy Quarterly* 16, no. 3 (July 1999): 249-75.

Trueman, Carl R. *The Creedal Imperative*. Wheaton: Crossway, 2012.

Tyson, Paul. *Returning to Reality: Christian Platonism for Our Times*. Kalos 2 Eugene: Cascade Books, 2014.

––––––. 'Transcendence and Epistemology: Exploring Truth via Post-Secular Christian Platonism.' *Modern Theology* 24, no. 2 (April 2008): 245-70.

––––––. 'Truth.' *Dictionary for Theological Interpretation of the Bible.* Edited by Kevin J. Vanhoozer. Grand Rapids: Baker Academic, 2005. 818-22.

Vanhoozer, Kevin J. 'Theology and the Condition of Postmodernity: A Report on Knowledge (of God).' In *The Cambridge Companion to Postmodern Theology*, edited by Kevin J. Vanhoozer, 3-25. Cambridge: Cambridge University Press, 2003.

Vidu, Adonis. *The Same God Who Works All Things: Inseparable Operations in Trinitarian Theology.* Grand Rapids: William B. Eerdmans Publishing Company, 2021.

Von Balthasar, Hans Urs. *Theo-Logic: Theological Logical Theory.* Vol. 1, *Truth of the World.* Translated by Adrian J. Walker. 3 vols. San Francisco: Ignatius Press, 2000.

Vos, Arvin. *Aquinas, Calvin, & Contemporary Protestant Thought: A Critique of Protestant Views on the Thought of Thomas Aquinas.* Grand Rapids, MI: William B. Eerdmans Publishing Company, 1985.

Ward, Thomas M. *Divine Ideas. Cambridge Elements: Religion and Monotheism* 6. New York: Cambridge University Press, 2020.

Ware, Bruce A. *God's Lesser Glory: The Diminished God of Open Theism.* Wheaton: Crossway, 2000.

––––––, ed. *Perspectives on the Doctrine of God: 4 Views.* Perspectives. Nashville: B&H Academic, 2008.

Weaver, Richard M. *Ideas Have Consequences.* Expanded edition. Chicago: University of Chicago Press, 2013.

Webster, John. 'Perfection and Participation.' In *The Analogy of Being: Invention of the Antichrist or the Wisdom of God?*, edited by Thomas Joseph White, 379-94. Grand Rapids: William B. Eerdmans Publishing Company, 2011.

Westminster Confession of Faith. Carlisle, PA: Banner of Truth Trust, 2015.

White, Alan R. 'Coherence Theory of Truth.' In *Encyclopedia of Philosophy*. Edited by Paul Edwards. New York: Macmillan, 1967.

White, James Emery. *What Is Truth?* Eugene: Wipf and Stock, 1994.

White, Thomas Joseph. *The Incarnate Lord: A Thomistic Study in Christology*. Thomistic Ressourcement Series 5. Washington, DC: The Catholic University of America Press, 2017.

———. *The Trinity: On the Nature and Mystery of the One God*. Thomistic Ressourcement Series 19. Washington, DC: The Catholic University of America Press, 2022.

———. '"Through Him All Things Were Made" (John 1:3): The Analogy of the Word Incarnate According to St. Thomas Aquinas and Its Ontological Presuppositions.' In *The Analogy of Being: Invention of the Antichrist or the Wisdom of God?*, edited by Thomas Joseph White, 246-79. Grand Rapids: William B. Eerdmans Publishing Company, 2011.

———. *Wisdom in the Face of Modernity: A Study in Thomistic Natural Theology*. Second edition. Ave Marie: Sapientia Press, 2016.

Wink, Walter. *Engaging the Powers: Discernment and Resistance in a World of Domination*. Minneapolis: Fortress Press, 1992.

Wippel, John F. *Medieval Reactions to the Encounter of Faith and Reason*. The Aquinas Lectures 59. Milwaukee, WI: Marquette University Press, 1994.

———. 'Thomas Aquinas and Participation.' In *Studies in Medieval Philosophy*, edited by John F. Wippel, 117-58. Washington, DC: The Catholic University of America Press, 1987.

———. 'Thomas Aquinas on Divine Ideas.' In *Gilson Lectures on Thomas Aquinas*. Edited by James P. Reilly. Toronto: Pontifical Institute of Mediaeval Studies, 2008.

———. 'Truth in Thomas Aquinas.' *The Review of Metaphysics* 43, no. 2 (December 1989): 295-326.

Wood, William. 'Thomas Aquinas on the Claim that God is Truth.' *Journal of the History of Philosophy* 51, no. 1 (Jan. 2013): 21-47.

Subject Index

Scripture Index

288